UNDER
the GREENWOOD
TREE

UNDER the GREENWOOD TREE

A Celebration of Kentucky Shakespeare

TRACY E. K'MEYER

UNIVERSITY PRESS OF KENTUCKY

Copyright © 2024 by The University Press of Kentucky

Scholarly publisher for the Commonwealth, serving Bellarmine University, Berea College, Centre College of Kentucky, Eastern Kentucky University, The Filson Historical Society, Georgetown College, Kentucky Historical Society, Kentucky State University, Morehead State University, Murray State University, Northern Kentucky University, Spalding University, Transylvania University, University of Kentucky, University of Louisville, University of Pikeville, and Western Kentucky University.
All rights reserved.

Editorial and Sales Offices: The University Press of Kentucky
663 South Limestone Street, Lexington, Kentucky 40508-4008
www.kentuckypress.com

Cataloging-in-Publication data available from the Library of Congress

ISBN 978-0-8131-9883-5 (hardcover)
ISBN 978-0-8131-9884-2 (paperback)
ISBN 978-0-8131-9885-9 (pdf)
ISBN 978-0-8131-9886-6 (epub)

This book is printed on acid-free paper meeting the requirements of the American National Standard for Permanence in Paper for Printed Library Materials.

Manufactured in the United States of America.

Contents

Introduction vii

Prologue 1

Act 1: The Plot 39

Act 2: Putting Shakespeare on Its Feet 77

Act 3: In the Park 106

Act 4: "All the World's a Stage" 135

Act 5: Reviews and Reflections 169

Appendix: Methodology and Acknowledgments 191

Notes 195

Index 205

Introduction

On a hot summer night, with the sun just beginning to dip in the west, you find a parking spot along the Old Louisville side streets and make your way into historic Central Park, a sixteen-acre oasis of rolling hills, shaded paths, and playgrounds designed by Frederick Law Olmsted and opened to the public in 1904. Madrigal music beckons you onward, as does the sound of applause greeting a community arts group getting its chance on the big stage. Maybe you get some greasy goodness from a food truck or a literary-themed cocktail from Will's Tavern in the pavilion at the top of the hill. Then you make your way to a seat on the benches in the natural amphitheater at the center of the park. Before you loom the Three Sisters, a trio of massive trees that frame the stage. They draw your gaze to the deepening greens and blues forming a canopy above. Clang, clang, clang—like a town crier, a young intern rings her bell and announces, "Two more minutes!" Finally, the soothing baritone voice of Monte Priddy, who has been performing in the park since 1960, comes over the public-address system to welcome you to "your Kentucky Shakespeare." Actors take the stage. The light begins to fade. Planes fly over. Sirens blare in the distance. You lean in, ready to be transported back to fair Verona, a spooky moor in Scotland, a storm-battered isle, or a magical wood. This has been the scene in Louisville's Central Park on a summer night for over six decades, as Kentucky Shakespeare has brought audiences together to share some of the most beloved plays in the English language.

Under the Greenwood Tree: A Celebration of Kentucky Shakespeare draws on interviews with past and present cast, crew, and supporters to tell the story of the company and transport readers to the park.[1] What began in 1960 with a production of scenes from *Much Ado about Nothing* on a makeshift stage in Central Park has, in the past sixty years, grown into Kentucky Shakespeare, an arts organization with

viii   Introduction

a mission not only to perform the Bard's plays for free in an urban setting but also to enrich the broader community in Louisville and around the state and region.[2] The seed for the Kentucky Shakespeare Festival was the Carriage House Players, a theater troupe formed by C. Douglas Ramey in 1949 that rehearsed and performed in a carriage house in Old Louisville. The troupe did not have a tradition of putting on Shakespeare's works for its first decade. But in 1960, it presented several *Much Ado* scenes at an art fair and then the next year performed the whole play and added *Othello* and *Macbeth*, launching the annual tradition of Shakespeare in the Park. The Bard's plays have been performed there every year since, with the exception of the 2020 shutdown for the COVID-19 pandemic, making it the oldest free, nonticketed, outdoor Shakespeare festival in the country.

Over the years, Ramey and succeeding directors added educational programs that serve schools around the commonwealth and outreach initiatives that benefit a wide variety of constituencies in the community. Some of these initiatives include Shakespeare Behind Bars; Shakespeare with Veterans; Survivorship Shakespeare, for people living with cancer; and special performances for immigrants and refugees. In 2010, the broadening scope of the company's work led to a reincarnation as Kentucky Shakespeare. More recently, the company has endeavored to bring more people into the park, sharing the stage with local community and professional arts groups. Conversely, after 2014, they began performing indoor shows during the fall and spring at venues ranging from a warehouse behind the Play nightclub to the Bomhard Theater at the Kentucky Center for the Arts and the performance studio at Louisville Public Media, the home of the city's public radio stations. Over the years, the company has received local, regional, and national accolades for its performances and programs. Nationally, both the Folger Shakespeare Library and the National Endowment for the Arts have recognized the quality of the group's work in the community and on the stage. Closer to home, the company has won the Kentucky Governor's Award in the Arts and the Center for Nonprofit Excellence Pyramid Award for vision in the arts. Perhaps most reflective of the outreach mission, in 2017, Kentucky Shakespeare won the Arts Impact Award, designated for organizations that have a significant influence on their community beyond the stage. The company's artists have also earned numerous Broadway World regional performance and design awards.[3]

To tell the story of Shakespeare in Central Park, I have organized this book to mimic the structure of the Bard's plays. An opening prologue presents stories of the early life and career of members of the company, including descriptions of how they became theater artists and got involved with Kentucky Shakespeare. The story that follows is divided into five acts. Act 1 is the history of the company, from its roots in the Carriage House Players through changes in directors, the period many interviewees refer to as the "dark days," and the recent renaissance and expansion of Kentucky Shakespeare's programs. In act 2, the narrators describe how they make their art and how a season and a production come together. Act 3 catalogs the joys and tribulations of live outdoor theater. Moving outward, act 4 showcases the many ways the company brings Shakespeare to diverse constituencies around the city and region, as well as the partnerships it has formed as a result. Finally, act 5 contains the narrators' reflections on what Kentucky Shakespeare has meant to them personally and to the wider community. The appendix describes the oral history project that was the source for this book, as well as my methodology in editing the interview transcripts into the excerpts that appear here. The chapters are made up primarily of material from the oral history interviews, which is by its nature at times conversational and colloquial, with short contextualizing introductions in my voice.

The members of the company, from Douglas Ramey to the present cast and crew, have believed that Shakespeare is for everyone and have taken it as their mission to bring the drama, comedy, and joy of his work to diverse audiences. My hope is that this book will do the same. The memories shared in *"Under a Greenwood Tree"* can give students lessons about pursuing a career in the theater and bringing the Bard's words to life on the stage. Shakespeare fans can find descriptions of standout performances of their favorite plays in the unique setting of Louisville's Central Park. Arts lovers can take pride in the many ways the company engages with the community, from hiring local talent to partnering with other arts and social programs and fostering a sense of mutuality with the audience. Indeed, what comes across most notably in the stories about being onstage in Central Park is the deep sense of connection the artists feel with the audience, the joy it gives them to perform, and the energy they get back from the people gathered under the trees. From the very beginning, Kentucky Shakespeare has sought to expand that sense of community by bringing people to the park regardless of age, education, race, economic status, ability to get to the park, or other barriers. Their main mission—the theme to their plot—is to strive for inclusion in the seats, on the stage, and behind the scenes so that people can see a reflection of the diversity of their community in their whole experience of Shakespeare in the Park.

Prologue

The cast, crew, and leaders of Kentucky Shakespeare come from near and far. Some are actors who grew up in Louisville and recall being inspired by seeing the performances in Central Park when they were young. Others were brought to the city by an audition or the theater program at the University of Louisville. Their early exposure to theater, their education and training, and sometimes chance brought them to Kentucky Shakespeare and informed how they do their art. In this prologue, the members of the company, both past and present, tell the story of their personal journey to Central Park. The stories are arranged roughly chronologically, from early directors and actors to the young people treading the stage today.

Born and raised in Louisville, Bekki Jo Schneider began volunteering for the Carriage House Players while she was in high school. She was producer of Shakespeare in the Park from 1980 to 1985. Schneider passed away in 2018.

Bekki Jo Schneider: I am from Louisville. I went to a Catholic school. The nuns decided I was so backward that if I didn't do something, I would be shy forever. I had a boyfriend who auditioned for something, so I went to audition. I got a role, and he didn't. That was it. I've done theater for the whole rest of my life. Nothing but theater. In 1962, I started working at the Carriage House, which Doug Ramey ran. He did Shakespeare on the weekends in this carriage house that seated about fifty people. I auditioned and got small roles in *Macbeth*, small roles in this, and small roles in that. In my senior year in high school, my parents and my school allowed me to be gone usually one day a week to tour the colleges with Doug. I was there on and off after that as Doug needed me or if I didn't find a summer stock company I liked. He would call me every summer and say, "Will you do this show? Will

1

Bekki Jo Schneider in *Taming of the Shrew*, 1966. Unless otherwise noted, all photographs are courtesy of Kentucky Shakespeare.

you assist me? Will you do this?" Because he just trusted me. It was kind of catch-as-catch-can, different roles or different jobs. I built costumes for one thing. I choreographed some shows. It all depended on the summer. I learned about life, theater, his family, and parts of Kentucky. It meant so much to me because here was a man who did this for no money, survived his whole life trying to make it work. I found the passion of theater, and I fell in love with Shakespeare.

Another Louisville native, Monte Priddy began acting with Shakespeare in the Park in its first season and has been there ever since.

Monte Priddy: I don't remember being exposed to theater through high school. One of my teachers encouraged me and my buddy to try out for a play that was being done at the school. But we were scornful of that. We were not interested in that. Shakespeare wasn't something that excited me a lot. I remember asking one of my teachers when we were reading *Julius Caesar*, "Why are they acting as if it's so bad to be ambitious?"

Caesar's ambitious. I thought that was a good thing. Instead, I wrote poetry. One of my teachers gave me a lot of encouragement. She sent batches of my poems to the *Saturday Review* and a bunch of little magazines in Chicago, and the board of editors at the *Saturday Review* wrote back a nice encouraging letter, but it didn't go past that.

I went on to the University of Louisville [UofL]. They gave me a partial tuition scholarship. I was very serious about writing poetry. I got a lot of encouragement again from Dr. [Harvey] Webster, my writing teacher at UofL. I won one contest at the school, but then a couple of years later I was writing in a different style, and I did not win that contest and was discouraged by that. So I guess I was ripe to be seduced by the theater after that.

I had seen a couple of plays at the Playhouse at the University of Louisville.[1] Still, I was not thinking about being an actor myself. But an acquaintance of mine who was an actor, a very serious actor, talked me into auditioning to replace an actor who was dropping out of a show. Jim Bird, the head of the theater department at the time at UofL, was directing two one-act plays by a French playwright: *Antigone* and *Madea*. Travis Leech, who was in Speed Engineering School, had been cast as Jason, a very important part in *Madea*, and as the first guard in *Antigone*. He decided that was too much and he didn't want to do the first guard. So the acquaintance of mine, John Seitz, who later made something of himself, talked me into auditioning. I got the part, and it was a good experience. What I did was very well received. I got laughs, and I thought, "Hey, I like this."

Then, Doug Ramey, the director of the Carriage House Players, which became Kentucky Shakespeare years later, asked my adviser, Dr. Webster, to give him the names of some people he could recruit to be in the plays. One of the complaints or comments people made to him about Shakespeare was that they couldn't understand it. They couldn't understand so much of the language. He thought an English major might be a good person to play roles, if he understood it and spoke it clearly. I got a call from Doug Ramey inviting me to come over to the Carriage House to see a couple shows, and I did. The first show I saw was *Oedipus Rex*, with a man named Ewel Cornett who played Oedipus. He later became one of the founders of Actors Theatre. That made an impression on me.

I soon was offered a role at the Carriage House, and I liked it. It was sort of magical going on the stage: people pretending to play

Monte Priddy as Casca in *Julius Caesar* on a school tour, 1973.

characters and pretending to find themselves in interesting situations. That summer, I had a small but significant role in *Much Ado about Nothing*, which we did in Central Park. As far as I know, that was the first time we actually did a production in Central Park.

Doug liked me. I think he was impressed at my ability to speak Shakespeare and make sense of it. I didn't have any formal training. In fact, I probably would have been better off if I had left Louisville and got some formal training. But I did have lots of opportunities to be onstage and to do Shakespeare, and that was probably as useful as anything. I accumulated a lot of roles over the years. As a matter of fact, that is my main claim to fame, if you can call that fame. I've done so many characters, including lots of small ones, since I started out. In 1989, when Curt Tofteland took over as producing director, I made a point of trying to count them all up. I got close to ninety, and then I decided that was approximate enough.

John Gatton also grew up in Louisville. He acted with Shakespeare in the Park from 1962 to 1972. Later, Gatton became a Shakespeare scholar and professor of English at Bellarmine University.

Prologue   5

John Gatton: In 1958, at age eleven, I auditioned for a play at Louisville Children's Theater.[2] It was the first play in the season, and it was titled *Junket*. I wasn't cast, and I think I was very upset. What did I do wrong? But then for the second show, *The Red Shoes*, I auditioned and got cast. I was one of the children in the town. Then, it might have been Belknap Players or a student group at UofL, but somebody at UofL was doing a production of *Richard III*, and there are a few roles for children, young people. I auditioned for that and was cast as Richard, Duke of York, one of the princes killed in the tower. That show went up in February of 1959. We did performances in the playhouse, and then we took it to what was Eastern Kentucky State University, now EKU, in Richmond to do a performance. I worked with the Children's Theater from grade school into early high school, from '58 to about '63 or so.

My introduction to Kentucky Shakespeare had been a play that my father and I saw down at the Carriage House in 1961. The Carriage House did three plays in Central Park in 1961. In 1960, they had done a one-hour *Much Ado about Nothing* for an arts fair. In spring of 1962, the *Courier-Journal* had an ad for auditions for Shakespeare in Central Park. I got my dad to drive me down to the Carriage House. I don't know what I did for an audition. I think I was the youngest person there. But I got cast. I was fourteen or fifteen, I guess. In 1962, they did *Macbeth*. Doug was very cordial. He probably wasn't expecting somebody like me to show up. But here I was. I did ten summer seasons there.

Although he did some acting for Shakespeare in the Park under Bekki Jo Schneider, Hal Park's most important role was succeeding her as producer-director in 1985. He served in that role until 1989.

Hal Park: In Franklin, Kentucky, in those days when I was growing up, we had a public library called the Goodnight Memorial Library. They used to bring traveling shows through Franklin at the time. We saw violinists from Europe come through. Our community always did spring and summer festivals and high school plays and those kinds of things. I grew up seeing those things early on. We would get up and do our little dances and those kinds of things on the stage of the Goodnight Memorial Library. Then in high school, I was in the drama club. We went to a state tournament and did well there. I went on to the

University of Kentucky as an English major, but not a very convincing English major. I tended to gravitate toward all the dramatic lit courses that I could possibly take and eventually sort of gravitated over to the theater side of things. I came out with a liberal arts degree at the University of Kentucky.

I was working my way through college as a production stage manager at a dinner theater over in Winchester, Kentucky. I spent two years opening a show every five weeks as the stage manager and production manager and running the shows at night. All I knew was I could either move to Los Angeles, New York, or Chicago, because that's what you did. I had a couple of friends out in LA, so I said, "I'll go there." I crashed on the couch there and started applying my career as a production manager and technical director and film and theater and eventually graduated into directing and producing.

Shakespeare found me instead of me finding Shakespeare. I saw a lot of very bad Shakespeare during my early career in the theater. I didn't know that it was bad until I saw some good Shakespeare. The guy that really helped me understand what good Shakespeare was about was Warren Hammack, who was the founding director of Horse Cave Theater in Horse Cave, Kentucky. Warren and I had worked several showcases together out in LA, I as a stage manager and he as an actor. He finally got the funding to start Horse Cave Theater, which was going to be an Equity professional theater.[3] The night that the board of directors approved going forward with the first season in 1977, I was literally the first guy that he called. He said, "I think we have a theater. would you consider coming back and being our production stage manager?" Warren's vision was to do European and American classical theater and to try to create the opportunity for the audience in Horse Cave and Glasgow and Munfordville, Kentucky, and Bowling Green, and those areas to get used to the idea of watching classical theater. About year four or five was our first Shakespearean production. We did *As You Like It*, and it was there for the first time that I really saw good Shakespeare. At that point, I became a fan.

After leaving Horse Cave, I knew that I wanted to produce and direct, and I really didn't know where or how to begin to start doing that. So my wife and I moved up and hung out in Louisville for the summer. Bekki Jo and I crossed paths on several occasions at Kentucky Arts Council events or grant-writing workshops or whatever. She knew I was in town. Bekki Jo called and said, "Hey, could you play a couple of parts for me this summer?" I played Adam in *As You Like It*. I did another little part or something that summer. Then I moved to LA. Then three years later, I moved back to Murray, Kentucky. Bekki Jo knew that I was here, and that's when she reached back out again and recruited me to come back to Louisville. She called and said, "I'm getting ready to leave. I would like you to come up and interview for this job. I think you'd be the right person for it."

Raised in Louisville, Phil Cherry studied acting at Western Kentucky University and then returned to Louisville to perform for Shakespeare in the Park and other local theaters in 1980.

Phil Cherry: My stepfather was a concert pianist, Dr. Bruce Gordon Cherry. He took me around to see plays and concerts. He took me to see plays at the Kentucky Shakespeare Festival when I was eight years old, so I had a chance to see Mr. Doug Ramey and other wonderful actors of the day perform on that stage, as a child. When I first saw the Shakespeare performances, I was just trying to understand the storylines. We didn't have a television set until I was like five or six years old, so I was really excited about seeing live theater, and it was Shakespeare, so that challenged me as well. I loved it. My dad would tell me about the story, and we'd talk about the characters and the costumes and all of that. I was able to take it in, in a way that I think definitely made an impact on me. I didn't personally get into acting until many years later. But from the time I was eight years old, I always loved it.

Then while I was in high school at Ahrens Trade School, there was a drama teacher there who encouraged me to perform in a play. I thought he had made a mistake when I saw the casting. I went to him and said, "You got the wrong guy. I don't want to play a big role. This is the lead role!" I thought he'd made a mistake! He said to me, "No, I have not, Phillip." He said, "You have stage presence; you have a great voice." He said, "You're a smart kid. You can do this." I said, "It's a three-act play! I've only done, like, a scene here and there." He said, "Well, you can do this." So, in 1974, I ended up playing a role. My parents came out to see it; everybody was really proud of me. I learned that I could learn lines like that; I didn't realize I had that kind of memory capacity. He got me started.

I really didn't have a lot of confidence in my performing Shakespeare in my early years. The first Shakespeare play I ever performed

8   Under the Greenwood Tree

in was *Romeo and Juliet* in 1974 at Western Kentucky University [WKU]. I played Friar John. It was directed by a guy from the Royal Shakespeare Company who came as a guest artist at WKU, Patrick Tucker. He gave me a great deal of encouragement. I got over my fear of Shakespeare at that time and learned how to speak the language, somewhat. When I sat down with Patrick, I said, "I don't know how to speak it. It challenges me beyond belief." He encouraged me to look at the text. Shakespeare put everything he wanted his actors to know in the text. He made me go back and examine the text that Shakespeare wrote. He talked to me about the iambic pentameter, how to make every word sound the way that you connect the dots.[4] The subtext is there; it's right there. He worked with me so diligently on it. I watched the process. I watched him work with Mercutio, who was a very good actor, a friend of mine at Western. I watched him work with the kid who played Romeo, and Tybalt.

I was the first Black kid to play the lead role in a mainstage performance at WKU. I played Brutus Jones in *The Emperor Jones*. I didn't realize I was making history at the time. I just thought, "Wow, what a great opportunity." I didn't expect they would do a performance like that, a show like that, at WKU. Here's what happened: I also performed in a play there called *Ceremonies in Dark Old Men*, written by Lonne Elder III, directed by Pat Taylor.[5] It was an all-Black production, the first all-Black production at WKU. That opened the door for the following year. All the theater people said, "Wow, they've got a lot of talented Black kids over there." The theater department decided, "If we've got this kind of talent, let's do *The Emperor Jones*. Let's do a play with the emperor, get the dance department to dance." It was a beautiful show.

I joined Equity in 1980 when I was with StageOne. I was in a production with Curt Tofteland. It was *To Kill a Mockingbird*. Moses Goldberg directed that. I played Tom Robinson, and Curt played Boo Radley. In 1980, I was also in the Humana Festival of New American Plays at Actors Theatre. I was kind of busy in those days. I was in a play called *They're Coming to Make It Brighter*, directed by Jon Jory, written by Kent Broadhurst, and there were a lot of wonderful actors in it, some of them from the Negro Ensemble Company.[6] I also performed Shakespeare at Actors Theatre: *A Midsummer Night's Dream. Glengarry Glen Ross*, that was directed by Marc Masterson. I performed my own shows at Actors Theatre: *Voices of the African American Poets*, which was

Phil Cherry (*second from right*) and Georgette Kleier (*right*) in *Twelfth Night*, 2000.

directed by Karen Hunter. *Emperor Jones* was performed in the Victor Jory Theater, and I directed *A Raisin in the Sun*, which was also there at the Victor Jory Theater.[7]

I didn't return to the stage of Kentucky Shakespeare until 2001. I resigned as a faculty member of the Kentucky Governor's School for the Arts for the purpose of returning to the stage and doing some really good work with Curt Tofteland. Curt had already offered me roles and invited me to come to the company, to *return* to the company. I started out there in 1980. I came back in 2001.

A native of New York, Tom Luce came to Louisville after impressing Bekki Jo Schneider at an audition and has acted with the company since 1984.

Tom Luce: I started my performing career while I was on Staten Island, New York. I think I was five. For the Christmas program at my church, I had to read the passage that they made famous in *A Charlie Brown Christmas*: "Lo and Behold." When I walked out of the church after I had read it, I turned to my father and said, "You know, I remember," and I recited the whole thing from memory. I was five. I guess that was my first memory of performing.

10   Under the Greenwood Tree

When I got to high school, I took a theater class, and then the spring musical came along. It was *Anything Goes*, and I was cast as one of the "Chinamen."[8] It was basically that there just weren't enough men, so I kind of got drafted to do that part. I loved it. I did the musical the next year, which was *Where's Charley?*, which is a musical based on *Charley's Aunt*. It was very funny. I had taught myself how to ride a unicycle. I played Spettigue, who is this older guy who is pursuing who he thinks is this young lady, who is actually the main character in drag. I chase him across the stage one way, and then I chase him across the stage another way. In the script, it called for me to ride a bicycle across the stage. I said to the director, "I can ride a unicycle, so why don't I ride a bicycle one way, and then on the way back I'll ride a unicycle." It really was a great bit. It brought down the house, which I kind of loved. Very simple thing, riding a unicycle, but it worked. The picture in the local paper was of me riding the unicycle across the stage.

After finishing college in 1984, I was ready to go out into the real world. I went to the Midwest Theater Auditions at Webster University in St. Louis.[9] I went and auditioned and got a few callbacks. One of them was Bekki Jo Schneider from Kentucky Shakespeare. I was offered a contract, so I came to Louisville in 1984. When Bekki Jo called me to offer me a contract for *The Tempest*, she said, "Well, I want you to play this role in this play," and I swear I thought I heard her say "the third man" in *The Tempest*. I thought, "Okay, one of those roles standing there on the side with a spear maybe." I'm thinking, "Okay, that's the role I'm going to play: the third man. That's all right. I'm okay." There was another company I had been talking with at the time that had said, "We were thinking about casting you." I said [to Schneider], "Well, I have this other sort of semi-offer I want to try to find out about first." I found out years and years later that I had gotten sort of a reputation in her eyes as being arrogant, maybe because I wanted to hear this offer after she had offered me Ferdinand in *The Tempest*. I didn't know until I got the contract. I said, "Oh, okay, that's a pretty good part."

After studying theater in college in North Carolina, Jon Huffman came to Kentucky to attend the University of Louisville. Like Cherry, he has acted with the company on and off since 1980, alternating with a career in theater and film both locally and in California.

Jon Huffman: I was born in 1954. I grew up in Washington, DC. My dad was a Lutheran bishop, and my mom was a homemaker. Growing up in Washington, there was a lot of cultural opportunity, and we went to a lot of theater. I remember specifically Arena Stage, which was one of the very first regional theaters in America. I'm not sure if it predated Actors Theatre. It was run by a wonderful woman named Zelda Fichandler, who started Arena Stage and ran it for many, many years. That's where I saw a lot of theater growing up and where I took a lot of theater classes, way before I had any intention of going into theater.

I went to college as a premed major at a small liberal arts school called Lenoir-Rhyne University in western North Carolina. I went to my first science class, the first day of classes, and at the end of the class, the professor said, "Great. Well, we'll see you tonight for lab in the lab building." I thought, "Oh man, lab at night in college. That's not why I came here." I'm almost ashamed to say that as I was on my way to the lab, I saw a group of what I thought were really beautiful young women going the other way, and I thought, "I'm going to see where they're going." They walked straight to the theater and auditioned for a play, and so did I, and I quit my science major and eventually became a theater and English major. The play was *School for Scandal.* I got a role, and that really kind of set me on my way.

After I graduated, I came to the University of Louisville to the theater department. I was offered a master's degree in return for being in the UofL Rep[ertory] Company, which was a group of five actors who did three plays every morning in public schools in the region. That was what we did in lieu of teaching. Did that for two years. We were expected to write a master's thesis at the end of the time. I didn't really get along with the faculty too well, and they didn't really like me a lot, so at the end of the two years, I didn't write a thesis. I still don't have a master's degree, but it was great experience.

The theater scene in Louisville at the time was Actors Theatre. That was pretty much it. There was the precursor to StageOne, the Children's Theater. I don't know if it was a union theater then or not, but that was operating too. In the summer there was Kentucky Shakespeare, which was called Shakespeare in the Park then. I don't know if right then they paid very well. It was still being run by Douglas Ramey, the man who started it, with Bekki Jo Schneider as his assistant. Because it didn't pay or pay very well, I really had very little interest in it. I was interested in being a professional actor. When I got out of UofL, I was planning to move to either New York or Chicago. But then a couple friends of mine and I started a home repair company. We made a lot of money doing that for a while, and I thought, "Who needs theater. I'm a working man making a living." Eventually, about 1980, there was a recession. People quit hiring us. I thought, "Well, if I'm going to be poor, I might as well be an actor."

People kept telling me, "You should check out Kentucky Shakespeare because they now pay pretty well." That was true. I auditioned for Bekki Jo, I think in her second year of being the artistic director. This is a terrible story. I was cocky as a young actor, as young actors tend to be for very little reason. I had heard that this theater was run by this woman named Bekki Jo. I thought, "Oh wow, this is perfect. I can get a job there. I can dazzle her with my talent and get a job because she's obviously some Kentucky woman who came in from the hollers to run this theater." I'll never forget the first audition. It was in the Humanities Building at UofL. I thought, "Well, I'm going to nail this." I came in, and she was in there with a couple other people. She was barefoot. She had on short shorts and a flannel shirt. "I've got this. They will never have seen an actor like me." I auditioned. I did a couple of pieces and started to walk away. She ran up to me, and I thought, "This is perfect; she's going to beg me to be in her company now." She said, "What's your availability this summer?" Because I wanted to nail this job at that moment, I lied to her and I said, "Well, I've got a lot of other offers. I'd prefer to stay here, and I'd prefer to work with you, but I've got these incredible offers at these other theaters, so I'm not sure." She looked at me for a moment, and she said, "You know what, you should take those offers," and she turned around and walked away. I was terrified. I thought, "Oh no, she beat me in this. I've blown it." I never underestimated her after that. Eventually, she offered me the job, and I took it. She let me know that I wasn't going to pull one over on her.

Another Louisville native, Georgette Kleier has been an actor for Kentucky Shakespeare, as well as for Derby Dinner Playhouse across the river in Clarksville, Indiana, since 1984. Kleier was also the head of the Theater Program at the Youth Performing Arts School in Louisville.

Georgette Kleier: My neighborhood friends and my sisters and I would create theater. We created this town in our garage. It was called Garabe. We would hang sheets to denote different things, like the general store or the hardware store, the beauty salon. We would have a theater inside this town, with sheets hung up for curtains. Our first production was *Hansel and Gretel.* Then the theater moved inside during the winter into the basement, and we did things like Christmas reviews where I would sing "Let It Snow" and do a little dance number and make my sisters throw snow on me as I was doing my number. So that's what I did as a child. I created. I always knew that I like creating different worlds than the world I inhabited.

I did not take lessons or anything. We were working-class people. That's why I think I was driven to volunteer at Actors Theatre. I don't even know how I heard about Actors Theatre, to be honest. I ushered at Actors Theatre for two or three years in high school, so I could see plays for free. My first play was probably something like *One Flew over the Cuckoo's Nest.* To see Adale O'Brien do her work onstage multiple times was just really impactful for me.[10] Watching her is really what sort of solidified it for me in terms of theater. And in terms of what I later pursued, which was directing, watching how Jon Jory could visually construct theater was just awe inspiring to me.

I started with Kentucky Shakespeare in 1984. I wasn't in the park with Bekki Jo, but I was part of a group that Jon Huffman was also a part of, that did their first stint in educational Shakespeare, or Shakespeare for students. We did staged readings. The one that I can remember doing is *Macbeth.* I can remember doing Banquo in *Macbeth,* and I'm sure I played other roles. This was Bekki Jo's beginning of the educational component, a focus on education with the company. Shortly thereafter, Bekki Jo bought Derby Dinner in '85, partners with Carolyn Lamb. So I go, as does Jon Huffman, with her to Derby. I continued working with her there for years. She was a mentor. It was a family. It was a time in my life where doing theater was completely joyful. Completely. It didn't feel like work at all. Not at all. We all became very close. I can't tell you how many people have bought houses because of Bekki Jo. Lots of actors have been able to buy a home because of her. She was a mentor to all of us. She was like a surrogate mom to us. When I adopted my son, she threw me my baby shower. Even just talking about her makes me still emotional. It wasn't even about what she did onstage for us in terms of directing. It's what she did outside of that.

Curt Tofteland began acting with Shakespeare in the Park in 1980 and became the producing director in 1989, a position he held until 2008. He is also the founder of the Shakespeare behind Bars program.

Curt Tofteland as Richard II, 1993.

Curt Tofteland: My first experience of live theater was in a very small elementary school in Martin, North Dakota. We did little skits, and in church we did different pageants, so I had early experience with it. When I was in middle school, one of the actors in the high school play was ill, and they wanted somebody to stand in, and I volunteered to do that. That was my first experience with a three-act play, and I really loved it. After I graduated from eighth grade, the school that I went to had an amazing music teacher. I had played in the all-school

Prologue   15

marching band, starting trumpet in third grade, so music was a big part of my early life. Dennis Moser was one of my mentors. I played trumpet and French horn for him in the band, but I also was asked by him to sing in the choir. That's where I discovered formal singing. He also did a yearly musical. I got my first experience in a musical playing Mayor Shinn in *The Music Man*. It was a nonsinging role, but the next year I played the lead in *Cabaret*, and that sort of solidified the fact that I really loved musicals. I love music. I love theater. I love combining them.

When I graduated from high school, I went to the University of North Dakota. I was in their fine arts school in the music department, where I majored in vocal performance. I got my BFA in vocal performance theater and creative writing–poetry. I knew in undergrad that I would go on for a graduate degree. I would get an MFA, a master of fine arts. That was back in the early seventies when there weren't that many MFAs around, and I assured my dad that the MFA would give me the opportunity to be qualified to teach college.

My first season out of graduate school was with the Oslo Repertory Theater in Sarasota, Florida, and I spent nine months touring three productions all through that area. Then I went on an audition trip taking Amtrak. You used to be able to get a six-week Amtrak pass. I set up about twenty-five auditions all through the Midwest and the East Coast. One of the places that I came was to Louisville, primarily because I wanted to audition for Moses Goldberg at Stage-One but also for Jon Jory at Actors Theatre, which was then beginning its journey into being one of the top-notch regional theaters in North America.

I was offered an acting position at StageOne, then called the Louisville Children's Theater, by the artistic director Moses Goldberg in 1979. I took the job and moved to Louisville. I started my career with Kentucky Shakespeare in 1980 as an actor in the summer company, and I was in all three plays. That's when I fell in love with the work and Shakespeare in Central Park.

Born and raised in Houston and Austin, Texas, Casey Clark arrived in Louisville as a lighting designer at Actors Theatre. Though she has worked for theaters in Florida and locally at the Palace Theatre and Derby Dinner Playhouse, since Curt Tofteland's tenure she has reserved time in the summer to design lights for Shakespeare in the Park.

Casey Clark: My mother was a patron of the arts. She loved fine art, music, and particularly performing art, so I was exposed to a lot of it when I was young. We went out to a lot of things. I think the first place she took me was a children's troupe called the Pied Piper Players. We did a lot of that. The first lighting that I did was as a child at a summer camp at the Houston High School for the Performing Arts. I was probably ten or eleven. It was a camp. Get your kids away from you for a week. I sort of forgot about it after that and went on to other things.

I went away for college at Dartmouth. I majored in English with a concentration in Shakespeare. But then I needed a work-study job. One of my friends hooked me into a job as a stagehand at our college art center. I got interested in the lighting aspects of stagehand work, although most of what we did was music recitals and concerts and other things. I started taking some classes in the drama department as electives. That's where I got into stage performance and design. What does it take to support that performance? What does it take to light it? I was also really interested in architecture at that point, and theater architecture and acoustics interested me a great deal. But you know, once I got my hands on some lights, it was all over. I liked it so much that I went back to graduate school at the University of Texas–Austin and got an MFA in it.

I came out of graduate school in 1990, and I needed a job, so I got a job at Actors Theatre of Louisville. I worked there as an electrician for two years and then as the mainstage board operator for one year. I got to watch a lot of designers at the top of their game coming through there. I got to see their process and their work. I got to do some design work while I was there, which was really valuable to me. Then I left there and became a freelance designer. I worked at different places here. For Shakespeare. I worked at Derby Dinner Playhouse. I ended up moving to Boca Raton, Florida, and got to work with a modern dance company for about a year and a half, which was fantastic. Then I wanted to come back here. I had reached the point in my life where I wanted to buy a house. It's really hard to do that as a freelance artist. The banks just don't like you. So I took a job as the director of production at the Palace Theatre, and I did that for fifteen years. I've had these sort of day jobs, if you will. But I've always stayed with doing Shakespeare in the summer, and anybody that I work for knows that there's a week that I disappear for the first tech for Kentucky Shakespeare.

Donna Lawrence Downs grew up in Pennsylvania, outside of Pittsburgh. After graduate school, she came to Louisville to do costume designs for StageOne in 1992 and soon got introduced to and began working for Kentucky Shakespeare.

Donna Lawrence Downs: I've never been taught to sew. I just kind of knew how to do it. When I was little, I'd make lots and lots of doll clothes with toilet paper and aluminum foil and Saran Wrap, until I could use scissors. Then I started using fabric. It was the sixties, so it was lots of cool Emma Peel from *The Avengers* or Barbara [Feldon] from *Get Smart* outfits from TV that I'd make for the dolls. Because I've been able to sew, I was pigeonholed into doing costumes or makeup in high school. It was, "Can you do this?" or "Can you fix this?" When I had home ec in seventh grade, it was funny because everyone else was making a pillow and I was making a vest and a blazer and a pair of pants. [*Laughs.*] A little ahead of the curve.

I got involved in theater more in undergraduate school. My education was really trial by fire. It was a really small undergraduate school that I went to, California University of Pennsylvania, near Fallingwater. I was an art major for a little while. I broke my left hand, and it stopped me from being able to do pots and weave. The two things that I really loved to do, create fabric and create pottery. I put those things on hold, spending more and more time in the theater because my boyfriend was there. [*Laughs.*] But I think what it really might've been that attracted me was the collaborative part of brains coming together to do a puzzle.

I got an unsolicited offer for graduate school at Penn State, which I took. I worked at many theaters in Pittsburgh over the years, making unexpected strides in my career. I worked at the ballet, and I worked at Shakespeare and other places like that there. It was about my fifth or sixth job doing theater when I was like, "I could probably make a living doing this. I have these skills at a weird part of life. I should just use them instead of doing it as a hobby and sitting at a desk all day." I have a lot of friends who knew since they were five they wanted to be in theater. That was not me.

My introduction to Kentucky Shakespeare was a very convoluted thing, really. The director of StageOne's wife was the money person for Kentucky Shakespeare at the time, which was the fall of '92. When I moved here, my apartment wasn't ready, so I stayed with them for

18   Under the Greenwood Tree

seven weeks. She was telling me about Kentucky Shakespeare and how cool it was, among other things. I appreciated their artisticness and fun atmosphere in the office, so I spent more time at Shakespeare. I started doing more projects for them, like the money bags they use during the show, when the actors come out in costume during intermission and collect money. The bags I made twenty years ago—they're still using them.[11] That was my first foray into getting involved in Kentucky Shakespeare.

Doug Sumey grew up in Kansas and got his professional start in theater there at the Heart of America Shakespeare Festival. In 2000, Curt Tofteland recruited him to take over the education program at Kentucky Shakespeare.

Doug Sumey: I went to Indian Creek Junior High, and I did *Bye Bye Birdie*, *Annie Get Your Gun*, and *West Side Story*. Then in high school I was a sports kid, but sports kind of started to drop off, and theater took its place. I did anything I could to be in the theater in high school. That's just where I immersed myself. Then I went to undergraduate university and got a business degree only because my parents were business-related people. But they always said, "We'll support you with whatever you want to do." It was a couple years after undergraduate where I realized I don't really want to be in the corporate world. I went to my folks and said, "I'm going to quit my job; I'm going to start serving tables and auditioning around Kansas City. How do you feel about that?" With a big gulp, they said, "We support you and love you for what you want to do."

The first Shakespeare experience that I had was when I got a call from the producer from the Kansas City Shakespeare Festival saying, "Would you come in for an audition for the role of Paris in *Romeo and Juliet*?" The reason why he knew to call me was because he knew my theater professor in college. He had recommended me for the role. So, I went in for that audition, and I got the job, and I worked for a summer—I think it was 1994—as an actor for the company. The next season, I did another year as an actor in the company.

The next season I started working in the education program, running their Camp Shakespeare program. I did that for about three years. We wanted to expand our work into the school communities and alternative school communities. We were really excited about bringing Shakespeare to students who might not otherwise get Shakespeare.

Doug Sumey speaking to the Globe Players, 2004.

20   Under the Greenwood Tree

My boss at the Heart of America Shakespeare Festival knew Curt Tofteland, who was the producing artistic director at the Kentucky Shakespeare Festival, and asked him to come to Kansas City and do a full-day workshop for the teachers that I was working with. He and I hit it off, and he had a position open: education director at Kentucky Shakespeare Festival. He offered me a position, and that's what brought me to Kentucky.

After growing up in Pennsylvania, where she discovered a love of theater as a child, Tina Jo Wallace pursued a career in North Carolina. She came to Louisville in 2000 after an audition with Curt Tofteland, and she acted in the summer productions and worked in the education program. She has since acted and run the children's program at Derby Dinner Playhouse. She is married to Matt Wallace.

Tina Jo Wallace: I remember going when I was very little to Fulton Opera House, which is in Lancaster, Pennsylvania. They did *The Wind and the Willows* play. I remember going to that and being like, "I want to do that! I want to do that!" You grow up watching TV and movies, but seeing it live and seeing their skill live was so impressive. I was always then creating stories. I was writing sock-puppet dramas. In fifth grade, I talked my principal into letting me write a version of *The Night before Christmas* and cast all second graders. I went and held auditions with the little kids and cast the show and had a full-on performance for the parents at night. My mom and I made props in the middle of the night. I don't know why the principal let me do it, but I should've known then that I would eventually get into directing and not just acting, because I produced the entire thing!

I did community theater. It might've been sixth or seventh grade that I had a drama teacher who did community theater who was like, "You should come and audition for this!" My parents would take me to practices and all of that. I was involved in another community theater when I was in high school. I knew that's what I wanted to do by the time I was maybe in ninth grade. I knew I *loved* it all the way up. I was one of a few kids that consistently worked at the community theater— because there's not always shows with kids. But if I wasn't in a show, I volunteered to do props, lights, sound. I would do whatever I could to hang out there. My parents all along the way were like, "You should go for it if you want to do it. If you don't end up doing it, then that's fine, but if you love this, go ahead and study it! Do what you want to do." Their encouragement is probably why I said, "Okay I'm going to try this. I'm also going to minor in education so if I don't get a chance to make money doing theater, I can at least maybe teach it."

After college, I went right to North Carolina. I had a friend, Joanna Gerdy, one of those actors who did community theater with me in Pennsylvania. She was extremely talented and loved to direct. She had moved to North Carolina to work for this children's theater. I went down on one of my breaks and auditioned for them and got hired as an education intern. Then I eventually got put on the tour, and I toured for five years with them. I did five years at the children's theater, teaching, touring, acting.

Then I wanted to do something other than children's theater. Not that I don't love it still, but I wanted to have some other experiences. I wanted to try some other genres. I had worked for a community theater in North Carolina called Chickspeare, which was all women. We did all women playing all the roles. It kind of gave me a taste for the stuff that I had gotten to do in my Shakespeare studies in college. I went to a Unified Professional Theatre Audition in Atlanta.[12] It's like a cattle call audition, where you have a number and you audition for hundreds of companies at a time. I met a bunch of different theater directors, who called me back. I ended up working at a dinner theater in Michigan. I also met Curt Tofteland, who was at the time the producing artistic director at Kentucky Shakespeare. I was working at a theater in Michigan that Christmas, and at the end of my contract, he asked me on my way back to Charlotte to drive through Kentucky.

I don't know the exact monologue I did for him, but I know that it was from *As You Like It* because I had done *As You Like It* with Chickspeare. I thought I knew this inside and out. When I got into the callback with Curt, he just started asking me questions, great insightful questions about the character. Things that I had not thought of, and here I was *so* smart. I might have been twenty-six or something. He asked me questions, and by the time I left the callback, I had a completely different take on the character than what I had done in my performance in North Carolina. It made me know here's a place I can grow; here's a place that I could learn. That spring I came to do the education tour first. That was the spring of 2000.

Tina Jo Wallace (*center*) and Matt Wallace (*right*) in *A Midsummer Night's Dream*, 2001, their first season in the summer festival. A foreshadowing of things to come.

A self-described "theater kid," Matt Wallace grew up doing community theater in Bowling Green, Kentucky. After a brief career in Chicago, he also was lured to Kentucky by Curt Tofteland. He began his career with Kentucky Shakespeare as an actor in the summer of 2001—when he met his wife, Tina. He has served as producing artistic director since 2014.

Matt Wallace: I have four younger sisters. I got into theater at a really early age directing my sisters. I would practice being the priest and giving communion wafers at home and reenacting that. I think it started with a lot of puppet shows. We would turn our refrigerator box into a puppet theater. I would direct the neighborhood kids. Then, when video cameras came out, I would write and direct and star in—and let my sisters costar in—various movies. I would cast many of the neighborhood kids. I even have some video of me. My mom took it. You can only see through the window, and you can't hear what I'm saying, but I'm probably all of nine or ten, and standing around a group of neighborhood boys, and have a script, and I'm directing them. I'm telling them what to do. Probably not directing them well. We built the set in my garage, and I was controlling all aspects of the creative part of the production.

Prologue   23

My dad took me to audition for the community theater around eight or nine. It was *Alice in Wonderland*. We didn't really have many opportunities in school, so he took me to audition for the community theater, and I got cast in the role of the March Hare in *Alice in Wonderland* and just fell in love with that. I really loved community theater. Here I am growing up in Bowling Green, Kentucky, in the early eighties, and I did some sports, some soccer and basketball, a little baseball, but I was discovering that what I wanted to do was the arts. There were so few kids in the community who really wanted to do that. I was going to the community theater and being around all these adults who were doctors and lawyers and assembly-line workers and who really, really, really wanted to do this. They really wanted to be there. They weren't doing it for a paycheck, and it was this melting pot of the community. I was one of the very few kid actors that got to hang out with them and go to the cast parties. *The Foreigner* and *Brighton Beach Memoirs* were my two really big roles in the seventh and eighth grade. Those are pretty great roles to do.

For me there was never any question in my mind: I wanted to be an actor. There was never one other thing I wanted to do from when I was little. My parents were middle class, working class, but they supported this kid in Bowling Green, Kentucky, who wanted to do that for a profession. I got my first taste of real training at the Governor's School for the Arts, where I met my mentor, Liz Fentress. It's a three-week intensive program, so I got some more serious training. For me, it was also about being around young people who were serious about this, and they were not ashamed. I've talked about this very often, about being in the closet as an actor growing up in Bowling Green. Some of my friends were, "Oh, you got to go to play practice?" Like it's this dirty thing. So I would keep it quiet. The Governor's School for the Arts opened a whole different thing. "Oh my gosh! I'm not the only one who wants to do this as a career!" For me, it was eye opening.

We had a great regional theater in Horse Cave, Kentucky, called Horse Cave Theatre. It was nationally renowned. It was featured in the *New York Times*. Warren Hammack founded that theater and operated it with Liz Fentress, who was my Governor's School for the Arts teacher. That was the professional theater in Kentucky that we knew of because Actors Theatre was too far away from Bowling Green. We would sometimes take field trips there. I saw *Taming of the Shrew* and maybe *Romeo and Juliet*? So that was my first taste of enjoying

24   Under the Greenwood Tree

Shakespeare. Not quite understanding everything that was going on but thinking it was cool. Sophomore year in high school, I remember us wearing sheets—togas—reading *Julius Caesar*, standing up in front of the class. I remember I was not particularly a fan of Shakespeare at all, even in college, though we had a great Shakespeare teacher, Bruce Longworth. It just didn't click with me. I just don't think I was great at doing Shakespeare. I don't know whether it was immaturity or my self-consciousness as a young actor and just not trusting the words. I think getting so caught up in the poetry of it—that sort of turned me off, which really informed how I teach Shakespeare now.

I went to college at the Webster University Conservatory of Theatre Arts in St. Louis. After college, I did my first extended professional contract at Horse Cave Theatre, hired by Liz Fentress, my former Governor's School teacher. What was really cool about that was I was working with all of these professionals as I was getting ready to move to Chicago to be an actor. Horse Cave was a four-month contract. I knew I was moving to Chicago with my girlfriend at the time. We moved there and did some shows, worked at a coffee shop as my day job. Very often, one way for actors to make money doing theater is through educational theater, very much so in Chicago. There was this company called Healthworks Theater; they're not around anymore, unfortunately. I auditioned for a play called *The Wizard of AIDS: Aware Individuals Deserving Survival*. It was AIDS educational theater, and this was 1996. We had another show that was educating about safer sex and HIV. It was really opening my eyes to theater that *does* stuff.

There was this company called Dolphinback Theatre that was founded by people from Webster. I auditioned for a show. They did really good work. I ended up becoming the artistic director of this small, storefront theater after doing a few shows—probably a $20,000 per year budget. I was producing, directing, getting my friends to do stuff, putting on shows, mounting them. I learned so much about fundraising and audience relations, about commissioning playwrights. We got Lee Blessing, the Pulitzer Prize–nominated playwright, to come to Chicago. We housed him, and he premiered a new play of his with our little theater company. I did all that about five years.

I had auditioned for Curt Tofteland a few times because he would come down to where I went to college. He had offered me to do a two-person tour, but I was at Healthworks. I had this day job, and I couldn't leave. I always loved my auditions with Curt because he was so engaging and I loved how he worked with the language. He had this actress, and they needed another person to do a two-actor tour with her. I couldn't, and I turned it down. That was Tina Jo, my future wife. But I couldn't do it! So I stayed in Chicago. But I was ready to take a summer away, and I worked out that I could leave for the summer, and I auditioned for Kentucky Shakespeare. I got my first offer in 2001 to play Lysander in *Midsummer Night's Dream* and Dumaine in *Love's Labour's Lost*.

Originally from Texas, Paul Owen came to Louisville as a costume designer for Actors Theatre and through his work there became a nationally recognized set designer. He redesigned the Central Park stage for first Tofteland and then Wallace and did set design for the summer productions beginning in 2010. Owen died in February 2021.

Paul Owen: After high school, I didn't know where I wanted to go, but I knew I wanted to do something, and my dad suggested I study electrical engineering in college. Along the way a teacher—like so many of us—grabbed me in the hallway in a junior college in Borden, Texas, and said, "I want you to be in this play contest, and I understand you act." I said I was in the senior play in high school and that's it. She said, "Well, you're hardly old enough to do anything else." In order to please her and get her off my back, I said, "Okay, I'll do that." Then she took me under her wing and got me a scholarship for my junior and senior years of college at the University of Houston. I did a scholarship in technical theater, and I was acting in all the productions.

I was drafted into the military and was gone for two years. Finally, in 1960, I came back to Houston and went to work at the Alley Theatre as a young technician. The founder had been disappointed with the person who was supposed to be doing the design things. She said to me, "Well, then you just do it." I said, "I don't know how to do it," and she said, "Figure it out." I didn't know how to draft. I can't draw. I can't sketch. I can't paint. I had a friend who was close to the stage manager at the theater, and he was an art student at the University of Houston. I asked him if he thought he could be a visual secretary. I didn't know how to express design. Even if I had an idea in my head, I didn't know how to do it or demonstrate what that idea was for a director or an actor. I would say what I was thinking as to what the design of the costume would be or what the design of the set would be and lights. And he drew that. For two years, he was my visual secretary. By that time, my wife had taken a mechanical drawing class in college, and she had a drawing kit. We had three triangles and a drafting board and a T square, and she knew how to use those, and she taught me how to use those. That's how I became a designer. I designed all the sets, costumes, and productions for the Alley until I left there in 1970.

I had a friend who was at another organization that was created as part of the growth of the regional theaters. I called him, and he said, "I think I know exactly where you need to go. Jon Jory's in Louisville, Kentucky, is trying to save a theater there." He said, "Jon Jory is looking for a costume designer." I called to get in touch with Jory, and we talked, and I came out and took the job here as the resident costume designer with the possibility of designing a couple of sets. That was the first season.

I knew Curt Tofteland and his wife. She worked at Actors. He wanted me to design some form of stage house for him and oversee its construction. That was about twenty-five years ago. I designed it and built it, and then it stayed a part of the park up until, I think, maybe three or four years ago. Then I started designing a little bit more because I was retiring from my career at Actors. I left Actors in 2009, and so I think I started designing and working with Matt in 2010. That was a relationship that continued.

Born and raised in Louisville, Gregory Maupin received his training at the University of Louisville and the Dell'Arte International School of Physical Theatre in Northern California. After meeting and marrying Abigail Bailey, he moved back to Louisville, where the couple started the Le Petomane Theatre Ensemble. Although he had done some educational-program work with Kentucky Shakespeare earlier, he began steadily acting with the company in the summer productions in 2014.

Gregory Maupin: My theater memory is based in trees because the first show I remember seeing was by the Blue Apple Players, who used to take things around when I was in Catholic school.[13] When I was in first grade, they brought a Saint Patrick's Day show—some kind of nonsense with a leprechaun. It had probably only two people in it, maybe three. They no doubt had some kind of fat little tree piece laid out. If I saw a picture of what the set looked like, it would look like one of the many crap sets I did in the educational tours. But in my memory, I see this knotty oak tree, literally growing out of the floor of the gym at the Saint Helen School. That is my memory of it. Someone chased the leprechaun, and it would run off and change clothes and be like a third character or whatever. I remember very clearly this chase around this very real tree, though there's no way it could have possibly looked like that. I know what their budgets are. It stuck with me. I enjoyed that sort of thing. But I didn't see Kentucky Shakespeare. I was in the South End [of Louisville], and it was more of a hike. I didn't go until I was a teenager when they did the Henriad.[14] That was my first experience.

Thoughts of being a performer didn't hit me until I auditioned for the school play when I was a junior in high school. It was *Brigadoon*, and I got a bigger part than I expected to, the snarky best friend. He doesn't have to sing or dance; he just has to deliver punch lines, which was like, oh, fine. We watched old movies, so I had seen the Gene Kelly one a bunch. Then we did *The Music Man*, and I was the lead in that the next year. I went to UofL and started doing stuff in the theater department because this was fun, and I wanted to continue doing it. I just sort of didn't leave because of the enjoyment of it. I have weird skills; I know this about myself. There's a lot of very normal things that I am not capable of keeping attention on, and there's a lot of odd things I can do. Those are the people who end up in theater, I think. Us kinetic learners. I think it feels like a home there. The Island of Misfit Toys—that's the theater department.

I went ahead and got the BFA. Left, lived in Boston for a while, lived in Chicago for a while, lived in New York for a while, studied in Northern California for a while at the Dell'Arte school, which does commedia dell'arte clown melodrama and ensemble-built work. The other big life changer besides actually getting into theater was Dell'Arte. These were people who took it seriously, who took very dumb, comic-timing, physical-comedy stuff very, very seriously. That was when I, even having been at it for five or six years at that point, or seven or eight years, really started to take it seriously and want to do something with it. Not just a living but as an artist.

Abigail Bailey Maupin grew up in small-town New England and was introduced to theater through summer stock. After initially studying to be an opera singer, she switched to acting. While living in New York, she met future husband Gregory Maupin, and after they wed, the couple decided to move back to his native city. She too worked in the education program first but then joined the regular summer casts after Matt Wallace took over as producing artistic director in 2014.

Abigail Bailey Maupin: The first time I saw live theater was probably at summer stock theater. My parents were theatergoers and theater lovers. The first one that I remember seeing was *Oklahoma.* I must have been about four. It was in an old barn that had been refurbished into a theater, and the balcony went all the way around. My sister and I were hanging over the edge of that balcony right up next to the proscenium. I remember the guy playing Curly looking up at us and walking over and putting his hand on the edge of the balcony and sort of leaning up and singing to us for a second. I think that was it. I think that was the moment that both my sister and I were like, "Uh, he's looking at us." We feel now like we're onstage, because we were so close to the proscenium edge that we could watch the audience watching him watching us.

I started with musicals for the most part. It was a summer stock theater, so that's what would be available for kids. The von Trapps or *Annie Get Your Gun* or the *King and I,* when that was a thing that people still did. I'm a singer. I wanted to be an opera singer for a while in my teens. I went to the Boston Conservatory, so I have a degree in musical theater. Because it was a musical theater degree, they gave us a little bit of everything. We had to take dance; we had to take acting classes; we had to take individual voice lessons and music theory and group classes.

I started getting some Shakespeare there. We had one year that was a Shakespeare class, and then one of the teachers really focused on acting Shakespeare. That was when I first started going, "Oh, I like this." I personally think that musical theater actors have a good prep for doing Shakespeare because they understand how to phrase a song and how to interpret verse already. They also are used to performing in a very stylized world, where something like breaking into song and dance is just how that world works. Shakespeare does a lot of those same things. A lot of people who come out of musical theater are already used to the idea that this word is on this beat and so that means it's a little more important. For my senior year acting final, I did Lady Percy's *Henry IV* speech about "For God's sake go not to these wars." I remember doing it, and my teacher just looked at me afterwards and said, "Okay, you're done," and feeling like, "Oh my god, I got it right. I did that."

New York and the theater world make you believe as a young actor that that's the only place that you can be if you want to be a successful actor. I got there and did all the things you're supposed to do. Pounded the pavement, went to all the auditions, had some good work, joined the union. But I never really felt like I was getting anywhere, and it made me want to leave acting. Being a woman in New York was not great. I personally never had a lot of harassment or very obvious discrimination of any kind, but there's just simply not as much work.

Greg and I met in August of 2001. He was living in Chicago, and I was living in New York. We met in Boston. We had gone to two different weddings on the same weekend in Boston and we ended up staying with the same mutual friend. Because we were both there for the weekend, she and her roommate decided to throw a luau. Saturday morning, we both got up. When you're in someone's house and you're uncomfortable or whatever, you go in the kitchen; you just drink some tea or coffee. He and I sat there in our pajamas like, "What's your name again?" And we started talking. We had to go to these weddings, and the next day was the luau. Honest to God, other than the time that we were at the weddings, we have not stopped talking. He, after that weekend, decided to move to New York.

I eventually realized, and part of it was meeting Greg and him moving to town, "I don't want to do this. I don't want to be here. But I don't know where else to go." Greg said, "Well, let's go somewhere together and make a company." He didn't want to come to Louisville. He kept trying to think of other cities. Because there is that thing that sticks in you, "If I go home, is it giving up?" We finally said, "You know what? It's got an arts community. We can afford it. It's not so big that we'll be a drop in a bucket. But it's not so small that people don't go out in the evenings. You are from here, so you have connections." We've been here eighteen years now.

Gregory Maupin: We were in New York when we got married. That was in '03. We moved back here in 2004. We started a theater company, Le Petomane Theatre Ensemble. That was around from 2004 to 2014. After that is when we really started working with Kentucky Shakespeare.

Abigail Maupin: I can't remember who told us that we should do it or how it came up. Someone told us about the auditions for the school tour. That sounded great; we needed work.

Abigail and Gregory Maupin as Beatrice and Benedick in *Much Ado about Nothing*, 2017.

Gregory Maupin: As a married couple, we were attractive to them because: one hotel room. You don't have to keep up the whole boy and girl sleep separately. I'm sure that helped. We auditioned, and the gig started in January of '04 and lasted for the semester after that.

Abigail Maupin: We rehearsed with Matt Wallace because he was working at the company then and with Doug Sumey, with Curt Tofteland kind of putting together the tour. It had its ups and downs. Curt was working a lot with Shakespeare Behind Bars then. When Curt left, they were in the turnover years. Before Brantley Dunaway started his tenure, Matt came in to direct *Richard III* in 2010. We were both in that, and that was great. But that was it. We didn't perform again until he took over as artistic director in '14.

Gregory Maupin: Matt was like, "Hey, could you guys come do your six-person *As You Like It* on the stage at Kentucky Shakespeare?" I built masks so six of us could do Shakespeare comedy. We came back and

Prologue   31

did our *As You Like It*, set in the Old West. Le Petomane was about to end, and we were like, "This will be our last hurrah. We will perform our *As You Like It* on the stage at Kentucky Shakespeare. That'll be the end of Le Petomane." We do some weird little things on our own, but our primary thing is working with Kentucky Shakespeare in the last six or seven years now.

Amy Attaway grew up in Louisville and was engaged in the children's theater world from a young age. She studied at University of Evansville and spent several years working as an actress and director in and around Louisville, founding her own company, Theatre [502], and running the apprentice program at Actors Theatre. Matt Wallace invited her to direct for his first summer season, and in 2016, she became the associate artistic director of Kentucky Shakespeare.

Amy Attaway: My mom took us to plays a lot when we were little, my sister and I. She took us to plays at StageOne. That's pretty much what did it for me: seeing plays. I was in a production of *A Christmas Carol* when I was in third grade. I played Christmas Past, and that was so exciting. Ever since then, I have never looked back. I started taking lessons when I was little at the Summer Ursuline School of Music and Drama. We did musicals. I had my heart broken when I did not get cast as Brigitta in *The Sound of Music*. That's who I really wanted to be. I didn't get it. The next time you could sign up for which roles we hoped to play, we were doing the *Pied Piper* [*of Hamelin*], and I signed up to be the vice mayor because I knew he'd be funny. I was really funny. I had a funny voice, and I did all these ridiculous things. I was like, "Yeah, this is the stuff. Who wants to do the pretty-girl thing? I want to do the funny stuff." But turns out, that was not actually true at all. I spent most of the rest of my acting life being the ingenue.

When I was in high school, I met a lot of kids my age from other schools at the Young Actors Institute.[15] I went with some of them to see Shakespeare in the Park. We would take a picnic blanket and sit on the grass and watch Shakespeare. One of the big things that I remember that is close to my heart from that time is that Kentucky Shakespeare did the Henriad, which is when you produce *Richard II* through *Henry V* with the same actors following through in their roles. The actor who played Prince Hal was Jeremy Tow, who was one of my idols at StageOne. Art Burns played King Henry IV, who was another one of my StageOne idols. Both of them passed away while I was in college. Seeing their performances and knowing them as people, and having worked with them, having been onstage with both of them at StageOne and watch them work up close, and then seeing them work in the beautiful Central Park stage doing Shakespeare—that's one of my magical early theater memories. And it's my first Kentucky Shakespeare memory.

During that time, I did a lot of theater for free at night. There are a ton of small theaters in Louisville. Every Sunday in the *Courier-Journal*, there would be an audition section, and I just went to all of them. Sometimes I'd be cast, and sometimes I wouldn't. I started to work a lot with the Necessary Theater and Bunbury and other places, but mostly the Necessary Theater. I learned a lot about new plays during this time because Necessary Theater was focused on new plays and contemporary playwrights. Tad Chitwood and Susan Linville were the directors who ran that company. Tad gave me the opportunity to direct, and so I directed the play *Impossible Marriage* by Beth Henley. That was when I really got that I wanted to be directing, like, "Oh, *this* is the thing."

In 2013 my plan was "I'm going to freelance from Louisville and see how long that lasts me." I had two gigs out of town. I hadn't seen Kentucky Shakespeare in a while. I had met Matt Wallace once. We had met because Greg Maupin and I worked together to produce a staged reading of *It Can't Happen Here* around the something anniversary of that play. We had all these actors from all over town and people from the community. Matt was in it because he and Greg were friends. I met him at this cast of thirty. It was just, "Matt, hello. I'm Amy; nice to meet you. Thanks for being here. Thank you so much for doing this." So that was my first impression. I'm hearing, of course, from my theater colleagues, from my director friends in town, from everybody: "Kentucky Shakespeare is crashing and burning. This is horrible. Kentucky Shakespeare is crashing and burning." Then the switch quickly to "Oh, they got Matt Wallace. Oh, okay, great. Cool. I like Shakespeare. Yay. Matt who? Great, somebody is going to save that theater that I love. Fantastic."

I get back to town, and I'm waiting for my next freelance job when I got this email from Matt Wallace asking me to have coffee with him. I was like, "Cool. That's nice. I bet he's just reaching out to all the local theater folks in town. He's been working in southern Indiana for a while. So maybe he's just trying to get reacquainted with the local theater community." I put no pressure on this coffee. It was like, "Cool. That'll be a fun chat." He offered me a job to direct *Henry V*. It was so meaningful. I probably did say it without crying at that coffee—but who knows? I cry easily—how important *Henry V* was to me and Kentucky Shakespeare because when I was a teenager, I saw those two actors who were so important to me in it. I think I accepted on the spot. We did the whole audition process together in the fall, and the design meetings and the prep for the summer. Then we did the summer together, and it went well enough that he went ahead and asked me to come back even before the summer had closed. He asked me to come back the next year and direct *Taming of the Shrew*, which I did. Then, during that summer, he started talking about the idea of having me come on as associate artistic director. I was into it. He had to figure out the money part, of course. The next summer was *Winter's Tale*, then I started officially as associate AD.

After growing up in New York, Crystian Wiltshire came to Kentucky when his mother was transferred to the state by the military. As a student in the theater program at the University of Louisville, he was introduced to Kentucky Shakespeare and was a stage management intern in the summer of 2015. He got his start as an actor with the company the next year, playing Romeo.

Crystian Wiltshire: When I was in seventh grade, we were living in Germany—stranger in a strange land. My middle school at the time was on the military base. I go to the school, and the guidance counselor says to me, "You can either take, for your elective, a cooking class or a theater class." And I'm like, "I'm pretty sure I suck at cooking, but I don't know if I suck at theater, whatever that even means. Let's give it a shot." In that class, we ended up putting on a courtroom drama play, and I was the judge. The way they set it up was you have someone come out and say, "The Honorable So-and-So presiding," and I would walk out onto the stage. I'll never forget our first show. We did it during lunchtime, so the whole school was there. I walked up onstage after they said, "The Honorable So-and-So presiding," and I just remember getting this applause from so many of my classmates. My mom was there. It was really cool to hear "Oh my God, that's Crystian, that's Crystian!" Oh man, I like this! I like this a lot. I remember at the end of the school year, seventh grade, in my yearbook, my theater teacher wrote this star in the yearbook, and on top of the star, she wrote this really, really beautiful message, saying to stick with this, because she saw something in me that I didn't necessarily think was there. That was my first intro to this world.

When I was two years into college in Virginia, at Norfolk State University, a historically Black college, my parents were moving back to New York. I thought that that was really exciting because as an actor, it's like, "Oh, now I get to go back to New York; that's great." I got to New York, and I ended up not necessarily getting back in school as quickly as I wanted to. Next thing I know, my mom tells me, "Hey, the military needs me to go to Kentucky. If you want, you can come to Kentucky with me, and I can use your father's GI Bill to get you in school, and you can finish up your degree and keep up with your acting that you love so much and go from there." I initially didn't want to leave New York, because I really loved it. But I did want to finish school, so I decided to come out to Kentucky.

When I came to Kentucky, that first time driving to Louisville, it wasn't necessarily about finding theater yet. Because I was still in this place where it would be really nice to get back into theater, but I have no idea what the theater scene here is. I know of zero theater companies in this city; I know nothing about the arts in this town. I'm just here checking out the campus of the University of Louisville. I drove past the playhouse that they have. I just kept driving down Second Street, and I ended up at Garage Bar. That was the first bar I went to in Louisville. I thought, "This place looks really cool, and they have Ping-Pong tables outside, and I'm a master at Ping-Pong, so this city might be for me. I really like it."

My first exposure to Shakespeare was in English class in high school. We were watching *Romeo and Juliet* from years and years ago. I think this was the Zeffirelli film.[16] Honestly, it wasn't until I got to the University of Louisville where I really appreciated it, because of my acting teacher, Daniel Hill. We had a semester of just focusing on Shakespeare. That, combined with my time at Kentucky Shakespeare, has really helped me appreciate his work so much more than the high school version of myself did.

My start with Kentucky Shakespeare was not the typical way an actor would start a relationship with a theater company. At the University of Louisville, they have always done a really, really great job of keeping the students up to date on auditions and other opportunities in the community surrounding the campus for students to be a part of, whether that's Kentucky Shakespeare, or Actors Theatre of Louisville, or StageOne, or the Louisville Ballet. When Kentucky Shakespeare announced auditions, I was really excited. "Great, let me prepare my two monologues." My acting teacher at UofL, Daniel Hill, was an actor at Kentucky Shakespeare. I was like, "Okay, he knows what they're looking for." We got to perform our monologues for him, and I felt really, really prepared going into that audition.

I walked into that rehearsal room, and it was such a big, open space that it was very intimidating for me. I did not expect that. It was Matt Wallace and Amy Attaway sitting there. I introduced myself, and they wanted to know what pieces I was going to do, and I'm pretty sure one of the pieces that I did was from *Julius Caesar*. It was Mark Antony. I totally forgot the line in the middle of my audition. I totally froze up. Thankfully, I was able to get through one of my other pieces. So Matt Wallace was kind enough to work with me after my audition. He said to me, "I want to try something. I want you to go all the way to the end of this huge rehearsal hall, and I'm going to go to the opposite end. I want you to say the monologue that you know really well, say that one again. I want to make sure that I can hear every single word that you're saying." In the moment, I'm thinking, "Why does he want me to do this?" But afterward, I realized, "Oh, because if he's going to hire you to work at Central Park, he needs to make sure that you can be far away and I can still hear every single word that you're saying." Because clarity is at the heart of what Kentucky Shakespeare does. But at the time, I didn't know that. I didn't really appreciate that. I ended up not getting the job. I felt really bad, of course. But, you know, ultimately, I just wasn't prepared enough, and that's on me.

But at UofL, one of the technical staff, whose name is Charles Nasby, saw my work ethic. Because not only do I love acting, but I love the theater. I'm willing to help build sets; I'll paint the set; I'll clean up; I'll help with anything. I just love the theater and collaboration. I love it all. Charles Nasby saw that in me, and he also just so happened to be, on top of an employee at UofL, he also was the technical director at the time at Kentucky Shakespeare. He asked me if I would like to be an intern at Kentucky Shakespeare, helping to build sets, and things of that nature. I jumped at the opportunity. I absolutely wanted to. Through Charles Nasby telling Kentucky Shakespeare, "Hey, I know he didn't necessarily work for you guys as an actor, but I want him to be a part of my crew," I was hired on as a stage management and sound intern for my first year at Kentucky Shakespeare.

Once that summer ended, it was time for me to start school again. I still had a year left at UofL. I'm back at school, and then they announced that they're doing *Romeo and Juliet* for their spring tour. I think at that time they had also announced it would be a part of their summer season as well. I was like, "I feel like I'm a Romeo type. So let me just go in and audition." I got the call from them that they would like me to be Romeo in their spring tour. That spring tour would then blend over into the summer, so I was basically told very early on that, "Hey, we want you for the spring tour *Romeo and Juliet*, and you're going to be hired for the summer season." To me that was, yes, that's so exciting. But it's also, wow, this is a company that knows the amount of work, the sweat that I put in for them as an intern, and they saw my work ethic, and they know I'm always going to give it my best. That they were willing to trust me with a role like Romeo on their spring tour and on their summer stage as my first role, really, with the company, was really, really special.

Braden McCampbell grew up in Texas with more interest in athletics than the performing arts. He came to Kentucky with his family in his senior year of high school and then attended the University of Louisville. A faculty member in the theater program recommended he audition for Kentucky Shakespeare. He has worked for the education program and acted with the company since the summer of 2015.

Braden McCampbell: My first introduction to theater was being in show choir in middle school. We did the musical version of *The Nutcracker*, and I got to be the Arabian prince, partly because it's Texas and I was the only Black kid in the class and partly because I was the only football player that was interested in being in the production, so I was the only buff guy with my shirt off in the class. But that was one of the first productions that I ever really got involved in. All I did was stand there with my shirt off and lift a ballet dancer who danced around me, and then sang some songs with the rest of the choir. I was already an athlete, so I was used to being front and center for people's amusement and entertainment. But being in show choir for that little bit was one of those things where I was like, "This is pretty neat."

Prologue   37

I had an art teacher who got me interested in it. She was the teacher for show choir. Lynn Tyler and Marshall Wilson, her husband, who was the art teacher, were all about the arts. That's who got me into theater. Originally, it was just an elective. I'll take show choir; everyone says it's a neat class. That slowly but surely worked up into some other things that made me act out a little bit more—not in a bad way. I realized there was potential for doing something other than "I'm the jock. I'm from Texas." Then I ended up with a ripped Achilles tendon. So that kind of killed sports.

[My family moved to Kentucky for my senior year, and then] after high school I just went into working. I was trying to get my own place, do my own thing, et cetera. The transition came when I finally got to UofL, actually. That's when I started getting into acting, like full, dead-on acting. At UofL, my first performance was a Shakespeare play, *Much Ado about Nothing*, and I was Dogberry for that one. I actually did not like Shakespeare for the longest time. I was one of those kids who had to read *Romeo and Juliet* as a sophomore in high school. Reading Shakespeare in high school is god awful. Because the way they present it is this is a book that you need to read. Why? This is not a book. You don't read stage directions. This is a script, something that should be performed. It drives me nuts. That's frustrating as all hell to kids. It was to me when I was in high school. I hated it; I hated Shakespeare.

It was actually having the chance to do *Much Ado about Nothing* that changed my perspective on Shakespeare. Wholeheartedly. Working through the script, I immediately was like, "I hate this. Why are we doing this?" The teacher's like, "You're the comic relief." "Oh, I'm supposed to be the funny guy! Oh, that's what this means! It's a dirty joke! He's talking about penises. Aha! I get it now! This is great!" It's one of those little things where your brain finally clicks over to understanding the language, and that didn't happen until college because that's when I got the chance to see and experience people acting it out versus reading it. It's an entirely different thing seeing Shakespeare.

Then, I was taking the Acting for Majors class; they had Kyle Ware from Kentucky Shakespeare come. My teacher, Daniel Hill, was like, "If you guys really want to get in and make a name for yourself in the business, you need to impress this guy. Be ready to impress this guy." He had us recite just like we would in some auditions, where you don't know what you're reading for. You got a monologue ready, and you need to do sides.[17] He had us read *Macbeth*, and we had to do a little performance, a snippet of a monologue/part in a play, and then he had us do sides, like you would if you got a callback. But one of the things I've always realized about myself is that I try to react to people when I'm onstage. What is my partner going to do? I've never seen the scene before; let me go off them. I didn't realize I was doing it. For that one, I just worked off my partner because I had never read these sides before. What I heard from Kyle was "You're the only one of maybe two people who legitimately listens to their partner." I think that we did the Lady M[acbeth] and Macbeth out on the balcony bit where they talk about killing Duncan. Everyone else has this approach like "We're going to have a blowup; we're going to be angry," because it's the "Prithee, peace, woman! You will do what I say" bit. "Prithee, peace! / I dare do all that may become a man, / Who dares do more is none." It's that little bit. Where he's like, "I'm a man; stop saying I'm not a man." Everybody blows up at that part. Kyle was like, "You're the only one who is like, 'Am I supposed to be angry here? I don't know.'" He said he likes that. Long story short, that stuck with him, so he asked, "I would like you to come out for an apprenticeship." That's how I ended up with Kentucky Shakespeare.

Act 1

The Plot

"It was misting rain—a day I wouldn't want to spend sitting on a park bench watching a play. But I suppose the costumes and what-not attracted attention, for pretty soon we had a sizable audience. About three hundred people, I think. The guys came up from the croquet court. Women came in with their babies"—that's how Douglas Ramey recalled the 1961 performance of scenes from *Much Ado about Nothing* that was part of a summer arts festival in Louisville's Central Park. This was not the first appearance of Shakespeare under the stars in the city; that distinction goes to a production of *As You Like It* sponsored by "the ladies of the Flower Mission" in July 1895, when the park's land was still owned by the Dupont family. Tickets, which cost twenty-five and fifty cents, benefited the Flower Mission. In contrast, Ramey's 1961 production was free and ticketless. Indeed, there were no doors or gates or even chairs; the audience had to bring their own. More important, the performance inspired so much enthusiasm that "we decided to try more," and "then the next night, it really exploded." Exploded indeed: those *Much Ado* scenes were the start of an over sixty-year tradition of free Shakespeare in Central Park.[1] This chapter draws on the memories of past and present participants in the Kentucky Shakespeare Festival to tell the story of its origins, the development of the company over the years, some of the hard times when the future of the performances in the park seemed in doubt, and the renaissance and expansion of the program in the recent past.

Scene 1: Doug Ramey's Shakespeare (1959–79)

The development of Shakespeare in the Park from the performance of those first few scenes of *Much Ado* into an enthusiastically supported (if

C. Douglas Ramey as Macbeth, 1963.

sometimes with more love and praise than dollars) institution was the result of the "tireless cajolery, indefatigable optimism and sheer cussedness" of one man: founder and director Douglas Ramey. A native of Kentucky, Ramey tried out for his first play at the suggestion of Madelayn Douglas, his teacher at a junior college in Paintsville. Having caught the bug, he went on to act with a company in Illinois. But when the Great Depression hit, he moved to Chicago to work for Western Electric and sell magazines. Still,

The Plot   41

Ramey availed himself of opportunities in the city and received training at the Goodman Theatre of the Arts Institute. He returned to Paintsville to work as a recreation director for the Works Project Administration, a New Deal agency, and then moved to Louisville to do industrial training for Reynolds Metals. At that time, he felt the theater calling again. "I couldn't stay away from it," Ramey recalled. So "I started working out at the Belknap Theatre at the University of Louisville . . . and later helped establish the Clarksville Little Theatre. I stayed with that one for ten years." Then, in September 1949, taking the first step on the road that would lead him to Shakespeare and to Central Park, Ramey formed the Carriage House Players, named for the outbuilding in the "Old Louisville" neighborhood in which the new company studied, rehearsed, and performed.[2]

Several factors influenced Ramey to embark on a new adventure after a decade with the Carriage House Players. In the late 1950s and early 1960s, outdoor theater was a popular summertime draw for drama fans and casual tourists, with the local arts pages of the papers regularly listing and promoting shows around the region. While these included musicals and historic pageants, like *The Stephen Foster Story* in nearby Bardstown, increasingly Shakespeare was "the most popular playwright of the summer season," featured in a growing number of festivals around the country. Open-air Shakespeare had deep roots in the United Kingdom and United States, including, on this side of the Atlantic, free productions by the Federal Theatre Project in the 1930s. Then, after World War II, a postwar vogue for the Bard in natural settings spread throughout Britain, tapping into a nostalgia for a bucolic English countryside. That model jumped across the pond with the organization of the New York Shakespeare Festival, which started in 1956 and moved to that city's Central Park in 1957.[3] At about the same time, the Carriage House Players started including some Shakespeare plays in its indoor, year-round season. Their first outdoor performance was at the Kentucky State Fair in August 1959, when they put on an hour-long version of *Macbeth*, inspired by a similar performance at the 1933 Chicago World's Fair. By that point, Ramey recalled, his players "found themselves hooked on Shakespeare." Two years later, they brought *Much Ado about Nothing* to Central Park. Inspired by the audience's enthusiasm and his company's newfound love of the Bard's language and drama, Ramey decided to launch the first full summer season in 1962, and the Kentucky Shakespeare Festival was born.[4]

The choice to locate the productions in Central Park reflected Ramey's home in Old Louisville and his goal for the festival: to bring Shakespeare to

42   Under the Greenwood Tree

people who might not otherwise get a chance to experience his plays. The neighborhood, which sits approximately a mile south of the central business district, began in the late nineteenth century as a suburb for wealthy Louisvillians. The city annexed the land in 1868, and construction soon began on stately brick mansions, making the area a showcase at the time—and still today—of ornate architectural styles. In the early twentieth century, however, the well-to-do residents began moving out to enclaves on the outskirts of town, and by the 1930s and 1940s, many of the homes had been subdivided into boarding houses or apartments. With the postwar urban renewal of nearby neighborhoods, low-income and minority families—including both African Americans and immigrants—moved in and came to dominate the area. The onetime home of Louisville's leading families was now considered a neighborhood in decline.[5] The demographics of the users of Central Park had also begun to change. Though, like other public recreational spaces, Central Park had been designated as white-only since the early twentieth century, the entire Louisville park system had been desegregated by a United States Supreme Court order in 1955.[6] Ramey and his players, like directors and company members through the years, saw the changing racial and economic dynamics of the area not as an obstacle but as an opportunity: a chance to bring people of diverse races, incomes, and life experiences into the audience. Though there would be calls through the years for moving Shakespeare to other parks, being at the heart of the city would always be a key part of the identity of the festival and the company.

The new festival quickly attracted acclaim and support. In the first full season, the Carriage House Players put on *Measure for Measure*, *Othello*, and *Much Ado about Nothing*, the latter of which featured "dazzling costumes and dances" that impressed both audiences and reviewers. In 1962, they were back, once again offering *Much Ado* and *Othello*, while adding *Julius Caesar* and *Macbeth*. The performances remained free and ticketless. The money came instead from the Louisville Shakespearean Society; Louisville Central Area Inc., which raised funds from local businesses; and the city's Department of Parks and Recreation, which provided the stage: a circus wagon backdrop and cement-floored boxing ring. The festival attracted this support in part because its first years coincided with a growing interest among the city's elite in revitalizing Old Louisville, as demonstrated by the founding of the Old Louisville Association and Restoration Inc., two nonprofits committed to the historic preservation of the most impressive homes.[7] Despite the initial "makeshift" set and seating, the

The Plot   43

plays attracted "swelling" crowds as families spread blankets on the grass or brought chairs from home. After that first season, the city helped anchor the festival in Central Park by building a permanent amphitheater with a stage and room for five hundred seats. Meanwhile, the new Committee for Shakespeare in the Park took on the job of fundraising to pay the actors and other costs of production. For the next couple of years, Mayor William O. Cowger gave several thousand dollars of city funds to help allay those costs. The investment seemed worth it; by 1964, according to local newspaper accounts, the festival was attracting up to fifty thousand people over the summer.[8]

Not everyone was enthralled. The Kentucky Shakespeare Festival suffered both bad reviews and constant money troubles, and while the former gave way to more laudatory notices, the latter would last throughout the Ramey years. Almost from the beginning, arts reporter William Mootz used his reviews to call for restrictions on the audience and a new location for the festival. He did not particularly like the performances, focusing his criticism on Ramey's "graceless direction." He blamed artistic laziness and complacency for lackluster shows, and after the first couple of years, he bemoaned the lack of improvement in quality. But he directed most of his ire at the festival's Central Park setting. "Not even John Gielgud," Mootz argued, "could create an illusion" in the "hullabaloo" of "Fourth Street traffic, shouting teenagers, screaming kiddies living it up on nearby playgrounds."[9] The only solution, he argued, was to move to the city-owned amphitheater in Iroquois Park, a setting located five miles to the south and surrounded by a mix of older and more recently developed suburbs.[10] In 1966, Charles Vettiner, a member of the board overseeing city parks, endorsed Mootz's suggestion because the city lacked money to support free performances in Central Park. In that year, Mayor Kenneth Schmied cut the city's contribution to the festival, putting more pressure on the Committee for Shakespeare in the Park to raise it all themselves. Money problems continued into the 1970s. In 1971, for example, Ramey reported, "Last year, I got the company together and told them, 'We have no money, and we may never have any money. But if we're going to do the season, we have to get started. So if you're willing, we'll go ahead and rehearse the show, and if we get the money we'll have the show. If we don't . . . well, it's over.'"[11]

But the festival always had enthusiastic audience members, supporters, and players who were committed to keeping the shows free and in Central Park. Fans wrote to the paper urging others to "ignore the 'derogatory review'" and assuring people that, given the budget, the quality of the

44   Under the Greenwood Tree

performances in the park was "little less than a miracle." They also defended the audience, pointing out that Shakespeare wrote for a mixed crowd and that Louisville's "groundlings" differed little from those who shared the Globe Theatre with Queen Elizabeth. In contrast to Mootz, arts reporter Phyllis Funke painted an appreciative picture of the diversity of the audience, which included at one performance nursing home residents, a glue-press operator and his wife seeing Shakespeare for the first time, an Asian American professor at the University of Louisville and a young Black law student named Hulbert James, who in two years, as leader of a local civil rights group, would invite the company to participate in a neighborhood art festival. Coverage of the performances also stressed the size of the crowds, signs of neighborhood pride in Old Louisville, decreases in crime around the park, and the opportunity for wholesome recreation for low-income families in the area. The enthusiasm for the festival manifested in donations of time and money. The Committee for Shakespeare in the Park held splashy fundraisers with guest actors but also received small two- and five-dollar gifts from neighbors who appreciated the outlet for their children. The financial situation remained a nail-biter down to curtain time, but Ramey, the members of the committee, and other supporters managed to pull it together each year. One local journalist captured the spirit of the festival and Ramey's vision for it by saying, when "he sees people who have seen plays in New York sit side-by-side with people who have never seen a stage play before, he's convinced at the end of each season it's worth it."[12]

Bekki Jo Schneider: Doug Ramey was either working for a tobacco company or Reynolds Aluminum ... I don't remember which one. That's how he ended up here. He went to the Goodman School of Drama. Then he ended up here, working with the WPA [Works Progress Administration]. What came very first was in the 1950s he did *A View from the Bridge* in a bowling alley in Louisville. He just loved theater, and he made that work. The demand for theater in the fifties and sixties was not very great. Actors Theatre was not here yet. He led the way. You would average five to ten people a night at the Carriage House when you did the show. There was an Arts in Louisville club that was around the corner from the Carriage House. Many people belonged to that club. You would go in and discuss the arts. It was a typical sixties environment. This is what should happen; this is what shouldn't happen. But as far as theater in Louisville, except for community theater, not much else was going on until Actors Theatre came about.

The Plot   45

Carriage House Players was born from the idea of reviving Old Louisville. One of the ladies who lived there owned a house and was working with the mayor, so there was a chance for money. It was two or three people's ideas of how to keep this going, how to let Old Louisville benefit, and how to help Doug survive. Jack Clowes worked in government. He had written grants and things, and that helped. He was on their committee. Doug lived upstairs in the Carriage House. You changed upstairs, and then you came downstairs, and you performed on a stage that maybe was ten by twenty feet. There were electric cords everywhere. It was an adventure.

The first set in the park was a boxing ring. I didn't work with them that very first season, but it was whatever they could find. Then they had proved themselves enough that the mayor believed in it enough that there was enough money to build a platform type of thing and then build backdrops to that.

Usually, they did three plays a season. Maybe a history, a comedy, and then maybe something like *Julius Caesar*. *Othello* never raised eyebrows because it was outdoors. It was pleasant. It was in the city. You could come; you could leave. It didn't cost you anything. You gave people a chance, and therefore they didn't feel taken by either money or time or anything else. The first time he didn't [cast a Black man as *Othello*]. I really think the first time he did himself.[13] The first time I did *Othello* directing there, I did use a Black actor and had absolutely no trouble. In fact, I had less trouble there than I do at the Derby Dinner Playhouse. You leave when you want; you come when you want. If you don't want it, no one's taking your money.

He liked plays where [*laughs*] he could have some great roles. *Othello*, *Julius Caesar*, *Macbeth*. *Macbeth* was his favorite. He played Macbeth until he just couldn't play it anymore. He was good at Macbeth. One night we were doing a show and he came in from a different entrance. I was playing a witch. He came in from a different entrance, and he put his arm up, kind of behind me. I finished the scene, and I went off, and he said, "I didn't want to tell you, but that set piece was going to fall down." He held the set piece up and did the witches scene. That's just the way he was.

Doug usually found the actors locally. They were people who had enough training that when you said "Shakespeare," they knew what they were doing. Enough training, but they weren't brilliant. There were some college professors. One worked in a library; two were

46   Under the Greenwood Tree

professional actors from other places. Some of them had other jobs. I was a high school student. One of them had been right off Broadway. Very diverse because there was no place else to work. He would go to one bar and have his dinner almost every night because he could only cook on a hot plate in his apartment. That bar was called Cunningham's. Cunningham's had different rooms, and if you wanted to find out if you were going to be cast, you waited until Doug got in one room, and then you went to the next room and put your ear up to the door, so you could hear if you were going to get cast. I was honored to be amongst the group. Many of us learned tons by the people he used, by the sharing of ideas, and by that good old 1960s conversation after the show was over.

[After Vietnam,] when the "boat people" came over and were in Louisville and looking for housing, they would put them near Central Park.[14] They gave all the kids bicycles, so every day during rehearsal we had bicycles and kids. Doug would sit on the first three or four rows and talk to the kids in the neighborhood and explain what was going on. An audience is only affected by what touches them. Consequently, you have to speak to that audience. This is why I think many theaters fail. I run a dinner theater that makes, last year, $7.3 million. The reason is we listen to the audience. They don't want to see sad shows. They don't want to see shows they cannot pronounce. Right or wrong, they pay for it. It's for profit; therefore, it belongs to them. Doug Ramey felt the same about his Louisville Central Park audiences.

Jon Huffman: It began way before my time. In the late fifties and early sixties, there was a group of people who got together and decided we really need some theater in Louisville. These were people who had done theater elsewhere or had grown up here and gone away to do theater and come back. Louisville had a great tradition of touring groups coming through. But Louisville did not have a great tradition of resident theater companies outside of very amateur community theater groups. They were really just people who liked theater and would get together and put on a show, whether or not they had an audience. This group got together at a place they called the Carriage House, which was up on Fifth Street in Old Louisville. Out of this group came the people who started Actors Theatre, Kentucky Shakespeare, and who also did a lot of work over at the Derby Dinner Playhouse. Bekki Jo Schneider was the kid to these people. She would work with them after school.

She was in junior high or high school, and she would come over just to absorb what they were doing. To scrub the floors and wash costumes. To build things. Sometimes they would say, "Oh, by the way, Bekki Jo, Juliet can't do the show this week, so you're playing Juliet." She learned how to do theater that way. These people eventually were the foundation of most of our arts in town today. Just an amazing group of people.

Monte Priddy: It was called the Carriage House Players in the early years because the theater was in a converted carriage house on Fifth Street about fifty or sixty yards south from Memorial Auditorium. I was very fond of this carriage house because it was not very large. It was easy to be natural. That's where the magic happened. It was a two-story building. On the bottom floor was a theater space. On the second floor, Doug Ramey lived in one room. There was sort of a costume shop in another room, and there was a little makeup room and a little dressing room.

The theater really operated on a shoestring at that time. In fact, I'm not exactly sure how Doug made it go. He had some sponsors, I believe. There's Doc Hendon, Jack Clowes, and Mae Salyers, who was the head of a neighborhood organization. He relied on those contributors. The quality of the productions was uneven. Doug just had to get people anywhere that he could. There were people dropping out. There were people not available. One of the standards was a guy named Charlie Kissinger, who was in a lot of advertisements around town. He had a show on television in which he introduced horror movies. Charlie was a very funny guy. He used to make jokes about Doug calling somebody and saying, "I've got a role for you. It's got one great scene." That was the pitch. That was the attraction you would have. It's not a great role, but you have one great scene.

I remember the first time we did a full production in Central Park. We did *Othello*. At that time, the stage was in a slightly different location. Where the Old Louisville information center is now used to be known simply as the Shelter House. A wooden boxing ring had been set up down the hill from that. I remember doing the production on that boxing ring. I was playing Rodrigo, who is a funny character who has been exploited by the villain Iago. Iago, after causing a commotion waking up Brabantio, Desdemona's father, yelling that she had been abducted by Othello, was supposed to storm off the stage and leave me to deal with the angry father. The angry father did not show up.

Doug Ramey with early funders Mae Salyers and Jack Clowe, 1963.

I started yelling some lines myself. Finally, I had to go up the hill, go inside the Shelter House, and find the actor playing Brabantio, who was hiding in the corner. I said, "Come on, you've got to go." He said, "I can't remember my lines," and I said, "Well, you have to go. Say anything ... or, okay, don't say anything; just go on." Then I grabbed him and sort of dragged him down the hill. After that we got through the rest of it somehow.

It was very fun for me. I was a young man, and I enjoyed being onstage. I remember particularly in 1963 a production of *The Tempest*, in which I got to play Trinculo, which was a good comic character. We had a group of actors in from the theater department at the University of Kentucky that summer. Jack Johnson, who later went on to be in some movies in the 1970s, was a member of that group, and a girl named Pamela Brown. One of the theaters at Actors Theatre is named after her.

It was Doug Ramey's company. He was the producer and director in the early days. He was a very important actor in the productions.

He was still, nominally at least, the leader of the organization up until his death, which I believe was in the winter of 1979. Doug was an affable man, and he was an impressive actor. He had this wonderful bass voice, and he also had charm, which helped him in recruiting actors to work for him without making a lot of money for it. We were all fond of Doug.

John Gatton: Carriage House Players had been around since 1949. They hadn't been doing a lot of Shakespeare. They'd been doing [Henrik] Ibsen and modern plays, classical plays. Then in '60 or '61, they started doing Shakespeare. They were not a Shakespeare company. I joined in 1962. I was there when the stage was a boxing ring and the backdrop was a circus wagon. When you're sitting in the audience looking at the stage, the boxing ring and the circus wagon were to your right. They were a bit to the south, almost directly down from the pavilion. There were park benches. Some of the early actors were Doug Ramey, Diane Houghton, Richard Davis. That was an exciting time. We only did maybe two performances a week, and we might get rained out. But I was doing Shakespeare.

I liked the atmosphere of the Carriage House. It was on Fifth Street, south of Kentucky and Memorial Auditorium. Mr. Ramey lived upstairs. The stage was a concrete floor. There were platforms like a thrust stage. I think the chairs were folding director's chairs. In the summer, it was hotter than Hades. You'd go in and rehearse, and then you'd come out on the sidewalk on Fifth Street to walk up and down to cool off! The facade of the Carriage House was very nineteenth century. There was a metal ring, for tying up your horse.

Doug had his company of players: Liz Hoerth, Dennis Preston, George Hendon, Monte Priddy, who is still around. He's wonderful. I met him at that audition. He is the oldest surviving member. The voice that welcomes you at the beginning of the play, the recorded voice, is Monte's voice.

Doug wanted to have Shakespeare for people who couldn't afford it, who couldn't see it, for the people who lived around Central Park. We attracted a lot of kids, and maybe some yelled at us or made fun of us, but there were ones that were there for the summer, and they would come back. I'd love to run into one of those to see if they remember any of that. What influence, if anything, did those summers around a group of crazy people putting on Shakespeare have on them? Doug was encouraged sometimes to move out of Central Park and go to Cherokee. They don't have a space. It's wrong. They can come to us. We took plays to Shawnee Park. We took *Twelfth Night* out to Iroquois Amphitheater. All this was free. We took a play to Jenny Wiley State Park.[15] Doug had a school bus. We took the school bus to Frankfort. We had a folding stage. We set it up in front of the capitol. Doug was all about getting theater to people. He was from eastern Kentucky. We were doing repertory theater. A different play every week. At one point, we had an eight-week season. We did four different shows, a different show every week, and then we repeated.

I had wonderful big-name scholars as Shakespeare teachers in college and grad school, but I learned more from Doug Ramey in the park than I ever learned from them. Doug said Shakespeare was both an actor and a playwright. He knew the energy that the actor playing Hamlet and the actor playing King Lear would need to get through the last part of the play. He gave Lear and Hamlet a break. They don't show up for part of act 4. Doug would say, "I can't prove this, but they can sit down. They can go backstage and have a bonbon or something, and then they come back. Maybe not completely refreshed, but they're ready for the sword fights and the carrying of Cordelia and the emotion and all the rest of it." That was something else I liked about Doug. He knew his Shakespeare. He could sit on a bench in the park and say, whatever the line was, "The meter was off." But he wasn't somebody who stressed the iambic pentameter. He didn't want to hear the strict meter. He wanted to hear the conversations. He wanted the audience to be able to understand what's going on. If you're sacrificing clarity for the meter, then they might not get it.

He didn't trick up the shows. Well, one time *Much Ado* was set in a Spanish locale, and we had Spanish vests and whatnot. But most of the time it was tights and tunics and togas and sandals and all the rest of it. Well, when we did *Julius Caesar* [1972], in the part with all the conspirators, we all had white togas and we had to get sort of shoulder to shoulder because projecting from the back of the amphitheater there was this film footage of the assassinations of Robert Kennedy and Martin Luther King. I don't know if that worked or not. I'm not sure it was really necessary, but it was an interesting choice. I liked Doug's approach to Shakespeare. I liked his passion about it. I liked his demeanor. I think maybe I saw him get angry once or twice over the ten years that I was there. Very patient.

The Plot   51

Sometimes it could be fly by the seat of your pants. One time he came downstairs before a play started, he looked around in the audience, and he saw somebody he knew, and he came over and said something like, "How do you feel about playing Hamlet tonight?" I got a call in about 1964, early '65—I was still in high school—about two days before they were going to do *Macbeth*. It was Doug. "Are you free on such and such night? We need somebody to play Donalbain. It's one scene. It's about five lines. His brother Malcolm gets all the big parts." I said sure. The actor playing Malcolm walked me through the blocking. I did my lines. I don't remember staying for the curtain call. But that's in some ways the manner Doug had to work.

Later, he lost the Carriage House. It was bought by the Sons of the American Revolution, which had a big building on Fourth Street. They tore the Carriage House down.

Hal Park: Doug Ramey started it as a labor of love. Even when it was kind of ragtag and barely able to get up, it was done out of regard and respect for the art form and done out of regard and respect for the community of Louisville. That's why it has lasted. It's the oldest surviving free Shakespeare Festival in the country, and that's no small accomplishment, and it took a lot of people and a lot of good souls and a lot of help from the community to keep it that way.

Scene 2: New Directors, New Directions (1979–2008)

During the twenty years after Ramey's death in 1979, the Kentucky Shakespeare Festival had three producing directors with different styles who led the company in dissimilar directions. Ramey's handpicked successor was Bekki Jo Schneider, who had worked with him both onstage and behind the scenes since she was a teenager. She took the reins at a time when few women were in leadership positions in professional theater. Artists with the company in those years recall her ability to make a night in the park into a party, staging creative, fun events that drew large crowds to the performances. By her retirement in 1985, average attendance had gone from 350 to 850 people a night, the festival had added extra weeks, and the budget had climbed from $35,000 to $150,000 per season. Her replacement, Hal Park, a former actor with the company, came back to Louisville after having managed other Kentucky regional theaters. Park introduced more educational programs, supplementing the plays. He hired

52   Under the Greenwood Tree

the first dramaturg—Stephen Schultz, an associate professor of theater arts at the University of Louisville, who gave preperformance lectures—and organized a weekend-long Shakespeare Institute with events all around town cosponsored by a wide range of community partners. Park also created a high school apprenticeship program designed to help local young people learn the ropes of backstage theater work. In 1989, Curt Tofteland, another former actor with the company, stepped in to replace Park. Cast members recalled Tofteland's unique approach as a director committed to an ensemble style of rehearsing. His most significant contributions to the development of the company were the expansion of in-school performances and workshops that visited schools in nearly every county of the commonwealth and the creation of Shakespeare Behind Bars, a program that assists incarcerated men at the nearby Luther Luckett Correctional Complex to analyze and perform the Bard's plays.[16]

Monte Priddy: Doug stopped acting with the company in the early 1970s. His health was not good for the last nine or ten years of his life. But the show went on. He had people helping him as his health deteriorated. I was not there in '79. I found out that winter Doug had passed away. I came back in 1980 when Bekki Jo Schneider took over. She offered me the role of Falstaff in *The Merry Wives of Windsor*. Bekki Jo was there directing until '85.

Bekki Jo Schneider: When Doug died, he had basically left me the theater and said, "You can run it." For years and years and years in Louisville, being a woman in theater was easy. But being a woman in theater management was unheard of. There were very few women in Louisville, and very few women in the country, who either own their theater or manage their own. I think probably because women choose families and it's a full-time, over full-time, job. The five years I was producing, I would tie my son to a park bench so that he wouldn't get away. He was about four or five. He would watch the shows. [*Laughs.*] One day, I went to his school, and they were studying the alphabet. They said, "Your child has come up with a weird answer." I said, "What is it?" They said, "We were talking about words that begin with *M*, and his word was *Macbeth*." And I thought, "Oh, I'm doing everything right."

It was pretty exciting. When we did *The Tempest*, we flew people from the trees. We did all of that kind of stuff. That's pretty easy. The challenging ones are things like *Macbeth*, where it starts out dark but

The Plot 53

it's only six o'clock. Those are the challenges. Of course, my favorites were *Hamlet*—I did Ophelia—*Taming of the Shrew*, which I was supposed to do but came down with a problem with my gallbladder. I loved *Julius Caesar*; it is by far my most favorite of all. *Macbeth*. Just so many. *Twelfth Night*. We tried to do all those various ones and in fact were sure to throw in a history at least every year, or every other year. Audiences don't like histories as well; they don't want to think. Doug would do them. He would do the histories. I love Shakespeare's women, like Beatrice. You have these really, really fleshed-out roles.

The mayor lived directly across the street. On our opening nights, we would have parties at his house and invite the people who'd given us money. Then we would do things like have a bagpipe group lead us over to watch the show.

I left to buy Derby Dinner Playhouse. It had been going for ten years. I had so many friends who said, "I'm so embarrassed that you've given up real theater in order to build commercial." And I said, "I totally understand, but I want the money."

Jon Huffman: My first season was surprising to me because not only did it pay really well for those days but there were some really wonderful actors. Most of us were in our twenties. We did *The Tempest*. We did *Hamlet*, and I don't remember the third show we did. I was surprised and proud and pretty amazed by the level of talent. I discovered Bekki Jo was a really wonderful director, as well. Her vision was to create a professional company.

I think the best thing she did besides being a great director, besides attracting great talent, was how she was able to make the Louisville community involved. Whenever there was an opening of a show in Bekki's day, there were TV cameras all over the place. We were on the news every night. The feeling that the viewers had when they saw what Bekki would say and do on television was, "Hey, we're having fun in Central Park; this is a carnival. This isn't Shakespeare; it's like an amusement park. It is great theater. Come see us." I was amazed in those days. There were nights that we would have two thousand people in the audience. Now, this is before cable TV. This is when not everyone had air-conditioning in the summer, so there was an excuse to get out of the house. There was much less going on. We were the thing to do in Louisville on a summer night. It was really amazing, fantastic. I remember one night looking out and thinking, "There's only a

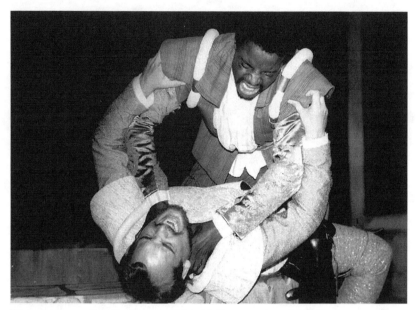

Victor Love as Othello (*top*) and Jon Huffman as Iago, 1983.

thousand people here; do we have to do a show?" That was really arrogant and stupid, but that's how exciting it was in those days.

I remember a time many years ago when Bekki Jo was the producer, and I can't remember the show we were doing, but we were young actors at the time. We decided over the course of the season that each night we would insert into the meter—the iambic pentameter, the rhythm of the poetry—each of us would try to insert the word *banana*. It was so much fun. If you do it right, the audience barely notices. One night I had a line that began "by yonder moon," and I said, "Banana moon," and no one noticed.

Georgette Kleier: The thing that Bekki Jo did so well is that she knew how to create this environment of fun. Even when I wasn't in the park in shows, I would go to the park and see them. It was simply fun. There's no more magical place than being on that stage once dusk begins to happen. It was quite amazing and quite moving.

Hal Park: I give Bekki Jo a lot of credit for really trying to help this company begin to stand on its own legs. Under Doug Ramey, God love

Bekki Jo Schneider handing off leadership to Hal Park, 1985.

him, it was always a catch-as-catch-can operation. He had somehow, out of his sheer will, willed it to stay around for twenty years. Bekki Jo brought a level of professionalism and fundraising to the production. It was still pretty ragtag, but I appreciated what she was doing with the festival. It showed me that there were people doing pretty good work out there in the park, and that was a good thing.

Bekki Jo would raise as much money as she possibly could from January to April or May, and then she would throw the show on. They would borrow a little money from the bank, and then they would spend the last half of the year—August, September, October, November, December—trying to raise money to pay off the note from the bank. My job as a producing director was to try to turn that around, and we did. By the time I left, we were closing the books on the previous season in September and then raising money October through March for the upcoming season. So we were paying our bills off by the end of that time, and we did that while I was there. As a producing director, what you do is you close the season and in September you start writing grants. We kept regular office hours, Monday through Friday, trying to raise money, having board meetings, reaching out to the community, sending out mailings—blah, blah, blah, blah, blah—into January.

By February, we were out auditioning. I would go to the Southeastern Theatre Conference and the Midwest Theatre Conference.[17] I'd go up to New York, and I'd go to Chicago. I'd hold local auditions here in Louisville. That was all about February and March, April. Meanwhile, we're raising money. By April, you're sending out invites to people. You're gathering your team together, the designers and the craftsmen and the actors and the guest directors and everything. Getting them ready to go. May is where you kind of put the bow on everything and get it all tightened up. Then come June, I'm through as the executive director.

There were successes and failures, of course. But the major success in the four seasons that I was there was we paid off all the debt of the company. I was there for 1985, '86, '87, '88. At the end of 1988, the company was in the best financial shape that it had ever been in. We had about a third of our funding already secured by the Fund for the Arts. We had a pretty strong fundraising program underway. Our debts were paid. We raised the money to terrace the audience and to put in the first lighting battens. We had updated all the electrical. I purchased the costume trailer, the tech trailer, even the little trailer in the back where they run the show from. The theater was in very good shape by the end of 1988.

We raised audience attendance up to around twenty-five or twenty-six thousand a season. When I first got there after Bekki Jo gave it over to me, I think we hit sixteen or seventeen thousand. We got it up to twenty-six thousand. We had what we call the Shakespeare Weekend, which was the final weekend of the season when we would put all three shows, one on a Friday night, one on a Saturday night, and the third one on a Sunday night.

We got our first National Endowment [for the Arts] funding ever during my time there, and that was a mixed blessing. It came with a lot of strings attached, shall I say. But we got it, and it was helpful, and I made sure that it supported the plays and not just the ancillary programming that went along with the plays. We had twelve productions, and we got twelve really nice reviews. That was back when the two papers were both reviewing shows. We raised our attendance. We definitely elevated the quality of the production. We did some really cutting-edge kind of stuff, and we paid our debts. We paid our debts, and that was good.

It fell apart after the summer of '88. We literally went from being in the strongest financial shape in the history of the organization to being in the worst financial shape in the history of the organization by March of the next year. It was very short lived. So that was a disappointment. We had done it. We'd reached it. We couldn't sustain it. I had a falling-out with the [board of] directors and chose to resign because of things that were going on there that I didn't agree with. Curt Tofteland, bless his heart, came in just before the start of the 1989 season and really had to try to pull something together and on a shoestring, unfortunately. I was sorry that that happened. It didn't have to go that way, but that's what happened.

Curt Tofteland: I took over as producing artistic director of Kentucky Shakespeare in 1989. The company was on the verge of bankruptcy, and I had one part-time bookkeeper. So that's how I started. It was a summer season only and in deep financial doo-doo. There's a lot of fundraising that has to happen because we are free. We give our product away. We have no earned income. That's one of the reasons I created the education program, because it became our earned income. We marketed it to the schools, and the schools paid for it. That paid for the expenses of sending the actors there. There was always money left over that I could use for the summer season. The summer season has always been the big black hole when it comes to economics. We've always needed money, and we've sometimes done things on a shoestring and a prayer. Much less so in my era because after Doug came Bekki Jo Schneider, who was a protégée of his, and she was a better businessperson. Doug was not a businessperson.

I was fiscally responsible. I can do the art because that's my specialty. But I also have a left brain, and I'm a fiscal conservative, and I don't make art unless I have the money to make the art. I make the best art with the money that I have. We're going to put something out there, and it's going to be creative, and it's going to be an artistic experience. But one year the budget might be $10,000 more or less than the year before, so you're always dealing with how to make art with a limited amount of resources.

Phil Cherry: Curt Tofteland gave me many wonderful opportunities with Kentucky Shakespeare Festival. I worked with other directors there as well, but I worked most with Curt. His process was totally different than a lot of directors I had worked with. He was all about ensemble. He was all about getting all the actors together, and before we would even pick up a script, we would be communicating verbally and nonverbally but not speaking the words of Shakespeare. The ensemble process dealt with the elements of performing. We would do our ensemble exercises that would help us relate to each other and feel good as a team. He was very much a stickler in that a lot of actors thought, "Wow, Curt's tough; I don't think I can work with him." He ran those ensemble exercises every morning before anything else happened on that stage. And some days it was hot. We worked over there at Saint Philip Neri's, and that church had no air-conditioning.[18] If there was [air-conditioning], Curt wouldn't allow us to turn it on anyway because he wanted us to get acclimated into the heat of working in the park. I think that's a good idea. I thought that was great. In the eighties when I worked over there with some other directors, we rehearsed out there on that hot stage, in the sun, and it was brutal. I was glad to be in Saint Philip Neri's with no air-conditioning working with Curt Tofteland. He strengthened everybody's minds before they'd pick up their script. Marsha Tofteland, his wife, was almost at every rehearsal. I learned a great deal of my exercises, ensemble exercises that I do with my students even today, from Curt Tofteland, doing ensemble. Not just from Curt but the ensemble circle. Anybody could bring in any exercise that they knew and teach it to the ensemble. We were doing amazing things.

Georgette Kleier: Back in the day, with Curt, you were required to be there all day. All, all, all day. As long as the rehearsal was, even if you had one small scene that he didn't get to until the afternoon, you were called at ten. Everyone was expected to do a group warm-up. That was the expectation. We did that, and then we just watched other people work. The idea was that we were all part of the creation of the piece. We would be in this pretty beat-up, pretty hot rehearsal hall and watch other people work. We did whatever we were brought in to do that day, and then if we were finished, we went and sat down and continued to watch people work until five. It was a fairly long day.

There was this sort of expectation that you were privileged to get work with this company. I did always feel that, that it was a privilege to be able to be a part of this company. I didn't take it for granted at all.

When I was doing *Romeo and Juliet* that summer, 2000, was when I was adopting my son, Miguel. My husband, Michael, was doing summer stock in New York, so I was here alone. We were rehearsing *R and J*, and I got a call that all of my papers, my adoption, all of my stuff had been lost in a fire. That was in the throes of one of Curt's rehearsals. I was so afraid to ask, but I needed to go and figure out what I needed to do to start that process over. He let me leave when I found out, which was really gracious of him. I was really thankful, because my initial response was "Oh my God, I'm not going to be able to leave and do this." That was during the rehearsal process. It was really wonderful because he did understand that he *needed* to let me go do this, to get all this stuff done, and I needed to be able to go to these government buildings and all of that. He was able to be generous as well, when he needed to be, in terms of people's time, and understanding that life happens outside of your rehearsal hall.

Tina Jo Wallace: Curt used to do something that was very different. I forget what he called it, maybe a renaissance run, where we would come in, we do table read, we talk and stuff, and then he would leave rehearsal, and we would do a rough staging of the show, the actors themselves, creating and showing it to him two days later or something. I remember just *dreading* that renaissance run! We didn't know what we were doing. We were making it up! There was value in that the company got really close really quickly because we all had to work together and create something. But it wasn't the same process as you do normally in a professional company. It was very different.

He also usually started the rehearsal process, before even the renaissance run, with what he called monologue work, and it wasn't necessarily from the show. He would have the actors come in and bring a monologue, and he would work through the monologue with them, in front of everybody else. He would work with you and give you notes and shape the monologue with you, and the other actors would watch! That was an interesting process because you would see how he worked. You'd also learn a lot about the actor who was being the guinea pig up in front of everybody. You learn a lot about their thought process and how they worked. It was very education driven. I feel like we had very, *very* professional shows when we were there. But it started out different than most processes do. Of course, at the time I was just nervous and excited and open. I feel like I learned a lot from that different rehearsal process.

60   Under the Greenwood Tree

Scene 3: "The Winter of Our Discontent"[19]

By the end of Tofteland's tenure, the Kentucky Shakespeare Festival slid into its "dark days." In the mid-1990s, the company performed just one play in the summer, and there were rumors that the festival might be removed from Central Park altogether. Tofteland justified the changes by pointing to the declining population in Old Louisville—from 35,000 people down to 12,500—and noting that for those who had moved to the suburbs, the trip to Central Park was just not appealing. Attendance was suffering. Donations were also falling, with the Old Louisville Neighborhood Association cutting its support by two-thirds. Because at that point the festival did not receive financial support from the city or county, Tofteland argued that free performances in the park might no longer be sustainable. Members of the acting company, on the other hand, blamed the director's preference for the educational and prison programs over being outdoors in the park setting.[20]

Morale declined further when Tofteland retired and the board of directors broke the tradition of hiring a new producing director from within the company or region. Instead they reached out to New York City and brought in Anthony Patton, the director of Ballet Hispánico. He did not last long. Finances continued to deteriorate, and Patton left in 2010 over "strategic differences." At that point, the board reached out to the West Coast and hired Brantley Dunaway, looking to him to revitalize the company. In summer 2013, Dunaway bragged that his fundraising efforts had put the company on solid financial footing. But he also suggested creating a ticketed summer festival to compete with similar events in Stratford, Ontario, and elsewhere, a threat to the cherished tradition of free Shakespeare in Central Park. Moreover, his directing approach alienated many of the key players in the company, some of whom accused him of abusive behavior and financial mismanagement. Indeed, the local public radio news station discovered that employees had filed a long list of complaints with the board of directors. Ultimately, a messy conflict between Dunaway and his wife caused a scandal that brought the festival to the edge of collapse and an end to his tenure in 2013.[21]

Monte Priddy: Hal Park was there about '85 to '88. Then Curt Tofteland took over in 1989. We had for years done three shows a summer. After Curt had been there for a year or two, he reduced that to two and then one show a summer. It was simply a problem with economics, paying for it. They did a lot of tours of schools. They played a lot of local schools. That paid for itself. But the productions in the park did not pay for themselves. We needed to raise a lot of money for that.

Jon Huffman: Curt's vision was very different than Bekki Jo's. He hated working outside. He hated the location. He really was into educational theater. He began the educational arm of Kentucky Shakespeare, which is very valuable and does great work all over the region today. But he did that at the expense of the summer program in the park. I worked Curt's first season and decided, okay, this is different, and this is not what I'm looking for. I didn't come back for eighteen years. I did other things. I came back in his second-to-last season, and it was really different. We were only doing one show in the summer. We only ran it for three weeks. There were only four of us getting paid, which I didn't know when I started. I was told everyone was getting paid. If I had known I was one of the few getting paid for what I was doing, I would've taken something else because I would've felt guilty. But it was not a pleasant experience.

Abigail Maupin: We did the spring tour in 2004, and it was good. In the midst of that spring, Curt announced that their summer show was going to be *Othello* that year. We auditioned for it.

Gregory Maupin: At some point, they canceled one of the shows. There was going to be an *Othello* and *All's Well*. I'm not sure what the financial reason was but they canceled *All's Well* and decided just to do *Othello*. That was sort of the beginning of the one-show summers. They had three-show summers in the past, and then they were two-show summers for a long time. I think the finances for the second show falling through for *All's Well* happened at the beginning of one-show summers that lasted for quite a while.

Abigail Maupin: I got cast as Emilia for that summer production. We started rehearsals and immediately had a couple bad things happen: The actor playing Brabantio got hurt. He ripped his Achilles tendon or something in rehearsal. Greg came in to play that.

Gregory Maupin: Also the guy playing Iago . . .

Abigail Maupin: Just ghosted us, really.[22]

Gregory Maupin: He wanted to have a weekend off for a potentially very lucrative short-term audition. He would just leave town for two days and come back. Curt said no and he left town anyway. Except, he didn't come back. He just decided he would go and do this other thing. The whole cast shuffled. Jack Lewis was playing Roderigo, and he became Iago. David Kranowski ended up playing Roderigo. I came in to play Brabantio, which I'm still slightly young to be playing fifteen years later, but that's what shoe whitener is for.

Abigail Maupin: I had some issues with Mr. Tofteland that summer. I know I'm not the only woman who ever has been treated poorly by Curt Tofteland. It culminated in a situation where I was feeling very humiliated and feeling like I was being lied about to other people. That was very much part of his need for control, and a need for control that I only ever saw him exert over women, other women and myself. I want to say that was really, in my storied career, my long years of being an actor, that was really the first and worst. So, after *Othello* was over, they asked us to come back and do the school tour again in the fall. We said, "No, we will not work for your company as long as Curt Tofteland was there."

Gregory Maupin: Well, in fairness, what we actually said was we would happily do the educational tour if we know that we will be working just with Doug Sumey and Matt. Doug very reasonably said, "You realize that is an unreasonable request." We said, "We do realize that is an unreasonable request, but we wanted to go ahead and make the point of making it anyway." We didn't really work full on for the company as actors again for the next six years.

Jon Huffman: The board of directors, when Curt left, with his help, decided the only way to bring in a new artistic director was to look out of town. They found a guy from New York and brought him in, and it turns out he had lied on his résumé and what he had done and who he was. It was a terrible experience. Then they said, "Okay, we'll go the other way," and they hired a guy out of Los Angeles who bragged about all the movie stars he was going to bring and didn't. There were some money problems I don't know much about except it was a mess.

Honestly, the last production I did before Matt took over was [with] the previous administration. I did a production of *Measure for Measure* that was god awful. It didn't work and got very low numbers in terms of audience. We were all kind of embarrassed to be onstage every night.

Monte Priddy: Anthony Patton was here for just one year as director, producing director. Then Brantley Dunaway came in. The organization was taken over by outsiders when Brantley Dunaway arrived. He made a point of not hiring local people, or if he hired a few local people, it would be at reduced pay and reduced status. He insisted on Equity actors, union actors. You would think this would make the production better, but I didn't notice much, in fact, if any, improvement.

Tom Luce: Toward the end of Curt Tofteland's tenure, Kentucky Shakespeare had really gone downhill. That's the only way you can really describe it. They had always done three shows during the summer. There was even one year, or actually maybe a couple years, where they did four shows during the summer. But he had cut it back to two shows, and then it was really just one show, and it wasn't even a full production. The quality of the productions had really, really, really gone downhill. He had hired a lot of out-of-town actors, which was fine. That's how I got here. I can't really say that's a bad way to do things. But there was just so much local talent that wasn't being utilized, and as a result, the quality of the productions really went downhill. The audiences were really, really, really down. So financially it wasn't quite where it needed to be.

When he left, they hired a guy from New York. There were several of us who wrote to the board of directors and said, "Please hire Matt Wallace." He's an actor himself. He's a good actor, but he also likes actors. Because there are a lot of actors who go into directing, producing, who might have a little resentment toward actors who haven't given up the dream, so to speak. Matt was a fine, fine actor, and he's a great director. This might be hearsay. It might not be exactly how things happened. But Matt was the second choice. Apparently, this guy from New York had lied on his résumé, is what I heard. He got fired after one year. We thought, "Great, Matt was the second choice, so now Matt is going to be it." But, no, they hired Brantley Dunaway from California, from Los Angeles. If you recognize the last name, it's because he is Faye Dunaway's nephew. I talked to a board member.

64   Under the Greenwood Tree

They said, "We realize we made a mistake, but we did it because we were looking for pizzazz"—that was the exact word he used. That's why he got hired.

I auditioned for him one year, and he started whistling in the middle of my audition. I've heard this from other people who've actually been cast. He just treated them with disdain. He was there for four years. They were still only doing one show per year. He was hiring a lot of his friends from LA and paying them a lot of money. Apparently, his wife had an affair, or was having an affair, with the leading man in the play. When Mr. Dunaway found out about it, he had a confrontation with his wife. She responded by filing a restraining order against him a week before the season ended. What that meant was he could not be x number of yards from her, which meant that they could not be in Central Park at the same time, which meant they had to cancel the final week of the summer season that year. It was quite a fiasco.

Brenda Johnson is a longtime volunteer who manages the merchandise table at every summer performance.

Brenda Johnson: Dunaway was charging money for front-row seats at a theater that was always supposed to be free. He brought in these special chairs, Adirondack chairs. He did stuff like that. Why he was ever allowed to do stuff like that, I don't know. So that's the first time in all the years that I did not go at all. I didn't go see the play; I didn't volunteer or anything. It hurt a lot of people's feelings, especially people who lived in that neighborhood who went there all the time. It felt like it was their park, and to me it was a real disappointment. That board of directors let something disgrace something that had been so wonderful for that area, that neighborhood.

Abigail Maupin: When Curt was leaving and Matt should have gotten the job at that point, I pretty much closed the door. I had been working with Matt a lot at Derby Dinner, doing kids' shows for him. He was directing a lot there. I took that very like, "They've made the wrong decision, and they're idiots." I get very het up about these things. I was like, "I'm not going to see shows there. I'm not going to be auditioning" and blah, blah, blah.

The Plot   65

Gregory Maupin: It's not this new guy's fault. But then we met Anthony Patton. I swear, when we met him, we had just finished a show at the Rudyard Kipling, and he literally came in and he was wearing a turtleneck and a tweed jacket. [*Laughs.*][23]

Abigail Maupin: It was Louisville in the late spring, which is hot. You should never judge a person on a thing like that. You should never judge a person for wearing a turtleneck and a tweed jacket, but, man, it was hard not to. He had this sort of air like he was a professor from Yale Drama School and not that he was the facilities manager of a dance company on Long Island, which is what I understand is actually true.

Gregory Maupin: He was trying to present impressiveness. I understand that that can be effective in certain places. If you have chosen a life in the theater, you get used to a level of pretentiousness, which I'm sure we both also have in our own way. It certainly can be turned on when you need to. You don't take things like that too hard. We got a snoot, whatever. The checks still clear. But it was after the 2004 summer that we developed our graph: the x and y axis of total jerk and real mensch and terrible director, genius. Bad to genius, sweetheart to evil. There's the unspoken axis of "How much are they paying you?" You'll work in the quadrant of someone who is a sweetheart and an okay director, and you'll work in the quadrant of "He's a jerk, but he does magnificent work." You'll figure out a way in those quadrants. You'll hope for the sweetheart, good director. You just learn to never again work in the "This guy is a hack, and he's also a jerk" zone. I don't need to do that.

We had a bad taste in our mouth after some of the stuff that happened when Patton was here. He was only here for one year for all kinds of apparently shady reasons on his part. We didn't go to the shows. Then he was gone. In 2010, Matt came in to do *Richard III* because it was sort of an interim time. We were all set to audition for Brantley Dunaway, but we were not getting a good vibe. Brantley was supposed to show up in September and showed up about two weeks before *Richard* opened and started to undercut the whole production in a lot of ways. A lot of weird, silly ways. It's very common for the director to give your standard opening night pep talk thing, and on opening night, he said that he would like to do it. He called us all in a circle. None of us knew him. We had barely been introduced to him. He was not particularly socially forthcoming with anyone in the cast that I'm aware of. He was then like, "Fuck the blocking. It's just you here in this moment." It was your usual actor claptrap, but coming from a stranger, it's super strange. There was a moment where he said, "I know some of you probably have your process, so if you want to go . . .," and before the sentence was finished, five people just peeled off at a run. [*Laughs.*] Abigail's legs are a lot shorter than Dathan [Hooper]'s, but they were together on that way out.[24]

Abigail Maupin: Brantley Dunaway just came and took over something that was not his place to take over.

Gregory Maupin: He wouldn't make eye contact with any of us, in a way that I took as none of us are ever getting hired here. It's so common in so many businesses. New guy comes in; new guy brings in his people. That's how things go. We were like, "Well, so much for that." Then we kind of didn't follow any of it until the great implosion.

Matt Wallace: I really, really wanted to be the artistic director of Kentucky Shakespeare. I applied in 2008 when Curt was retiring and they did a national search, and I made it toward the end of the process. I was in the top three or something and didn't get it. There was a person from New York who was here, and he left after a year. Then they were going to do another search, and I said, "I want to throw my hat in the ring." They said they didn't need to see me for an interview. I knew at that point my dream of that was gone. I'm like, "They're going to hire another person. I'm never going to get a chance at that." I had to let that go emotionally.

That was where Curt and I asked permission from the board of directors to take Shakespeare Behind Bars independent. It wasn't being valued like we thought it should. God love Matt Thompson, the board chair at that time, who let us take it. We got to take Shakespeare Behind Bars, and we created a not-for-profit. That and Derby Dinner Playhouse is what I did in those three years. I'm so glad I didn't get the job, because I spent three years building a not-for-profit, producing the Children's Theater Series and directing at Derby Dinner Playhouse, and being mentored by Bekki Jo Schneider for three years at a for-profit theater. Working with Curt Tofteland, creating a not-for-profit, creating a dozen programs for the incarcerated, writing

The Plot   67

grants to employ myself, and gaining *all* of these business skills that I was doing for three years. Being totally fulfilled artistically. Learning about customer service. Directing more Shakespeare plays. Spending *years* on Shakespeare, days and hours, dissecting it with Shakespeare Behind Bars.

But it was hard to truly say goodbye to Kentucky Shakespeare. This is where I met my wife and proposed to her. It was truly a dramatic breakup. I threw away everything I owned of Kentucky Shakespeare. I think I kept one shirt—from our first summer—but I had to get rid of it all. I emotionally just had to distance myself, particularly as I would hear changes that were made in the company that were the *opposite* of what was in my heart for the vision of the company, like charging admission for the first five rows. Those were twenty-five dollars a seat, and you would have bar service and food service. Those were really things that just struck to my core. That made it so much easier to leave. Oh, so the board wants *that*? Or you want to hire this type person, and you want it to be this? That makes it easy. But emotionally, it was very hard just to know the summer was coming around. For three years, we didn't come in the park.

When I resigned from the board, that was the summer before Brantley Dunaway had been hired. They asked me to direct the fifti-eth-anniversary production of *Richard III*. That was sort of my farewell to the company. It started as a really special experience because I got some of the old band back together! [*Laughs.*] Some of the people that you see on the Kentucky Shakespeare stage, right now, those are some of the people who also hadn't been working with the company as much anymore. I said, "Well, you want to come back? And you? And hey— and you!" We did it the way we wanted. I felt like it was this love letter saying goodbye to Kentucky Shakespeare. We got a real live horse in the production! I called in every favor I had on that production. That was my farewell.

Amy Attaway: I hadn't seen Kentucky Shakespeare in a while. Period. I had met Brantley, and I had seen a show his first summer. Michael DeWhatley had been my intern at Actors Theatre, and then he was the production manager at Kentucky Shakespeare that summer in 2013 with Brantley. I was out of town, and Michael and I were still in touch. He's my friend, in addition to having been my intern. He starts texting me, "This is, this is terrible. Something's really wrong here. There's no money, and no one's talking to each other. And no one seems to be in charge. There's this big set. There's a fountain. I don't know what I'm supposed to do." I'm like, "I am in Washington State. I can't help you. Go get 'em, tiger; you can do it!" I kept saying, "Who else is there other than Brantley?" And he said, "Well, there's this Rob [Silverthorn], who's the director of operations." I said, "Can this Rob person talk to the board? Is there anyone that you can go to who can take it up the ladder?" Because this sounds terrible. This was the beginning of the summer. When the shit actually hit the fan and they closed the show, then I'm getting, "There's no plan for how to get this set off the stage. What am I supposed to do now?" I was like, "I'm so sorry. I can't help you." So that was what I knew about the big crash-and-burn summer, just Michael's text messages. I was literally across the country. I was sad because I've had those beautiful memories of Kentucky Shakespeare when I was a kid, and I've loved the mission even then, before I was a part of it. I was like, "Man, that used to be a really good theater. That's really sad." That was my reaction.

Scene 4: Renaissance (2013–present)

But the story has a happy ending. Searching for a new producing director after Dunaway's abrupt departure, the board looked within and to the longtime cast member recommended by previous directors as well as many of the players: Matt Wallace. Once in charge, Wallace brought a new energy to the company and drew back many disenchanted local artists. He launched an ambitious 2014 season and started hearkening back to the Bekki Jo Schneider years with preshow performances by local arts groups, community outreach, and a festive atmosphere. People associated with Kentucky Shakespeare, from board members to actors to costume and light designers, remember the next couple years as a rebirth of Shakespeare in the Park.

Gregory Maupin: It was my understanding that Bekki Jo Schneider and Curt both almost literally went with one hand on each of Matt's shoulders and shoved him forward to the board and said, "This guy. We two former artistic directors say this is the direction that you should be going in." The board went, "We will consider that." Twice. And didn't do it until the third time. I was shocked, frankly, that it worked out the third time. But it did, and I'm glad.

Jon Huffman: Throughout this period, I had moved back to Louisville from Los Angeles and worked full time mostly as a writer. I had occasion to talk with some of the board members at the time, and I kept telling them Matt Wallace is here and wants this job. It's his dream job. All he wants to do, and he's perfect for it because he knows the town, he knows the talent, and he's a brilliant guy. It took them a while. I wasn't the only one saying this, by the way, to board members. Finally, they offered him the job. When the financial situation was in shambles, when they were an inch from being sued by all their creditors, and when it looked like it was going to crumble and disappear, Matt Wallace came in with this enthusiasm and his vision and his genius and took it over.

Matt Wallace: Cut to three years later when the company was having some public turmoil and going through another time of transition. I remember hearing a lot about bits and pieces of the things over the past three years and mainly just being really sad for the company and thinking, "Is this going to be the end of it?" They canceled the run early. It was smeared in the media. There are different allegations of things that have happened or what's going on. I turned from "Oh my gosh, that's juicy; what's going on?" to "Oh my God, this is *sad*. This is horrible! This is going to be the legacy of Curt and Bekki and Doug Ramey and all these people." I remember reaching out to the board chair at that time, and all I said was, "Is there something we can do in the community?" Some of us were talking about just doing a reading of Shakespeare somewhere. There was a movement of some other people who were saying, "Well, let's do Shakespeare in the Park in other parks," or "Let's go do something!" I remember them asking me to be part of that, saying, "Do you want to do *this*?" I was like, "No, I don't want to. It's not just doing Shakespeare in *a* park that's important to me. It's Kentucky Shakespeare Festival. It's Shakespeare in *Central* Park."

Anyway, I did not expect that he would say, "Do you want to come and talk?" The board chair called me in to meet, and he was more or less asking me if I wanted to be the producing artistic director. I'm just floored. Here's that dream job that I always wanted, but now I've got my own life. We had built up Shakespeare Behind Bars and Derby Dinner Playhouse and all of that. I have two children. It was really weird timing. Do I want to open this box? Do I want to go back to this? I love this company so much, but I need to see what the damage

70   Under the Greenwood Tree

is. I asked a lot of questions. I asked to see a lot of stuff, to see how bad the financial situation was, and it was pretty dire. They asked me if I wanted to be the *interim* artistic producing director. I said, "Absolutely not."

I remember telling one of the board members on the phone, "I think this might be the stupidest thing I've ever said, but I want you to vet me. I want you to do a full search. Open up a search for this position. Because if I get this, I want to get it the right way and I want to make sure you're vetting me." Because the other two people, I don't feel like they were vetted, and that was the problem. "So please vet me, talk to people, whatever. Let's do a search the right way." Then they did. It was quick! I interviewed, and I remember telling them that one of the things I wanted to do was get rid of the Adirondack chairs. [*Laughs.*] I wanted to embrace our mission and get back to serving people!

I think that's not the direction that some of them wanted to go. I think they sort of had this vision of the company, and the strategic plan was to buy this building down on Fourth Street and do an indoor theater and maybe do ticketed shows. The strategic plan at that time, that I read, was to become a destination theater and a tourism hub. I said in my interview, "I don't think you can become a destination tourism hub by doing one play in the summer." That's what was going on. The company was doing one play in the summer for three or four weeks and a student play for a week. When I interviewed back in 2008, I had printed out a rehearsal schedule because I *knew* we could do three plays in the same amount of rehearsal time we were doing one. I had that outline. When I came back to it, it was that same thing. I think we can do this with one company. This is just like the company used to do in the old days! They'd do three shows.

That first year in Kentucky Shakespeare was the worst year of my life. They offered it. I accepted it. Then I really started to uncover what I was walking into, and it was much more than what I thought. I remember first trying to find my way to the office. There were all of these programs blocking the door from the canceled performances. We had a small staff of two or three who had been through a lot. I really tried to give them a voice and to take care of them and at the same time assess where I was. I uncovered *more* money that the company owed than I thought. I was clearing the desk and asked one of my folks here, "What's that?" and they said, "Oh, that's one of the lawsuits." It's a lawyer writing to us for payment on a two-hundred-dollar bill.

I'm like, "Okay, pay that!" It was like digging out. I remember at the end of my first day at the end of July 2013 just being so overwhelmed. I didn't know if I could do it. It was just devastating realizing how deep in trouble this company was. I remember having to answer the phone from all the media asking about me getting the job. I think that's where a lot of the actor skills kicked in. I had to smile and, "Well, we've got a lot to do, but we're going to roll our sleeves up, and we're going to . . ." [*Laughs*] while *it's on fire*! I discovered in that first week I think one hundred thirty thousand dollars in debt that hadn't been paid, including payroll taxes to the IRS that hadn't been paid.

At the end of that first day, I went to Tina, and I said, "Let's just go to the park." Tina and my two daughters met at the park, and we got ice cream and went back out there, just to be there and connect with, why are we there? My daughter Anna ran up onstage. She was tiny, like two or three. She ran up, and I said, "Go do some Shakespeare onstage!" She ran up onstage and said, "Let slip the dogs of war!" [*Laughs.*] It was that battle cry that gave me some energy.

Then each day I was just trying to do as much as I could, trying to chip away as much as I could. Trying to reach out to the community and, hopefully, restore some of the reputation. I tried to meet with the neighborhood councils and to be authentic and passionate about what we're doing. I was trying to be inclusive and transparent. At the same time trying to quickly and quietly clean up the mess. To *not* say, "Oh yeah, we owe—" but "Guess what? We're going to get on a payment plan with the IRS and get in good standing." Okay, check! We're in good standing. Okay, let's get the board rallied around "let's clear that debt!" Okay, within that first year—boom—that's gone! I knew right away we had to roll up our sleeves and get earned income coming in, so I used my old booking-manager skills from Chicago getting some quality educational programming, getting that earned income coming in. I knew that we were really on the ropes and had to do something— had to do something *big*. It was time to implement that plan of doing the three plays plus the guest partners. I knew we sort of needed to come out with something bold but something we could achieve.

It was a very scary time. I had a lot of health issues. It wore me down health-wise and anxiety-wise. I think the only thing that got me through was just thinking, "I'm going to give this one year. This isn't my life." I wouldn't sleep, and I would wake up dry heaving many mornings, just not knowing if I could do it.

I met with some of my stakeholders and just said, "Okay, here's the budget, here's what we need to raise, here's what it's going to cost, and let's do it!" In November, we announced that we were doing eight productions that year. It was going to be our three professional productions, student productions, four guest productions. We got to that summer season, and we decided to partner with the Food Truck Association, so we added food trucks. We refined the bar. We had the full Brown-Forman bar. We added the preshows and all of those things. We were trying to make it more inclusive. I started to really think about what's keeping people away, and one of them was [people having trouble] hearing, so we added wireless microphones that summer. So those were the first big changes we made. That summer we went from forty-eight hundred audience members in 2013 to twenty-seven thousand audience members that summer. It worked! They came!

What's so fun about coming back together is all those people who ended up working with us. The theater community at that point was just so broken with Kentucky Shakespeare. During that off period, many of the actors were jobbed in from out of town and the designers were jobbed in. A lot of money was spent bringing outside talent, so in that fall, we had a welcome-back barbeque. We got Mark's Feed Store in the park, and *anybody* who had worked with the company came out.[25] We told some stories, and I sort of gave my pitch that I needed these people. There were some great pictures because I was very thin because I was so sick! [*Laughs.*] God, I looked good.

Tina Jo Wallace: We talked *so* many times about, well, if we were ever running it, what would we do? We dreamed a lot. We talked about ideas and things that could happen. What if we did this? We had a lot of time to imagine what would happen if one or both of us ever went back there. But because of the times that it *didn't* happen, that he didn't get the job, we kind of were resigned that we weren't going to be there. It was very sad for me because that was like our home. Not only did we have a connection with it through our mentor, who we were working for at Derby Dinner—Bekki Jo—we *cared* so much about the company and kind of hated that we weren't involved. We had just kind of had settled ourselves to it, so when he got the job, there was this final "Oh my gosh, finally this seems right!"

It was so stressful that first year. It was very hard. Not for us personally. Not for us as a family. It didn't affect our family. It was just so

The Plot   73

stressful for Matt. I'm just really grateful that we got through that! There were days where he was like, "I can't be there. I don't think I can do this." We worked through it, and he went back the next day. But that first year, with financial things and finding out things that needed to be fixed and things that were problems—bad will had been generated. He was trying to fix *all* of that in a quick second. It was *extremely* difficult. But he did it! Slow and steady. He is still working and fixing and hoping to make everything better every day. But that first year was—I won't lie—it was a mess! [*Laughs.*] It made him physically ill. But he made it through, and it is healthier than ever now.

Tom Luce: When they offered Matt interim artistic director, to his credit, Matt said no. "If you want me, I will be your artistic director. But I will not be your interim artistic director." He took it over. Because Mr. Dunaway hadn't been paying some of the bills he was supposed to pay, there was a pretty significant deficit when Matt took it over. Matt turned it around. He turned around the quality of the productions, number one, and went back to doing three productions per summer. He treated his actors with love and care. Just turned around the quality, turned around the finances. It's always probably going to be a difficult thing to keep such a huge thing going. But he's just done such a fantastic job with that.

Matt made it his, I wouldn't say his mission, but he hired as many local actors as he could. If the casting needs required a specific type, he was not opposed to hiring somebody from out of town, but he made every attempt to have most of the company be local. It was easy for him to do because all the local actors just had nothing but respect and love for him. If he asked do you want to come work for him, you're not going to say no. In [the] past couple years, it's been ninety to ninety-five percent of the company, including crew, have been local. And the audiences have started coming back. I know the audience numbers had dwindled. If you look at it from the early nineties to before Matt took over, it's a steady decline in audience numbers. From almost the moment he took it over, the numbers have just started climbing again.

Abigail Maupin: I did not go back until the summer of '10, when Matt directed *Richard III*. I had been working with him on and off on other projects. When he was going to take over and do that production that summer, he pretty much called me and Greg and said, "You guys going

74   Under the Greenwood Tree

to come be in my play?" And we said okay. He did make us come in and audition. He said, "I have to do it rules-wise. I'm not allowed to just ask people to be in it. So can you come do a monologue for me?" Yeah, of course. We did that show, and it was lovely and fun and was one of those things that made me go, "Oh, right. I do love Shakespeare. I love working with Matt. I love being outside in this amphitheater. I'm in love working with this particular group of people." Matt and Amy are very good at getting groups of people together who are lovely to work with, which makes a huge difference. That happened, and it was like, "Right, my love for it is back." But then he did not get the artistic director job, and we felt a little, I don't know, loyal. "Okay, it's not going to be Matt; then screw you." We went and did some other work here and there and did some other things, and then when '14 rolled around and he took the job back and he was like, "Okay, guys." Ring, ring, ring. "Hello? You coming to work with me again?" We all know of course we are.

Paul Owen: [After Matt took over,] we rebuilt the Central Park stage. We were eliminating the stage house and taking it a little bit at a time and reexamining it to make it more part of the park itself, of nature. For instance, we created wings for actors to be able to get on and off stage without being seen. There are hedges that are a combination of structure and AstroTurf. They look like hedges. They are scenery, but they don't look like scenery. They look like part of the park itself. We wanted to incorporate the three trees that anchor the stage house. The stage house more or less covered and put the center tree into a different perspective, and now it's much more dominant. That was important. I left it in the experimental stage, and it is sort of up to Matt and designers that he has which way they want to take it.

Amy Attaway: That first summer was magical. The audiences were huge. Everyone was so happy. The company was so happy. Matt has so much energy, and he's so positive. Everyone felt like we were on a mission together that first summer. I was pregnant, and it was the first trimester, so I couldn't tell anyone that I was pregnant. I was sick and miserable, but I was still on the journey. I was in the mission with everybody. This company of actors is incredible. That was palpable. The next year, both of the successive years after that, everyone just felt more stable. The tech side of things continued to get more stable. The designers haven't

The Plot

Ariel flies in *The Tempest*, 2015.

changed much, but I could see just as director that the people in the room were more comfortable and took more ownership even as we went along, which was great. Some physical things like the sound system got better. We got that new truss the year of *The Tempest*. That was a huge deal. Brian, my husband, advised on that a little bit because he did the flying.[26] That feeling of being in the park, when the audience is there, and the feeling of hearing Shakespeare's words with the crickets and the cicadas and the very happy people has never changed. It's just gotten better.

Georgette Kleier: I think that this idea of creating an experience beyond what happens on the stage for people, Matt has done that really well. This idea of the preshows and all of that that he's got going on, and community involvement, and bringing in other companies to do work, that is creating an experience that goes beyond just the presentation of the play. I think he's done that really well. I do believe that that's what Bekki did. I'm sure her way of presenting Shakespeare was gleaned from her mentor, Doug. I think that Matt has a direct sort of mentorship from Bekki in this particular piece of it, this idea of creating this event that goes beyond just the play itself and creates something really fun that people want to be a part of. Matt has really honored Bekki Jo with that idea and then taken it even further now with creating this whole evening that involves the entire family instead of just people coming down at promptly the beginning of the play and promptly leaving after. People are down there an hour and a half before, having dinner, watching a preshow, walking around the park before they see the show. It's just a completely different fun environment. What a great way to experience Shakespeare, you know? My God, make it fun for everybody.

Jon Huffman: The renaissance was almost immediate in terms of the community's reception of what we did in the park. I think audiences really sensed that something new was going on. We were using a company made of mainly local actors but professionals who people know, who people have seen, and they wanted to see them do this. Matt is not only a great director and producer; he's also a great PR guy. He will get out, and his enthusiasm will bring people in. Today, you wouldn't even know what it had been in its final season when they had to close down before the season was over because of scandal, because of money problems. They shut it down, and it looked like Kentucky Shakespeare was ending. Six years later, it's a force in America in terms of Shakespeare production. I spoke to a couple last year after a show who come from Missouri every year. They don't know anybody here or in the company, but they come to our shows because they had heard such good things about them, and now this is what they do in the summer. They come see our shows. I'm floored when I hear those kinds of stories. Especially considering where it was just six years ago. That's the change that has taken place.

Act 2

Putting Shakespeare on Its Feet

Hal Park summed up how to present the iconic, and to some people intimidating, works of William Shakespeare: "If you have good craftsmen onstage who are speaking their words well and you have a director that's not covering them up with a lot of goop, the audience will get it." Each of the narrators elaborated on Park's insight, painting detailed portraits of their own and shared processes of creating the art that is presented to audiences, producing the most vivid insights into the experience of Shakespeare in the Park. This chapter begins at the beginning, telling the story of how the season is prepared, from the selection of the plays to the casting process and different approaches to rehearsals. That story culminates in the jitters of opening night. Directors and designers then explain how they create a vision and environment for the play and how the outdoor setting affects that process. Finally, the actors illustrate their practices for embodying the characters, emotions, and story. For all of them, from directors to costume designers, the creative process begins with Shakespeare's lyrical poetry and prose. Starting with the words, they build the world and welcome audiences into it.

Scene 1: Preparing to Play

Matt Wallace: Getting the season together is quite a planning process. I will have ideas of what I want to do a few years in advance. But that's all subject to change depending on what's going on in the world, such

78   Under the Greenwood Tree

as what other theaters are doing. I kind of have a rough idea for a few years of what I want to do, but that's also very flexible. The planning in earnest happens about a year in advance. I do try to secure the actors earlier than we used to and that other theaters do. For a summer, I might try in November and December to have auditions, callbacks, and by the holidays have those offers finalized so that I can try to lock them in. A big change that we've tried to make—and getting back to how the company started—is using locally based professional talent. There's so much good talent here; there's so many people who grew up here who are so talented and people who've chosen to relocate here. The past two summers, at least ninety-seven percent of our hires have been locally based. We want to keep that.

We're often casting three plays at the same time. I usually know [if I want them] within about ten seconds, with how they're playing the text. Our rehearsal process is pretty quick because we're mounting three shows. I'm looking for somebody who can handle the text and maybe get out of the way of the text. Someone who makes it look easy. That being said, I have no qualms about casting somebody who's never done a Shakespeare play. I think if you're a good actor, you're a good actor. We often cast people who haven't done Shakespeare. But if we can see that spark in them—and a lot of times it is "Do they fit the need of what we're looking for?"

Tina Jo Wallace: You're limited to a certain number of plays that were written. You have to consider what the audience has already seen, what they've seen recently, what we want to give them, but also that we have to get people there because if we don't get people in the park, then you don't raise money, and then you can't pay for the next season. It is a delicate balance to find the right number of comedies that are going to draw people in. Matt really cares about showing the audience something new that they haven't seen, or something they haven't seen in a long time, or giving them a different take on something that they've seen. He's looking at the next five years. He's not looking at this season. He's looking at, "If I did this this summer, then what other options do I have for the next five summers?"

[When it came to casting,] Curt had people he knew were interested and had worked there several times. Then every year he had open-call auditions for locals because you never know, there might be people who haven't had an opportunity to work there before. Matt does the same thing. He has open calls every year. Curt would call me in and say, "Okay, these are the shows we're doing this year, and this is what I have to offer you. You can play this part and this part." I was very lucky that I got to work and do some really amazing things. I also played small roles. Both Matt and Amy [Attaway] do a great job of making sure that someone's not playing a lead in three shows or a lead in two shows in a row because physically, that's incredibly demanding in the heat, in the summer, and in the short amount of rehearsal time that you have. You usually have one lead role in a show and then maybe one that's a smaller part in another show so that you're not carrying all the weight.

The hard thing is that there's some seasons where they might not have a role for someone who's worked with them before. But it doesn't mean they won't work there again. Matt particularly is very interested in diversity, and so he's always looking at that. He's trying to bring in new people and finding them either through local calls or reaching out to the region and saying, "Hey, we're looking for people; will you come audition?" It's not done in a week—that's a long process.

Abigail Maupin: When they tell us what the season is, generally, if you're like, "I really want to play Iago. Can I come in and read for you?" They're like, "Of course you can." They still hold open auditions every year. There tends to be, for the real fancy roles, a callback. I went in to read for Rosalind because I wanted to. But I think most of the time, they already have an idea of how they're going to jigger the casting for the summer because it's a repertory summer and that gets tricky. There's a lot of math that has to go into figuring out the season and figuring out who your company is, because we do have a regular company. Who's going to be available next summer? Who had a big part this summer? I know Matt and Amy try to do what they call big, medium, small. They try to give everybody something fancy and then something that's fun but not carrying a show. Then something that's "you've done enough work for the summer, you have no lines, you're just in an outfit." The spear-carrier stuff. They try to be good about that. Of course, the math doesn't always work. But I think the season idea comes first because we're working with a limited canon. You don't want to do *Hamlet* every other year. That would get old real fast. Although I don't think an audience would mind if we did *Midsummer* or *Much Ado* every year, because everybody loves those plays.

80   Under the Greenwood Tree

Jon Huffman: Usually in the December before, they have auditions for the upcoming season. We have a really, really talented group of core actors who have been with Matt and Amy for a while, and every year we cross our fingers and hope they'll ask us back, and they have so far. Knock wood. There are always other roles that need to be filled. Some actors move on, especially the older ones. We need to fill up those roles. They have auditions for those folks and for interns and things like that in December, and by February, the season, the cast, and crew are usually set and ready to go.

Let me tell you how rehearsals used to work. How it used to work, especially the years between Bekki Jo and Matt Wallace, when the money was not nearly as great for actors, the rehearsals were done around people's work schedules. Nowadays, you're considered professional. Some of us have other things that we do. I narrate books at the American Printing House for the Blind, so a couple days a week, I have conflicts. Mostly we rehearse on an Actors' Equity schedule. We rehearse eight hours a day, and it's usually from ten to six with a break for lunch. Because we do three shows a season, we're often rehearsing more than one show a day. One show in the morning, one in the afternoon. It depends on where we are in the season. To do three shows in the amount of time that we have, the rehearsal schedule is really tough. As an actor, you never feel like there's enough rehearsal, but there always is. You just have to come in prepared. You have to know the material. There are some actors who have memorized all their lines by the time the first rehearsal rolls around, but they are in the minority, and I am not one. But you have to be very familiar and ready to spend the time away from rehearsal working on plays. That's your job as an actor. It's really hard, but it's what we love to do. We moan and complain about it, but it's what we love.

Tina Jo Wallace: I'm a firm believer, and I know Matt is as well, that the prep starts *long* before you start rehearsal. The day you get told what part you're playing, or even the day you know what the season is, you start reading those shows and working on them. I do the same thing, regardless of whether it is Shakespeare or a show at Derby Dinner Playhouse. I start really early. I'm a firm believer that you come to rehearsal, if not off book, then at least so familiar with the text that that's not what you're worrying about when you're in rehearsal. You're worrying about playing with the other actors onstage and listening

Putting Shakespeare on Its Feet   81

to the director and being able to try different things than what you thought in your prep work. I find that a lot of young actors come in and they think, "Well, we'll learn our lines during rehearsal or as I go; that's how I learn my lines." But it's really hard to make choices when you're worried about "What am I saying?" If you really know what you're saying, then you can play and learn and *react*—and not be looking at your script.

Under Curt Tofteland, we used to start with table reading and working on the language and what we're saying, everybody kind of agreeing what's supposed to be happening in the scene and then putting it up on its feet. Then rough staging, getting the idea of where you're coming in and where you're going out. Then the actors get more specific about, "Okay, what is this moment?" Breaking it down and getting more and more and more specific. You don't jump into rehearsal and start a run of a show.

In the rehearsal space, there's an energy and an excitement. I remember us all coming in with our coffees and comfortable clothes. We used to rehearse in Saint Philip Neri Church off Woodbine Avenue. They would let us rehearse in there. We would come into the church with our coffee and our water bottles, knowing that we were going to be there from ten to six, working hard. Curt really believed in you coming and watching the other actors' process. So even if you weren't in the scene, you were still there. We came to camp out for the day. If you were up, then you had a more active day. If you were one of the ones who wasn't onstage that day, you were working on your script while you were watching what's going on onstage. We would pack our lunches and things like that. Because you got your paycheck on Fridays, on that day we'd usually go down to UofL campus and get Chinese or something. And we would go to the Mag Bar after rehearsal on Friday nights.[1] That was the closest place for those of us who were staying in out-of-town housing. I remember lots of hard work, lots of sweaty, hard days, but it made it all worth it once you were up there—completely worth it.

Matt Wallace: I'm really a fan of just doing it. I don't like to do a lot of table work. When we read through a play, I don't like to spend days at the table breaking down the text because I think the way that we're going to find it is by throwing it up on its feet and just *doing* it. Yes, we have to do the homework of "What are we saying? What does it *mean*?

How does it connect to *me?*" But remember that first and foremost Shakespeare was a *dramatist.* He was writing plays to be presented, not to be published. This was an oral society, so the words were written because of how they sounded and how they tasted when you said them. These things were published way after he was dead. If you know the context of what you're saying and you say those words and you're breathing deeply and making it important, you will *feel* what you're supposed to feel. You can get the *hell* out of the way. You don't have to color it, because the language is so brilliant. I know that's oversimplifying it, but I think so much for me with Shakespeare is just stripping it away. It's easier than people think.

Tom Luce: The first read through is always the most exciting part of rehearsal. It is not so much meeting new people, because Matt uses the same people over and over again. It's just reconnecting with people you haven't seen in a while. At the other end, tech week is always a challenge. But because of the climate that Matt creates, it's never too bad. He doesn't keep you there till three o'clock in the morning if he can get away with just running cue-to-cues.[2] Because he's just so respectful of your time.

Braden McCampbell: This past season, I still had to go in and audition, which is perfectly fine. You see everybody there that you've already worked with, you see some new people there, and you can catch up with the old people, even if you've missed a season because you were doing something else that summer. Then you go, "Who are the new people?" You can always tell them because they are the ones that are in their own little headspace, pacing back and forth like, "I hope I get this. I don't know what I'm going to do. I hope everybody's nice." And everybody else is like, "Hey, man, you want a cookie?" Not in a mean way, but, like, legitimately, "Would you like a cookie? I have cookies. Hate to see you be off by yourself. We're all cool here. It's okay; we're friends."

We have table readings, and some of us come in knowing the script all the way, ready to go. Some of us come in with ideas. I try to do a little fifty-fifty, which sometimes backfires. I can't say that it hasn't. But I like to see how other people respond or portray something. I find if I get myself off script and ready to go, I get stuck in these mannerisms for a character that might not be what the director wants. It's a failing

Putting Shakespeare on Its Feet　83

Amy Attaway leading the first table read rehearsal, 2015.

on my part. If I'm going to get off script and come in with all my stuff ready to go, then my brain goes, "We're going to do this like this, because this is how you've made this character. You've read it this way three hundred times." But then the director says, "Yeah. I don't know what you're doing. Why are you doing that?" So I try to memorize as much as I can and then get off script during the process. Most of us still have the script in our hand for the first two weeks, and then beyond that, we're ready to go.

Rehearsal normally starts at ten o'clock, and then it runs all the way until about five in the afternoon. It's a full-time job. Almost all of seven hours, depending on which scenes we're doing. It usually is a lot of time to get feedback, to run through the scene a few times, to go, "Okay, that clearly doesn't work; that choice doesn't work. How can I make that choice work this way?" Or "Hey, this will work if I just do the thing this way." It's all these little, little things. We try to start running through the show as soon as possible. The way that characters grow and change is absolutely amazing. One of the strangest and most wonderful things I've ever worked with and experienced is just how quickly things can change from one day to the next. Greg Maupin can come in, and he's done a character, and he's got the idea ready to go, and it's Greg Maupin, so it's funny or he's already got the lines drilled

84   Under the Greenwood Tree

into his head. Then Matt will say something like, "Hey, maybe we can do it like this?" Greg goes, "Ah," and his entire demeanor can change just like that. He's like, "Okay, we can dial that back."

Normally we try to start with a comedy. We never do the history first. We never do the tragedy first. The tragedy is normally the last thing that comes. We always have a preview on Thursday night before we even open it because we're doing it in Central Park, so it's not like we can stop people from coming by and watching. People are still going over their lines, working on blocking, because sometimes something gets changed once we're in the park. "Yeah, we can't see you behind this tree, we just realized. Make sure you come in from this entrance." That's one of the cool things about the park is it can totally change from night to night leading up to opening night. One year, one of the trees fell! "Oh, well, we can change the blocking now because you're not going to be behind this massive tree anymore."

The first opening night is pretty electric but also very calm. For the comedies, it's just, "Hey, we've already got it; we just need to live in the work. We just need to relax and do the dang thing." At least that's how I feel. We're cracking jokes and just keeping everything light. First night is normally not really the jitters for the comedy, because everybody's like, "Ha, we're going to be funny; the crowd's going to love us." One of the big things that we always all say to each other is, "Hey, the crowd has already decided to come." Yes, the show is free, but the crowd has already decided to come, which means they already like you. There's a bunch of stuff they could be doing in Louisville [on] Friday night, but they're here, so they've already decided to come see us. Just have fun, live your life.

So that's a comedy. It's real light; you're meeting up at the afterparty afterwards. But then we go to the history. The history's a little more stuffy because there's a lot more monologues, a lot more expectations. There's also a lot more pageantry and bigger costumes. We're double-checking each other. We're checking in because at this point, we've already been doing a show for a month now. I've got this. You've got this. You've just got to go out there and do it. We've done the work. Now it's just putting the show out there for people to enjoy. It's a little bit more electric. Okay, really be on your stuff, guys. Let's wow these people; let's not just softball a *Henry*. There's a lot more monologues. There's more little things that somebody's got to build up. You have to keep people invested. With the comedies, you can throw in a little

Putting Shakespeare on Its Feet 85

lewd gesture or something to make sure that people go, "Oh, that's funny!" But with the histories and the pageantry, there's a lot more investment and energy that goes into that one.

There's all the pageantry and ceremony for the histories; you get all of that with a tragedy as well, but the stakes are twice as high. With a history, it's like, "We're telling you about Henry V, kind of like *Game of Thrones*, but it actually happened," versus *King Lear*, where it's, "You know people are going to die, and things are going to go bad, but how? How are they going to go bad? Ooh, girl, hold my popcorn. I'm waiting to see how this goes bad."

The tragedies are the ones that we're like, "Okay. Get on your *shit*." Those are the ones that a lot of people come to see. They're the ones that everyone's expecting. They're the ones that everybody's like, "No, really. Be. On. Your. Shit." You have to be good. You have to get it done. All the shows get the same amount of love; don't let me make you believe that they don't. All the shows get a lot of energy and investment. But the tragedy is the one where you have to keep the stakes high. You have to make sure that everybody's feeling this intensity, this moment; things can go south in an instant. Because things can go south and usually do. That's the thing you have to try and convey constantly: "Hey, at any moment, things can go wholeheartedly sideways with this show, and we are going to make sure you understand that." Opening night for tragedies is always a little more, "Be on it. Be on it. Be on it." You have to keep the tension building throughout the entire show. At the end, it feels like you just ran a marathon.

Tina Jo Wallace: Opening night is the best and the worst. I always say, "After opening, I can have fun." Because opening is *so* stressful. It's self-imposed because you don't have to be like this. You want to be so good, and you know that there might be critics. It's not so much that you worry about what they say about you, but you want them to love the show so that more people will come see the show. There's that weight of responsibility. But it's also so exciting because you know that there's going to be friends and family out there and the die-hard Shakespeare fans that always come on opening. You want to make sure that they love this as much as they loved last summer. It's scary because usually in the park, you're doing tech right up to the last minute. It might be that you're seeing some things for the first time on opening, especially if you've had rain during the week and you haven't been able

Braden McCampbell in *Shakespeare in Love*, 2021.

Putting Shakespeare on Its Feet   87

to tech. We sometimes open a show and you're like, "I've never seen that light cue before, because we didn't get to work that." It's exhilarating and scary and lots of nervous energy. I've learned as an adult to use that energy to my advantage and not let it go against me and not hold me back or make me behave erratically or unlike I did in rehearsal. Even now there are openings where I'm more and less successful at that. But, after opening, even though it's such an exhilarating night and everybody feels so great, I always feel better the day after. You've gotten through it. You've done it with an audience. They've hopefully had a great time. Now you can actually have fun and enjoy it and not have all those extra nerves that come along with opening.

Scene 2: Behind the Curtain

Hal Park, producer and director: The producer's job is to pull the team together and to get them to work together with a single vision and a single goal in mind and to make sure that everyone is truthful about what they do. The producer's job is to basically not allow the words no or can't come into play. That doesn't mean you're stupid about it. It doesn't mean that you force it. But what you do is you have to solve problems, and those words simply go away. I can remember times when people would look at me and at Shakespeare in the Park and say, "Well, we just can't do that," and I would look at them and I'd say, "I've been in the theater for twenty years. *Can't* doesn't work for me. Let's figure out how we can," and we would. The producer's job is to be smart about the technicians and the craftsmen that you pull around you. I always look to try to hire people that could teach me about the craft. I never wanted to be the smartest guy there. I wanted to have other people who would challenge me about the work that I was trying to do.

Beginning June, July, and August, as a producing director you're having daily production meetings. We met every morning. We're constantly looking at budgets. I'm walking around in the costume shops and the prop shops and the rehearsals and keeping tabs on everybody and getting them up and getting them moving forward. I do all of that, and about an hour before the show, I would go back over to the Shakespeare office, and I would lay down in my office on the floor and take a nap.

If you do Shakespeare right, it's accessible to anybody. Shakespeare was essentially writing for an eighth-grade audience. That was the education level at the very most for the people that Shakespeare was writing for. If you do it right, the language doesn't become oblique. It doesn't become difficult because Shakespeare will tell you what he wants you to know. He'll tell you again, and he'll tell you a third time to make sure. In almost every instance, he'll say it once; he'll say it again. He'll say it a third time. We used to have little kids come down and sit in the front row. After playing in the fountain behind us, they come and sit down on the front row and watch the play. I'd go down, and I asked them, "Well what's this play about?" And they would tell me, "Oh, there's the mean sister, and here's the good sister, and this guy's kind of crazy because he's old and he wants the two sisters to love him, but they don't really." They get it; they would absolutely get it. That's what's so magical about being out in the park with people from all walks of life. That's why Shakespeare holds up after four hundred, five hundred years.

When directing, you have to have a through line, and in the case of Shakespeare, there are several through lines that you can choose. I always tried to find what was the one quote, what was the one word from the key character, or the one line that to me sums up the whole problem of the play. I would work really hard to find that, and I would direct toward that moment so that when those lines came out, everything that happened after that moment was the result of that piece. In the Scottish play, there is a moment where Macbeth says, "Time was, when a man's brains were out that was the end. But now they come back, and they haunt me, and they have lives beyond the grave."[3] I'm paraphrasing here. But that's where that character was. He was stuck between two world orders. If you look back historically on the play, it was set after the Battle of Hastings, in which William the Conqueror introduced the Christian mystique to the island of England. Macbeth was caught between two world orders. There was the ancient order of when a man's brains were out, that's all there was to it. Well, William the Conqueror said, "Now there's life after death. You need to be aware of what you're doing in this world because you will pay for it in the life after." To me that was always Macbeth's tragedy—that he found out he had a conscience. It haunted him, and it ultimately killed him. That's why *Macbeth* is a tragedy. I've seen so many productions of Shakespeare where Macbeth is just so evil and so mean and so terrible that by the end of the second act you're saying, "When the hell is this guy going to die? I'm through with him, going to be glad

Putting Shakespeare on Its Feet 89

he's dead." That's not what tragedy is. Tragedy has to make you care for the character.

In the case of *Julius Caesar*, it was the tent scene between Brutus and Cassius getting ready for the final battle. This is where the masks come off and they finally deal with each other and they say, "What have we done here?" A lot of people directed up to the "Friends, Romans." Okay. Now what do I do? We blew right through "Friends, Romans, countrymen," and whatever. Those were good, important scenes, but I directed everything toward that tent scene between Brutus and Cassius, which to me was the moment when those two had to face each other and realize what they had set loose. After that, all the battle and everything that happens makes more sense. So that's what I do as a director, long story short.

Matt Wallace, director: I think the shift from acting to directing seemed like a natural progression. I think there is always awkwardness when you're hiring people who are your friends. It's a different relationship when we were working for someone else. As an actor, I can be in the dressing room with them, complaining about things. I can't do that as much now. I think I've always enjoyed leading and trying to bring the best out of people and inspire people, and I hope it was a natural progression to this position. I think how I direct people and how I lead people is not in an entirely different way from how I interact with them as humans, as an actor too. It's very collaborative and hopefully empowering.

Amy Attaway, director: When I started directing, I was doing contemporary plays. I was doing new plays, commissioned plays, in-the-room-with-the-playwright kind of plays. And now, Shakespeare, the playwright, is not in the room. With Shakespeare, you have to see the director's work because there are a bazillion productions of *Romeo and Juliet*. It's been on the stage somewhere every day for the last 450 years. Everyone has an idea of what *Romeo and Juliet* is. No matter what, people are going to see how you have done *Romeo and Juliet*. This is *your* interpretation of *Romeo and Juliet*. However, one thing that I take from my new-play life into Shakespeare that feels right, that feels like it was not a hard transition at all, is that I believe in the words on the page. I believe in trusting the words on the page. I believe in trusting the playwright's voice, which is, dare I say, not unique to me. I believe

90   Under the Greenwood Tree

it is a feminist way to approach directing. I don't like to put myself at the top of the pyramid. I don't like to be the center of the circle. I want the playwright's words to be the top of that pyramid. I really do see my job is making sure that we're all paddling the canoe in the same direction.

Additionally, very important to me is recognizing and enhancing and highlighting the strengths in every artist that I'm working with. If I feel like that lighting designer's doing their best work, that's very exciting to me. Or I've never seen that actor do that thing before. That's very exciting to me. This is an example: Greg Maupin is playing Lord Capulet in *Romeo and Juliet*, which is not his wheelhouse. The friar is his wheelhouse; the kind, comic buffoon is his wheelhouse. I've never seen him play anything like Lord Capulet before, and he hasn't, in his recollection, played anything quite like that before. Greg's a colleague whom I respect so much, and he knows so much about Shakespeare, so getting to work with him on a new part of his acting persona was really exciting. This is what gets me jazzed about directing, is that I get to be in a room with all of these smart, exciting human people and we get to make a thing together.

Georgette Kleier: Matt is fabulous, and I'm not just saying that because he's the current artistic director. They all have this thing about work. Bekki Jo's thing was always "Do the work," and then Curt's was always "Let the text do the work." And then Matt, his do-the-work philosophy is now much more broad because the company is very much invested in social justice and very much invested in equity. They are doing the work on that. It's about the work of the community. Matt's incredibly imaginative, but he doesn't dictate to the actors. It's very collaborative. His whole thing is about making people feel like their contribution is valued. It starts from the top like that. You have that kind of leader, and then the whole company sort of feels that way.

Amy, boy, she can coach actors. She had a very diverse group in the park tour of *Romeo and Juliet*. You've got twenty- and twenty-three-year-olds. Then you've got me [who is past retirement age]. You've got Abigail and Greg Maupin. But she was able to coach us each very individually. It felt always very specific to that person. I learned from her as a director. I learned from watching her to help inform my directing, because she had that specificity but without ever telling anybody what to do. She's able to get the actor to realize it on his or her own.

Paul Owen, set designer: [As a set designer, I get brought into the creative process] once the shows have been selected. I get scripts and audios of the plays, and I know who is directing which ones. Then I will go into conference with them separately, and we talk about the play. We talk about their impression and the direction they want to take it. If they want to do a circus in 1920, then that's one approach, and that's a whole other way of looking at *A Midsummer Night's Dream* or something like that. Then I go away, and I work on the design. I'm designing all three plays at the same time because they're occupying the same space. Then I arrive at what I think is the solution, or we may have more conversation. There are never doors shutting down on creative thoughts. When I think I have a solution for the summer, I get together with Amy and Matt and lay out what I'm thinking and what shape it's going to be and how we're going to alter and change the environment in order to accommodate that. Whatever timetable Matt is on and the workers or interns or technical director, whenever they go to work, then I'm ready to demonstrate and give them drawings, and the process begins, and the construction begins. Then we're in it together, and we go to the technical rehearsals, which include putting lights and costumes and all those things with the actor onstage. The whole process takes place collectively pretty much from the time the play is selected.

My interest as a designer is for the directors to express their feelings and thoughts because they have a reason for choosing the plays they have. Whatever those reasons are, I need to know what they are. I need to know what their goals are, what they want to achieve, and what their feeling is. Then I can be constructively helpful in making those kinds of things a reality. That's true of any play and working with any designer and director. It's a mutual examination of the material and what allows the material to be performed. It's a give-and-take. It's very much a shared process, and then the path is set before the rehearsal begins regarding what it's going to look like. All of that has been presented not only to Matt but the actors as well so they know what their home is going to be like.

In our collaborations, everybody knows what the budget is. If necessary, you begin there. You listen carefully to what the director's idea is and begin to see what he is talking about, or she is talking about, and go away and think about it and see how much of it you can achieve and whether it's useful in relationship to other plays that will be taking place in the same environment. Then you go back with possibilities.

92　Under the Greenwood Tree

It's never, "Well, you can't have that" off the top of your head. You have to investigate and see what can be achieved. That's part of the whole process. It's a puzzle. When you've got it and you see it in its final stage and it's ready to turn over to the audience, that's the best part.

Casey Clark, lighting designer: As a lighting designer, your first responsibility is to make it so that the players can be seen. That's at its most basic level, but pretty much anybody can do that. As you get deeper into it, you're illuminating an environment for the play. Even designers begin with script analysis, with dramaturgy, just like the actors do, just like the directors do. Because the script is the source of everything that needs to be communicated by this play. Everything that needs to be expressed. In an ideal process, the creative team starts together. With Kentucky Shakespeare, Matt and Amy will both talk to scenic first, which makes sense because scenic is under more constraints in the park than we are. Costumes and lights are a lot more flexible. So that makes a lot of sense. But it's better if the entire creative team starts together because certain looks or effects might involve scenic and lighting. For example, no scenic designer is going to do a painted backdrop unless the lighting designer is going to light it. Honestly, if you've been in the business even five minutes, you may well be a person who can make a comment or an assessment on an idea from another department. It is truly collaborative or should be, and that means everybody. If you have everybody on board from the get-go, you should ideally come up with a very unified visual production.

When I start to work on a play, I know that being outdoors and being in this space outdoors affect my process. As much as I really, really, really want to light the first hour of the show, I turn on lights, and you don't see them. Nobody sees them. I think we can start seeing lights a little bit right before intermission. Then intermission happens, and by the end of intermission, it's dark. That's when we actually get to see the lights. I know not to put a lot of resources into the boat scene at the beginning of *Shakespeare in Love*. It's a beautiful night scene.[4] It's lovely. There's a little light on the boat; there's a light at the dock. It's gorgeous. It could be really fun. But it's going to be in broad daylight with a western sun beating in. I cannot help with that, so I'm not going to put any resources into it. In *The Tempest*, there's the storm. If you're doing that indoors, you're going to put a lot of resources toward making it look bright and sound right and be huge. Out here, they can

Putting Shakespeare on Its Feet   93

make it be huge with sound and actors and sails and whatever else, but not lights. I know to concentrate on the second half of the show with my resources. But I don't dare only concentrate on the second half of the show in terms of my script analysis. I have to know why that storm is important. I have to know why that boat scene is important. It's a question of allocating resources to acknowledge daylight.

Donna Lawrence Downs, costume designer: There's a lot of challenges for designing for the park. Money is always a thing. There's never enough, and there's never enough time. It is a challenge making a full complete show three times a summer. It's a challenge being outside. We've been almost flooded out. We've had thunderstorms. It's been very cold. It's been so hot that people would pass out. There are people in period clothing, and there's only so much I can do about that. *Julius Caesar* and parts of *Romeo and Juliet* and *Othello* are the only three shows I've designed where I didn't feel like I was swarming anybody because they used very lightweight fabrics. Every other show I always say to myself, "I hope nobody passes out. I hope there's plenty of water backstage." We have to bring all of our amenities with us. We have limited dressing room space, and we are outside with the elements and bugs and things like that, which are a bit of a challenge but expected. When you say you're doing Shakespeare in the Park and it's outdoors, none of these things should be unexpected.

It is challenging to get clothing. I prefer to shop locally when possible. There are some really wonderful stores here in Louisville. I have to buy a lot of things online, which sort of sucks in a way because I can't see things before I buy them and I can't hold things or feel them or smell them before I get them. It is odd to say *smell*, but one of the things I have to think about when I'm at the park is some fabrics just stink [*laughs*], and heat doesn't help. If I can't wash it, then I can't use it. How are they going to do hair and makeup in this heat? No amount of Aqua Net is going to make hair stand out in some of the fabulous summer humidity that we have here.[5] A big challenge is the fact that when the show starts at eight o'clock, we have natural light, and by nine fifteen, we have artificial light. The sun's going to do what the sun's going to do. We had a freak storm that came through and knocked down a tree that had been for years and years and years sheltering stage right. The tree's gone now, so half of the house is in much stronger intense light at eight o'clock than it had been before.

Donna Lawrence Downs introducing costume ideas to the cast, 2014.

The first year of designing Shakespeare was a learning curve. I designed a lot of stuff that I couldn't really necessarily produce at all. *Midsummer* was my first show. We built about eighty percent of what you see on the stage in three weeks or five weeks, depending on how much time we have. It's pretty crazy. Generally, the actors have an idea about their costumes when they go into rehearsal. I'll show them design pictures, not necessarily ones I've drawn. I give them an idea of what they're going to be wearing.

We did *Much Ado* a couple years ago, and it was set in 1810, and we designed all of those costumes because we had to build everything. The Henrys and histories are pulled from previous shows. When the actors come in, we fit them in appropriate pieces. I generally build all the women's wear because my women are generally small and I'm trying to build up strong pieces so [Kentucky Shakespeare can make money by renting them out]. It's also harder to buy women's things that would require more alterations. Men are more generally shaped [the same], so I can buy and alter for them. In cases like *King Lear*, which we did last summer, I had many conversations, many more than I normally would before production, about expectations. It was very important to Jon Huffman [who played Lear] that he was part of the process, and it was very important to me, because his transformation is the story. We spent a lot of time

Putting Shakespeare on Its Feet 95

talking about things and coming up with ideas and working together to get what he needed out of it and what I needed out of it and what Matt needed out of it onstage. Another great example of collaborative art.

Scene 3: The Players

Crystian Wiltshire: [Getting started as a stage management intern] had a *huge* impact on the way that I carry myself as an actor. I could see the actors that [didn't] need me to call a line. I could see the actors that needed a little more help, because they were maybe mixing up some text and putting a word in the wrong place, or an actor that totally did not know their lines at all and just needed me to really help them get through rehearsal. I saw all different sorts of artists and how they prepare. That helped me shape how I choose to prepare now.

Being on the other side of the table as an intern, I could just sit there and watch Matt Wallace or Amy Attaway direct scenes and really get something special out of their actors. I can sit there and watch and say, "I see how they got that out of them." So those are experiences that a lot of actors don't necessarily get to have, because their job is just to get up onstage and be prepared as best they can to rehearse the scene. They don't necessarily get the opportunity to watch an entire rehearsal from ten a.m. to six p.m. As an intern, I'm there before they arrived, and I'm there after they arrived, and I'm seeing all the work that's being done. It was a really nice time for me to be a sponge and just soak in all the different ways that all of these really talented people prepared for the work. And I got to see it all culminate on the stage every night. I would never trade that experience.

John Gatton: When I teach Shakespeare, I try to get my students to start—it sounds like heresy—but I discourage them on a first reading to bother with all the footnotes. Get the plot. Who does what to whom, when, where, why, and how. Did Shakespeare's audience understand every word? Probably not. But the stories are up to date. They are modern. The costumes, the language, they're all different. But love, hatred, greed, envy, generosity, punishment, everything is in there. Even in those great tragedies, *Lear* particularly, there is this notion that as human beings we must go on. Lear comes to the bottom and then finds the strength to say to the storm, "Pour on; I will endure." It's how we get through the day.

96   Under the Greenwood Tree

Then the stories are told in amazing language: poetry and prose. Yes, there's meter there. But Shakespeare is not a slave to that. People say, "Well, the language is so old fashioned." Well, yes, it's Early Modern English. But go to a festival anywhere of Shakespeare and look at the crowd. They're not Shakespeare scholars. Are they understanding every word? No. But listen to the reactions. The laugh lines will get the laughs. The serious parts might bring forth a little sniffle or a tear. The old boy works now. My soapbox is when I don't think the director is trusting the playwright, when the director thinks he has to put his or her stamp on it or has to trick it up in some fashion. I'm not a purist. I don't have to see every show in tights and tunics and togas and sandals and all of that. But trust the script and get the people to speak clearly. They still work.

Georgette Kleier: How do I prepare? Read the play; read the play. I read the play several times. Greg Maupin [our dramaturg] is so good at giving you a lot of [the information] that you used to have to get on your own by looking up every word you don't know the meaning of. Am I using formal second-person pronouns, am I saying *you* or am I saying *thee*, with *you* being the formal and *thee* or *thou* being the informal? You try to pick out all those clues that help you understand that character's status, their relationship to other characters. If it's in poetry, I scan it; I still go back to scanning.[6] I do iambic pentameter. I go *tadum, tadum, tadum, tadum, tadum* [*tapping chest in rhythm*]. Then if it doesn't match up, then you go, "Oh, that's odd." I circle it. I wonder what Shakespeare's doing there because it doesn't match up. We know he is clever enough to have done it on purpose. I do research in the time period if a director is doing a specific one.

If it's poetry, if it's iambic pentameter, memorizing is easy, much easier than prose. Much. Because you've got a rhythm, so if you're off, it doesn't match the rhythm. A lot of times, you have rhyme; that helps you. The beginning of *Romeo and Juliet*—"Two households, both alike in dignity / In fair Verona, where we lay our scene"—that is a sonnet. You're dealing with strict iambic pentameter. You've got the rhyming couplet at the end. It's much easier than memorizing the nurse's prose, where she just goes off on tangents. Every actor has their own thing. I record it on a phone and listen to it in my car. I listen to it when I walk. I record my cue line, and then I record my line, and then I listen to it.

Tina Jo Wallace: I would say to someone who hasn't done Shakespeare, just don't be intimidated! [*Laughs.*] Give it a try. It's really the same with any piece of work that you're working on. It's about what are you trying to do? It's the same questions that you ask yourself—what are you trying to get from the person onstage, and what are your strategies for doing it? Don't worry about the language. Learn your scansion and learn all the technical things.[7] But then you kind of throw them away, and you just try to get what you want onstage. I think it's much easier than we make it. It's written so well that you just have to say the words. Sometimes I think actors get in the way. They think they have to use an accent or they have to be heightened in some way. Unfortunately, I see some Shakespeare done with very broad strokes and almost like they are *orating*. It's really much more human than that. You don't have to do that; [it] gets in the way.

Abigail Maupin: For Shakespeare, I start with the words. I'm a big fan of the idea that Shakespeare is directly from the page. There's a lot of interesting books and videos—John Barton's video series from the seventies—about dealing with the verse and being able to look inside it and at the clues that it provides as to simple things like stage directions but also things about what is my character's emotional state, right in this moment.[8] You can get that from punctuation, from monosyllables versus polysyllables, that kind of thing. Shakespeare is always, first and foremost, what is coming out of my mouth. Not only what do those words mean, but how do they feel in my mouth? Where do I need to breathe? Does this line of verse end feminine or masculine? As I end this line of verse and I move into the next sentence, am I building on that previous thought? Does my character need to search for a word? I feel like there are so many clues that are just written right there. Once I start to get that, I feel like a lot of character stuff just starts to happen on its own.

Then you always make choices, because the director has chosen a concept for the piece. Doing *Much Ado* in the Regency would be very different from doing *Much Ado* in Elizabethan or whatever.[9] Part of that is physical accepted behaviors, rules of etiquette. When do I curtsy? How deep do I go? Oh, this dress has a very fitted bodice from my top of my hips up to my neck. I just can't move the same way I usually do. So how do these people move? All those little tweaks. Who can I look straight in the eye? Who am I deferring to? Do I treat the king

98   Under the Greenwood Tree

or queen differently? Our *Othello*, when I was the duke, was set in the modern period. In it, I was dressed like Senator Elizabeth Warren with my power suit and my sneakers, and that's how I dealt with my assistants and how they treated me. There's a subtle difference from that and being Queen Gertrude in *Hamlet*, who has a lady's maid, who I asked to sit next to me when I was dead on the stage to keep the bugs off me. [*Laughs.*] Gertrude is very much ignored and sort of taken for granted by the men in that play in general. Your setting really changes up a lot of that. Your costume changes up a lot of that.

With Matt and Amy, a lot of those decisions are up to the actor. They want to see what you're bringing to the table and then work with you to find what the strongest choices are. A lot of that has to do with your other actors as well. Who am I onstage with? What is our character relationship? What's happening in the moment? With Matt and Amy, we have a lot of freedom as actors to explore it a little bit before we get to a point of "That's what works. That's what we're sticking with."

I'm a big stickler for consistency. The reason we have a rehearsal process is that we make discoveries and then we decide how we as a group are telling the story. The audience deserves from night to night to have that same story told. The struggle as an actor is how do I keep it fresh? How do I not just zone out and say the words and make the movements and phone it in every time? For me, that means that we go deeper, that I find small ways that change it for me, that keep me present, that keep me focused, that keep me listening to my partner. Even if that's just yesterday I got up and I stood on my left leg. Today, I'm going to stand on my right leg. Sometimes it is saying a line and hearing it differently and going, "Oh, wait, wait; *this* word," and punching something else, or hearing a laugh in the audience and saying, "Oh, okay, they're with me on this tonight." Sometimes it's just how your partner is reacting to you as you're doing a scene. I know a lot of actors—and I feel like this is a thing that comes out of film work, where you do a take and then you change it up—who keep themselves fresh by completely doing something differently. In theater, that is dangerous because now you've screwed up somebody else's performance because they had other expectations of where this was going. Sometimes the stage manager or the crew is trying to do things off what you're doing. You don't know if you've screwed them up. Sometimes it changes how the audience is seeing the story, and I don't think that's fair to anyone.

The real challenge, and to me this is part of being a good actor, is how can I be present? A lot of it is about focus. You have your training that teaches you how to present it, to say it, to move it, to do all those things in a way that the audience, if you're having an off night, the audience doesn't know. You have your tricks to say, "Okay, well, I'm supposed to be weeping here. I have no tears tonight. So I'm going to fake it till I make it." I know how to move my body, and I know how to make my voice sound like it. I can put a hand up to my eye, and they'll go with me. I've come offstage some nights like, "That was the worst thing I ever did," and sometimes my fellow actors respond with, "That seemed the same as it usually does." Okay, and then sometimes it's the opposite. I come off, "Oh my God, that was incredible. I just felt like I was right. I was in it," and people say, "Oh, well, you know, I saw something in your eyes going on, but it was great. Good job." Yeah, I'm thinking that it really seemed the same to you, didn't it? Yeah. Okay. Well, that's all right. That's the goal: consistency. Comedy much more needs to have that consistency because so much of comedy is math, timing. We have to wait this long and then the spit take, and then this guy who gets hit with the spit take has to shake it off.[10]

When we did *Twelfth Night* in the Bomhard Theater in '16, I was Olivia. I had already in other productions played Viola and Maria, and they were super fun. But Olivia was one of those moments when I was like, "Oh, I get to be the pretty girl!" Then I said, "Ooh, she's hard though. How do I make this funny?" I like that challenge of how to make things funny. Because that's hard. Just thinking too much about comedy sometimes makes it not work. But at the same time, there's a math to it. I know how to do that. I know how to dig in and figure out how to make the comedy work.

I love the big emotion of Shakespeare. But you're not playing the emotion; you're playing the words. I'm a Virgo. I'm very practical and organized. I'm very analytical. I love that with Shakespeare, you get to break it down. You count your beats. You figure out where your commas are and how you're going to breathe. Once you get into all of that brain work, you just let the words come out. It's built so that the emotion happens, and you don't have to manufacture anything. I adore that. It's so much fun. And the situations are insane. What's more fun than playing make-believe as a grown-up person and getting to throw yourself headlong into planning to kill your father or dying yourself extravagantly? The rage and the grief, those are just fun to let loose. We live in a world that has civilized rules about how we all behave with each other, and absolutely blowing up at someone or suddenly having intense grief in the middle of a public place is generally frowned upon. Getting to get out on a stage and let her rip, yeah, so much fun.

Phil Cherry: Nothing's ever the same for me. It's not like, "Oh, this is routine, and I have been doing this for thirty years; I know what I'm doing." It's never like that for me. I get all my impulses onstage from other actors, so I was fortunate to work with a lot of really talented actors. Before I go onstage, the last thing I'm thinking about is my lines. I've seen actors on the sidelines looking through the script at the last minute, thinking about their lines, and I'm like, "Oh God, I'm glad I'm not one of those actors." Because I couldn't do it that way. That's what the rehearsal process is for. If you don't know your lines by the time the audience is there, looking at it on your break is not good. I was one of those actors: once I put my script down, it was down. I went out there [and the] only line I was thinking about is my first line. I wanted to make sure to get my first line down. I love speaking Shakespeare, and I can tell you right now, every monologue and soliloquy I've ever learned, I can still recite it.

Jon Huffman: There's nothing as satisfying for an actor, I think, as being able to express the thoughts that all of us have but using Shakespeare's words. It's a thrill. It's an amusement park ride. It's just fun. It's wonderful to be able to have those sounds come out of your own mouth and still make audiences understand what's going on. There's nothing like it.

As an actor—I hate to put it in such simplistic terms—all you have to do is learn the words. Learn the words, and that's how you do it. Because it's all there. I'm not very good at explaining how to do Shakespeare and make audiences understand it. When I teach Shakespeare, and it's not often because I'm a terrible teacher, I say, "It's just poetry." And people say, "But I don't know how to talk poetry and do that." I tell them, "Yes, you do." The first thing I do is tell them to tell me "The Star-Spangled Banner" because everyone knows "The Star-Spangled Banner." "Tell it to me." They start to sing it. "No, no, no, tell it to me. Speak it to me; don't sing it." They can't because they've never done that. But once they do, I say, "See, it's a story. It's a story about what happened one night and waking up the next morning and look what's there. That's all this is." Then we turn to the page, and we look at Shakespeare, and I go, "If music be the food of love, play

Tony Milder rehearsing for *The Tempest*, 2018.

on." What's difficult about that, you know? I'm in love. I want music that reminds me of it. Keep playing. It's a revelation to a lot of young actors. But honestly, if you learn the words and you understand them, you can make anyone enjoy it.

I've come to realize over the years that what I do, what we in my business do, is more of a calling than anything else. I don't mean to sound pretentious, but I look at it as a very noble profession. To be able to spend two hours a night roughly taking an audience of hundreds of people somewhere else, away from what they're used to, away from what's troubling them, and take them somewhere else and make them think about something else a couple of hours a night is a gift.

Braden McCampbell: I've always liked making people smile. That's the one thing that I did miss about sports. In sports, when you score a touchdown as a tailback and the crowd explodes, that's a rush; that's immediate pay. The crowd will interact with you. During choir, it's "We will sit here quietly, listen to you sing your aria or solo, and then clap because it was beautiful." And that's the extent of it. With acting, I realized I can have a whole thing with the audience if that's what the character is supposed to do. There are soliloquies in Shakespeare where you literally go, "Hey, I'm going to talk to you, audience members. Yes, you. I'm not talking to these characters in this scene; I'm talking to you. I'm explaining—this is me explaining what is about to happen or what has happened, and this is just for you." You can turn and look someone in the face and make eye contact briefly, and they go, "Oh, you were talking to me." Their face kind of lights up. It doesn't always light up. Some people shrink down into their chairs. They're like, "Don't look at me, dude. Don't talk to me. Talk to someone else." [*Laughs.*] But those moments when you're talking to the audience, or you say something and the audience gets it, and their faces light up like are pretty epic, actually. That's what got me into theater, because of the interaction with the crowd, when you can feel like you had an interaction with them as a human being, versus "Ah, you liked my song; you all clapped. Woo, bravo."

Scene 4: The Blooper Reel

Sometimes, despite all the preparation and rehearsal, bloopers occur. While discussing their craft, some of the narrators brought up mistakes and ways of handling them.

Putting Shakespeare on Its Feet   103

Matt Wallace: I missed an entrance for *Merchant of Venice*, and it was closing night, and I'm the freaking merchant of Venice. The cast used to have this friendly competition of who could collect the most money at intermission, called barreling. We'd come around the amphitheater with bags to collect donations, and we would get really competitive about it. I'm backstage at the end of the first half talking to Phil Cherry, something about, "Well, I'm going to get more than . . ." And then all of a sudden there's a pause. And it was *me*. Bassanio is talking to Shylock: "Oh, here comes Antonio!" It was like a five-second pause. In that situation, you realize you can't come *running on*. I just remember walking on and, like, gesturing back like I was talking to someone on the rialto. That was not good.

John Gatton: One story on me: *King Lear*, it's our final dress. This is when Doug is playing Lear. I'm Kent. Tom Atwood is Gloucester. I have the opening line. We walk through a doorway upstage. We come to the center. We're talking, and I think, "Something's not right here." I have to stop and say I'm sorry. I've started a scene much further on when Tom and I walk on and I have the first line. Awful, I was very embarrassed. So we went backstage. "Okay, here's my line. Let's start again." Thank heavens it wasn't opening night, because it would have been a whole lot of exposition that we would have had to somehow insert into the play, including the division of the kingdom.

Tina Jo Wallace: Almost every production I've ever been in, there's been somebody at some point who's forgotten a line or got distracted and didn't realize it was their turn. If you do a run for six weeks, at some point someone starts thinking about their grocery list and forgets that they're onstage. I can't remember specific times, but I know there have been times where I'm like, "Oh, it's me!" I've been caught off guard. I personally try not to think about my shopping list when I'm onstage, but I know that that happens. [*Laughs.*] It's just human nature, especially if you're doing eight shows a week, nine shows a week. With other actors, you can see the look in their eye. They might not give it away to the audience, but you can see that this is not typical, something different is happening. You can usually ask them a question or say something similar to what they were supposed to say, where they're like, "Oh, *that's* where we are! Oh, I got it!" Sometimes, after six weeks of doing a show, there will be one word that you can't think of! That's

104   Under the Greenwood Tree

like, "I know it's something like *this* word"—and you say something similar, and it just goes on. But sometimes someone literally looks at you, and you're like, "You're not going to say your line. I know that's not going to happen." So you have to kind of think of some way to go around it.

There have been times where the audience for sure knew someone had slipped. Usually, they have no clue. It's seamless. When you're living moment to moment onstage, the minute something's different, it's like all your Spidey senses go off! And everybody's like, "Okay, how do we get this back?" Usually, the actors know long before the audience has any clue, and usually it can be covered. It's harder with Shakespeare—*much* harder with Shakespeare—because you can't just ask a random question because then all of a sudden you sound like you're not in the same world. So it takes a little bit more, um, cleverness. But for me, Shakespeare is harder to mess up because there is a rhythm and a rhyme to it.

Jon Huffman: Everyone forgets their lines frequently when you're doing Shakespeare. If I'm working on a play and there's a line that doesn't fit my mouth, if it just doesn't come out right, I'll sit down with Greg Maupin, the dramaturg, or Matt and say, "Listen, can we get rid of this line or change this word?" Shakespeare's not going to know, but this is hard for me to make work. They're usually pretty good about that. A lot of times, you'll have a word that maybe in one version of Shakespeare is a different word. We tend to use what's called the First Folio.[11] But maybe in other, later versions of it, he used a different word, or whoever transcribed it used a different word.

Ask any other member of the company if people forget their lines, and my name will probably come up. It's not that I forget lines so much, and it happens to everyone almost every night, especially with Shakespeare. You're in the middle of a scene, and you're acting your tail off, and there's a word that won't come. With Shakespeare, if you are in the middle of an emotional scene and there's one word that goes out of your mind, it ruins the line for you. It can really mess you up because each word is so important. It happens to all of us. Over the years, I have developed the—I hate to call it the ability; other actors call it "Huffmaning." I'm able to improvise in iambic pentameter until I get back on track. I couldn't do it now if you asked me to. But put me onstage during a show, and if I forget a word—and it's usually just one word. You're in the middle of the line, and you forget a word [and] that word messes up the next word. I have learned how to sort of compensate for that over the years.

Braden McCampbell: I used to beat myself up horribly for it, anytime I forgot a line. "Hey, I completely forgot I have to say something there. My bad, I'm sorry," or just, "Aw, crap." In the middle of whatever, your brain goes, "*And* we're thinking about ice cream! Oh, wait, we were supposed to say something after the sword fight. *Uh.*" Jon Huffman, who was my mentor—helps a lot when your mentor is somebody like Jon Huffman—he's got a cool little trick where if he goes up on a line, he will resay the line before it or some part of a monologue. He does it so smoothly that people don't realize he's resaying a line from something else. I've only caught it once, and I asked Jon O'Brien, [another actor in the company], "What just happened? Did he repeat that line?" He's like, "Yeah, we call it Huffmaning now." You never catch it. It happens at least once or twice, but he does it in such a way that nine times out of ten, you can be onstage with him and not realize that he just said the same thing twice to get back to a line that he lost.

Act 3

In the Park

There's nothing like a perfect summer night at Kentucky Shakespeare in the park. It's the second half of the play, and the sun's gone down, and you see the lights bouncing off of the amazing trees. It's just a really, really special, almost religious experience that you really can't get at too many other places.

—*Crystian Wiltshire*

I think that my final words would be . . . [*pauses*] Greg Maupin sweats way too much.

—*Crystian Wiltshire*

From the sublime to the ridiculous, company actor Crystian Wiltshire playfully summed up the spectrum of delights and difficulties of performing live theater in Louisville's Central Park. Early reviews in the local paper cataloged some of the latter, complaining of the distracting cacophony and disruption. But from the beginning, spectators, reporters, and participants also saw the atmosphere in the park—even the heat—and the diverse makeup of the audience as central to the experience and the mission of the company. The lack of an admission charge, or even a gate or doorway, prompted one reporter to note, "This is come-as-you-are, leave-when-you-like Shakespeare." The generally relaxed ambience invited an "audience . . . as colorful as the characters on the stage," made up of doctors, students, homeless people seeking shelter and distraction, assisted-living residents on a night out, "young lovers, girls in curlers," and, most often noted, children. Doug Ramey set the tone early, interacting with young neighbors and making sure they felt welcome. He even granted three young squires'

Audience, August 1967.

request to be knighted after an early performance of *Macbeth*.[1] Sixty years later, the diversity of the audience remains especially rewarding. For many of the performers, the ability to connect with the spectators and share the experience is one of the primary joys of being in the park. And in recent years, striving to be even more inclusive and welcoming has become a primary focus of the company. But as Wiltshire hints, there are also challenges to performing outdoors, including power outages, encounters with stray critters, sudden storms, and, as Gregory Maupin puts it simply, July. But the company (and audience) perseveres through those challenges. This chapter paints a picture of a night in Central Park, from the lovely light to the horrible heat, and ends with the narrators' stories about some of their favorite performances.

Scene 1: The Joy of Being in the Park

Jon Huffman: Last year, we did *King Lear*, and I was very fortunate enough to play the [title] role. My first big scene was up high on a platform. It was still daylight when we start. We start about eight o'clock, and it is still daylight. I discovered in this scene that while I was up there, I could plant myself so that the sun was a spotlight right on my face.

108   Under the Greenwood Tree

I was kind of overwhelmed by that. To be outside speaking Shakespeare, one of the greatest plays ever written, and the sun is a spotlight on me. It's just a wonderful experience.

In the park, you have people coming and going. Especially at the beginning of the evening, you have a lot of people who haven't quite settled down. But as the sun starts to go down, as the story starts to unfold, then this group of anywhere from five hundred to a thousand people start to really lean in. You've got hawks, and you've got owls, and you've got night critters, and you've got sirens in the background and airplanes overhead. But you've got people leaning in to hear it who get offended at the sirens, who get offended at the airplanes. It's kind of wonderful to watch them be drawn in. It's the same indoors, but outdoors you can see them better and you can feel them better. Much more. It's just a wonderful feeling to be able to take people for that length of time somewhere else. It's just a wonderful atmosphere. Especially in the sort of amphitheater we have in Central Park here, a natural amphitheater with the park benches.

Georgette Kleier: The performance part was a blast. It was awesome. There's nothing like being on that stage, absolutely nothing. Part of the reason people do theater is to have that dressing room environment, to have that group of women or men or both that you commune with for six weeks, eight weeks, two months, whatever the length of time is. But while the sense of community backstage is amazing and wonderful, the real joy comes from the shared experience with the audience. In the park, you start act 1 seeing their faces. You see them! They're right there! Then this sort of magic begins to happen as the evening progresses. You walk out after that break, and nine times out of ten, there's stars in the sky. And it's beautiful; it's stunning. And you go, "Gosh, I get to be out here and say these words, under this beautiful canopy of stars, and these people that I got to know in full light are now here with me in this very different, magical kind of place because of the lighting." Truly, truly, there's nothing like it.

Tina Jo Wallace: In Shakespeare, it's very frequent that you're talking to the audience, which is one of the reasons I *love* Central Park because you can see them and make complete contact with them. I think it's exhilarating. I know a lot of actors are very intimidated by that. They want to look above everybody's heads and not look in their eyes. But

In the Park   109

I feel like it's fun because every time you say that line—every night—there's going to be a different person that you're saying it to, and how they react is totally going to give you a different ball of energy. Not a complete change of line read but a different energy that will feed the next moment. I love it. Central Park is one of my favorite places to perform in the world.

Tom Luce: I love telling this story. I was playing Adam in *As You Like It*. I had a line where I say, "I may look old, but I'm young and lusty," and I would jump up and click my heels. I was barreling at intermission, and this father and his son came up to me. His son was maybe seven years old. It was very sweet. I was very shy when I was a kid, and I think acting kind of was my way of trying to get over that. The father was encouraging him to come and talk to me. His father said, "Go ahead, go ahead, tell him what you wanted to say." He said, "My favorite part is when you jumped up and clicked your heels." So I said, "Well, how about I do that for you here, now; just for you, I'll do that." I clicked my heels, and he got this big, huge smile on his face. They turned to start to walk away, and then he turned back around and ran and gave me this big hug.

Matt Wallace: We had these two little boys who saw every show. They lived in the neighborhood. Their parents didn't mind, and they were right there. They'd come follow us as we'd walk out of the park, and be like, "Well, that fight scene was different tonight," or "I didn't like that—you know, when you did *that* tonight!" They had an educated, valid opinion about everything that we did, and I loved it! I loved that these kids could see Shakespeare every night. They grew up with Shakespeare because we were there.

Robert Curran is artistic director of the Louisville Ballet and an audience member.

Robert Curran: It was the first time I'd seen a Shakespeare performance like that. I remember it being very hot. I remember it having a delightful mix of really, really quality performance in a very relaxed environment. There was nothing sloppy or relaxed or unprofessional about what you were seeing on the stage. But it was kids running around, dogs, and joyfulness out in a relaxed atmosphere. I remember really liking that. I love the transition from day to night that happens during the performance.

Volunteers Brenda Johnson (*right*) and Connie Harris, who greet visitors and run the gift shop at summer performances.

I love that. I feel like that's a really interesting evolution for the performers. As you get deeper into the story, you actually get more into a theater experience as you get into the dark. It feels really magical.

Tina Jo Wallace: I think a lot of us who go to theater, we see the same people. People who can afford to go to the theater and who enjoy theater; we see a lot of the same faces. But you go to the park, and you see people that you don't expect to see. I think there's value in that. I think there's value in the communal experience of everybody having the same experience together that are *not* the same. I love that. I feel like that's educational for everybody. There are studies that when you're watching a show, an audience will start to breathe together. Especially in musicals. They find this even when you go to watch a movie. When you watch *with* other people, that you start to have a similar heart rate and similar breathing patterns and things like that. Creating that kind of experience for people that are *with* people that are different than us, that we wouldn't necessarily choose to buy a ticket to sit beside, I think is *so* healthy for our community and *so* important.

Elizabeth Siebert, a student of theater and previous theater professional, has been a longtime audience member, volunteer, and member of the board of directors.

Elizabeth Siebert: To me, it's really that sense of community, that you've got all walks of life, all age and gender, all socioeconomic status. It really feels like a little microcosm of the whole world. I love it when the planes go over. I love it that you can hear the crickets. I'm not bothered when people talk. In fact, opening night there was an unhoused man who was at the park next to us, and he started talking. For half a second, I thought, "He's going to talk, and it's going to bug me." But then I realized within seconds that what he was doing was actually quoting the play. It made my heart swell because I thought, "I don't know his situation; I don't know how he's gotten to this place in life. But this is for him, too, because this is free." It was actually one of my favorite nights in the park. I got to hear him quote *Romeo and Juliet*, while we were watching *Shakespeare in Love*. It was great.

Casey Clark: It's one of my favorite ways to watch a show, personally, because I like the freedom of being outdoors. I like the freedom that I can get up and walk around if I want to. I love the park setting. It just feels more relaxed than when you go to the theater in an indoor space. The dress code is more relaxed, and the environment is more relaxed. Because we don't have a proscenium wall, or even really any backstage that we haven't built for sight-line issues, there's an immediacy to the relationship between the actors and the audience that I love. I love that actors not only come through the aisles, but certain places where you sit, you are conversation distance from them. It feels that way even when you're farther back because you can hear everything that they say, and I know that the actors can hear what the audience says. There's an intimacy to it that is inexplicable given the size of our seating area. Inexplicable. I don't know why it's that way, but it is.

Donna Lawrence Downs: The atmosphere of being outdoors is lovely because people can come and go and they can get a drink if they want to or go to the restroom if they want to, whatever. That sort of free atmosphere. We also get people that would be afraid to come to a theater or think they would never want to see theater. They can kind of stroll by and check it out themselves a couple times before they find themselves taking a seat because they're actually very interested by what's going on. We get a lot of people that come before we're open, in tech rehearsal. Usually, there'll be some little kids, and the little kids are fascinated by what we're doing and just want to sit in the house and watch. Even though we're still in tech rehearsal or whatever, they're glued to it. They just think that's the coolest thing. It gives them an opportunity to see theater, and if you're not equipped to see theater and be quiet and respectful, you're not losing anything. It's a great way if you have kids with auditory or other mental challenges to come and see it a couple of times if they can't sit all the way through one show. You have the whole experience without missing out and without costing a lot.

Georgette Kleier: The idea of making Shakespeare truly for everyone, and the fact that it's free, gives you an amazing feeling. As an artist, you feel like I'm doing something of value. I think I'd rather be doing Shakespeare, where the temperature gets to be ninety-something, than I would doing something comfortable inside an air-conditioned theater, because it feels much more a part of the community.

Scene 2: "Shall I Sweat for You?"[2]

Gregory Maupin: We have a common enemy, and that enemy is July. [*Laughs.*] I'm in Elizabethan-cut upholstery fabric, and there are mosquitoes on my face, and I'm supposed to be dead onstage, and I can't move. I can't swat this thing that I feel biting me right now. That's a memory from when I played Polonius in *Hamlet*. Microphone complexities and remembering the words when there is an airplane. July is the Axis to our Allies. Matt is our [Winston] Churchill, leading the charge. We have an uphill battle. It's sweaty out there. There are going to be days in the Bard-a-thon summers when we're going to be doing a show that is literally called *The Winter's Tale* at four thirty in the afternoon in July, wearing fur robes.[3]

Abigail Maupin: When we did the Bard-a-thon, there was a moment in the first act, in the midst of that July five o'clock sun, when Dathan Hooper, playing Leontes, had been out there ranting and raving in his winter clothes, and we got to the trial scene, and he had to go from the stage to up above, which is hotter, significantly. He was losing it. He had been drinking water every second he could, but he was so dehydrated that he crawled up the stairs onstage. The stage manager spotted him, and they had some Pedialyte backstage, so they put it in a goblet.[4]

Gregory Maupin: Neill Robertson, who was also in the show, delivered it to him on a little tray because we have these props around for other things. Dathan says he almost kissed him on the mouth at center stage once he realized that cold Pedialyte had been brought to him so he could finish the act.

John Gatton: Once we were doing *The Winter's Tale*. It was beastly hot, and people were in fur and whatnot onstage. Leontes early on has the line "too hot, too hot," and he read it just with a bit more emphasis, and the audience laughed because it really was. Another time, during that first production of *Hamlet* in the park, it started to rain. It started when Polonius was onstage talking to Ophelia and giving her advice. He came to the end of the scene, and the rain was getting heavier, so he said, "I need to fix that leak in the roof," and walked off. The audience laughed. We probably canceled the show. We didn't always. People would sit there with umbrellas if it wasn't too heavy and there wasn't lightning.

Braden McCampbell: Neill Robertson, he's normally my foil, or I'm his nemesis or something for a show. I was Benvolio, and he was Tybalt. When we have a sword fight, normally we manage to make sparks happen when we cross swords, in some form or fashion. We were Edgar and Edmund in *King Lear*. On the last show, it starts to rain in the final act, and we are trying *so hard*, so hard to beat the rain. But we have to get through this fight scene where we're fighting with staffs. We're brothers going at each other. We start circling. We're going, "Ha-ha, come at me, you fool," and all this other stuff. The first time our staffs meet, there is a bolt of lightning that goes off overhead at the exact moment. You can hear the crowd go, "Ooh." I'm like, "I'm glad y'all liked it, but that wasn't in the budget! All right! Thank you, God, Jesus, whoever did that one. We appreciate it!" Neill was even like, "Oh my gosh, did you see that lightning?" I'm like, "Yeah, I saw the lightning; that's why we paused." Ha. That was a big lightning. Are we safe with these, you know, sticks up in the air in the middle of the park? Mmm, let's get through this. But we managed to beat the rain for that show.

Braden McCampbell (*left*) and Neill Robertson in *King Lear*, 2019.

Scene 3: Other Challenges of Being in the Park

Matt Wallace: We had some power issues in the park that gave me a lot of this gray hair. It was my second or third year. We couldn't find out why something was short-circuiting in the lights. *Much Ado about Nothing* in 2017 ended up being the most attended show in company history. It was a Sunday night, and something tripped, and we couldn't get it back on. We tried to work the lights, and it kept tripping, and it kept tripping, and it was so stressful. We couldn't finish the play. Luckily, the run wasn't over, so people could come back and see it. But that was a low point for me, production-wise. I had to throw up my hands. I was sending out people during the show to Lowe's to buy work lights. *We're going to do this!* We had seven hundred people there!

Doug Sumey: The planes! We would always have to communicate with the airport tower to let them know that we're starting Shakespeare, and they would divert planes to another runway just so that they would lessen the traffic. Planes always go over Central Park. There would be the random plane that would go over. During *Midsummer Night's Dream*, the fairies were onstage, and here's this plane that went over, and the actors worked with it beautifully. They treated it like it was some UFO, extraterrestrial thing that they had never experienced. They ran in fear, all of them, and then came out when the plane went away, wondering if it had passed and if their lives were still in danger. The audience just ate it up.

Phil Cherry: You have to be tough to do outdoor theater. Sometimes, your audience interacts with the actors on the stage. I've had that happen. One night, I was performing, I think it was *Hamlet*, a guy came up and literally relieved himself on the corner of the stage, in the light. On the stage, basically, while we're performing. We as actors, anything happens in our space, we have to react to it. So it was kind of a terrible, weird moment, but the stage managers finally got him offstage, the audience got a laugh about it, and we paused the scene. I think this was *Hamlet* too: One night I was performing, one of the people on the stage had the torches going, and they lowered their torch a little too far, and the ball that was burning inside rolled out across the stage, and there was a big line of fire on the stage. During a performance. I was on the stage, I was playing Horatio, and I just kind of stepped the fire out as I kept on with my monologue, and the audience loved it. Got big applause. Hey, the show must go on. You just have to be keenly aware of what's going on, not just on the stage but at all times around you, when you're doing outdoor theater.

Scene 4: "The One with the Dog" (and the Squirrel)[5]

Tom Luce: Working in the park is wonderful. It's an Olmsted-designed park, [Frederick Law Olmsted] who designed Central Park in New York. It's a beautiful, beautiful park. You're working outside. Last summer, there was an owl that every once in a while you could hear in the trees behind the stage. At one point during a performance, it was in *As You Like It*, a dog just wandered up onstage in the middle of a dance. The dog was just sort of dancing with us onstage.

Monte Priddy: In *Midsummer's Night Dream*, when I was playing Bottom, who gets turned into an ass by Puck, I was wearing an ass's head that had been specially made for me. But it was not easy for me to see out of it. I had to move very carefully and point the ass's head in just the right direction before I could see anything. One night as I was pontificating, a

116   Under the Greenwood Tree

dog came up onstage barking at me in a very threatening way. I thought, "Oh no, oh no, this is where it ends." A big gray beast. But somebody finally came up and grabbed the dog by her collar and led her away.

Crystian Wiltshire: At the end of the comedies, we usually do a jig: a big group dance. The play ends, and we all come out onstage; we do a lovely dance, have a good time. The audience loves it; it's a great time. We're doing it one night, and it's going great, and then a dog—a little one, not a big one like Monte had to deal with—runs on the stage while we're all in one line doing the group dance. I'm a dog lover, so I got sidetracked by the dog, and I end up chasing it offstage. I'm just going after it, and we get backstage, and I unfortunately never really picked it up or anything; it was too fast for me. I eventually have to run back onstage and finish the dance without the dog. But that's, you know, it's live theater in a park. There's planes, there's dogs, there's people shouting at you for some reason, there's ambulances going by, there's cop cars going by because it's summertime and people are crazy in the summertime. There's always something going on. It's just such a fun environment to try and get through a Shakespeare play.

Casey Clark: We have lots of run-ins with critters: squirrels, and a couple of years ago we had the owl issue. We had an owl sitting in the stage-left tree that did not want us anywhere near that tree on the thrust. Art Burns played Henry IV in the series when Curt Tofteland did *Richard II* and then *Henry IV, Part 1*; *Henry IV, Part 2*; and *Henry V*. I forget whether it was in *Part 1* or *Part 2*, but Art had this big monologue that he delivers. Curt had him up on the platform above, up in the center. There were these big hardware cloth, sort of side-wing things up there that I bounced light off and shined the light in. It was very kingly and dramatic. He'd be just at the build point of this monologue, and every night at the same point in his monologue, it was something about his voice or his volume, a squirrel would run from the up-left corner of the truss, straight across to the center point. So now she's five feet above his head, in the center of the truss, yelling at him and making so much noise that he got to the point where every night he would stop and look up at her, and she's just *chittering* to beat the band. She is so upset with him. He would talk to her, and she would calm down. Then he would immediately turn around, back in character, and pick up his monologue.

We have that immediacy, that need to adapt to whatever the environment is going to bring you. That strikes me as very Shakespearean. Maybe that's the key to the outdoor thing. What do you do when a hawk soars across the stage? What do you do when you're doing the Scottish play and your sound designer has all of these lovely owl sounds and the real owls start to answer but not on cue?

Scene 5: Memorable Performances

Macbeth (1986)

Hal Park: I directed the Scottish play, and that was, I thought, excellent and meaningful. We actually chose to stage the battle that's only referred to in the beginning of the play. That's the very start of the play, when Banquo and Macbeth are on their way back from the battle and they talk about it before they meet the Weird Sisters. It was my idea to actually stage the battle and then start the play. I hired David Liang out of Northern Kentucky University. He's a superb stage fight director, and it really elevated us. The summer before, my wife and I had gone up to the Stratford Festival [in Stratford, Ontario]. They were doing *Lear*. I remember sitting in the audience, and when Lear reviews the troops on their march to battle, I counted how many actors they walked across the stage in front of Lear to try to get a sense of how many actors we need to stage a battle in *Macbeth*. There were sixteen actors who walked diagonally across the stage, and it felt like there were hundreds. I knew that I had to have sixteen actors onstage in eight pairs to really stage what would feel like a major battle, and that became my focus. We did it, and it felt like there were hundreds out there. I would say that my production of the Scottish play was probably one of my favorites.

Rosencrantz and Guildenstern Are Dead (2002)

Tina Jo Wallace: I've had some pretty incredible experiences with Kentucky Shakespeare, getting to play opposite my husband. I really *loved* doing—and this is not a Shakespeare show, but it is inspired by Shakespeare—*Rosencrantz and Guildenstern Are Dead*. That summer, we did *Hamlet* and that show together. Two different nights, obviously, but we did both of those in rep that summer. Matt and I played Rosencrantz and Guildenstern. That show was so intense. We never left the stage, either one of us. As a matter of fact, they built into our costumes these jugs of water, pouches of water because we just never left the stage, which is not typical for Shakespeare. You get these framed scenes; people come in and leave. You get to go off for a little bit. But because we were onstage the entire time, they built in the water bottles. I think Tom Stoppard, who wrote the play, is brilliant. That show was not just creatively challenging but emotionally challenging and so much fun. For our audiences, it was one of the first times they'd been given a non-Shakespeare show. Yet because they'd seen *Hamlet*, they identified with the characters and knew all the inside jokes that were going on. So that was a really exciting show to be a part of! We got some of the best response from doing that show, night after night. I could have done that for another six weeks.

Othello (2004)

Phil Cherry: I knew I was playing Othello a year before I played it because Curt told me the year previously, in 2003, that he was going to do *Othello* in the following season and that I was going to be the actor. I gave him a big hug: "Thank you!" He knew I wanted to play this role, and he knew that I had the chops for it, and he knew that I already knew ninety percent of the play because I've been studying it for a long time. So he knew I was the guy. All the cast, everybody in the cast, went to Curt and said, "Hey, Curt. Do this with Phil." I mean, everybody in the cast was really wanting to do this.

Othello was . . . [*sighs*] what an amazing, grueling role. I sweated off five pounds on the stage every night; I drank two gallons of water before every performance and didn't pee a lot, believe it or not. I mean, I was sweating that much. I drank a gallon at the first act and a gallon at intermission to get me through. We were performing in Elizabethan costumes. But it was my most amazing time on the stage over there.

The most amazing moment that happened while I was playing Othello, the actor playing Emilia lost her voice. Curt said, "We're not canceling. I will speak Emilia from the audience on a mic." Emilia was onstage, and I was listening to Curt's voice while I was playing Othello. Talk about exercises in focus and concentration—that was it!

It was always a challenge over in the park at certain times, with other elements coming in like airplanes and bugs, drunks sometimes.

I was always in a rush to get done with "Desdemona, down," before the planes come, because you don't want to hold that moment. I was listening for planes while I'm saying, "Put out the light, and then put out the light," and then I'm thinking, "Oh God, here comes another big plane," during my murder monologue. "Let me hurry up and get this scene over with before this plane comes!" Curt always encouraged us to kind of hold, pause the scene, because when the planes come by, you can't hear the words. That's a pause you don't want to take when you're killing your wife onstage. I don't want to pause then! I want to get it over with. I was fortunate to have a wonderful cast: Andrew Lincoln, Allie Silva—Curt directed it—the Maupins were in it, and they both played wonderful roles. Abigail is the actress I was talking about who played Emilia who lost her voice. But the show must go on! We were all in the mode of that, and Curt certainly was. Unless the weather would stop us, most of the time we found a way to continue.

Macbeth (2015)

Abigail Maupin: I played Lady Macbeth in '15. She was not a part I had ever thought about playing. I didn't think I was appropriate for it. And, frankly, she's scary. Matt said, "Okay, we're going to do this, and I want you to read for it." Okay, I'm not going to turn it down, but I'm scared. I did not want her to be a straight-up cartoon villain. I was very worried about how to find her humanness. That was something I very specifically started looking for as I was going through the script. What are the moments for her that are filled with real human feeling? Where is she scared? Where is she sad? What's her drive? Not just "I want my husband to be the king." But why? Why is it important for her? Why is it important for him? What is their relationship that makes this so important to her? That was something that I really started to scan the script for. I was working with Jon O'Brien, who I have a good relationship with, and we started talking about how can we find that? Because he was on the same page, and so was Matt. It started to become a group discussion about where can we find the moments that are about their love for each other? Everybody gets so into the gore and the murder and the fun of all of that because it is fun. But we revel so much in the Grand Guignol of it that we lose "They're doing this because they love each other."[6] I personally think that the child thing is important. There were many ways you can interpret that for yourself

Abigail Maupin and Jon O'Brien in *Macbeth*, 2015.

as an actor. But for Jon and I, we decided that it was we had recently lost a child. Because I was in my forties when I played it, she was panicking that it's too late and there will be no babies. That was her last shot at it. That gave us such a good connection to each other in grief and such an urgency.

The Taming of the Shrew (2015)

Amy Attaway: When I did *Henry V* and Matt was talking about wanting me to come back the next year, I was like, "Can I do *The Winter's Tale*? Please? I really want to do *Winter's Tale*. Can I do *Winter's Tale*?" Pretty presumptuous after my first guest spot, trying to suggest what I wanted to do. He said, "Yes," and I did eventually do that. But he said he wanted to do *The Taming of the Shrew* because it's a very popular, very known title. He wanted to keep up the momentum from the first year. But he said, "I can't direct that. A man can't direct that play." All right, then. That's pretty much how the conversation had gone.

The way I found my way into that play was with the Maupins. We worked together on it from the beginning. This is one of the things I love to do most is to work with actors on the whole process. With

Greg and Abigail, once I knew that they were going to play Kate and Petruchio, we spent a lot of time, the three of us, talking about how we could make it work. How we could make Kate and Petruchio not seem awful, first of all. To make them not feel horrible and to make it not so clearly a horrible, misogynist, abusive-husband play. Because that's kind of what it is on the surface.

It happened that Matt and I took a trip to Stratford-upon-Avon before I directed that play. This is before I was on staff. I got to spend a lot of time in the archives there at the Royal Shakespeare Company reading about old productions of *Taming of the Shrew*. I stole some ideas, which was fun. Then working with Abigail and Greg with the inspiration that I got from the archives, we figured out a way to make Petruchio and Kate equally misfits in their own way and to find a way to make that ending scene, that reconciliation scene, not so much "I have now decided that men are powerful and I should be subservient" but more "We have decided that we are both in our own joke. We are now going to show all of you how you need to stop taking yourself so seriously and be in on our joke."

The other thing that I got inspired to do from looking through the archives was to make it clearly a play within a play. I used the pieces that are normally cut, that I actually didn't even know existed until I started working on this play in earnest. I kept in the frame, and I leaned heavily into the Renaissance-ness of it—Greg, as dramaturg, was for that as well—and to lean into the commedia [dell'arte] bits of what was going on. We framed it so that the people coming to do *The Taming of the Shrew* were a commedia troupe coming to do this play for this drunk dude. I knew it was Greg and Abigail, and they have all the commedia skills. I knew I had great game, smart, young ensemble actors and the great Donna Lawrence Downs to do the costumes. I was able to talk about the commedia archetypes and do that without entirely making it over the top and stylized. Somehow, we worked on threading that needle.

Abigail Maupin: That was one of those moments when I was so glad that Amy is a very ensemble director. She and I and Greg spent a lot of time just talking about how we make this work for a modern audience. We eventually came to the place that at the end of the play, we wanted it to be sort of Kate and Petruchio against the world—that they find their connection and team up. It's not just Kate that is a shrew. She's

Abigail and Gregory Maupin in *The Taming of the Shrew*, 2015.

playing an expectation. Everybody has decided that she's the shrew, so she has been like, "Okay, fine. Then this is my behavior." But everybody in the play is doing that. Bianca is a terrible bitch. The beautiful younger sister who's all spoiled and lovely, she's awful. When dad's around, she's the eye-batting, sweet, sweet girl. So innocent, lovely. When she's alone with Kate, there's hair pulling, and they are terrible. It's all about your appearance and what everybody else sees and leaning into that. I think Greg and I were able to find the small moments, even from their first scene, when they're actually intrigued by each other. They're playing their masks. They're playing their expectation of behaviors. But a couple times, it was, "Oh, wait. You get me." So that by the end of the play, the whole big final speech was about the two of them pulling something over on everybody else. They are immediately like, "Oh, I see what we're doing here. Yeah, we're going to win this bet together." Her speech then becomes making fun of everyone else in a way that makes them embarrassed, that takes away their masks. "Nope." [*Pointing to three characters in sequence*] "This is what you play, and you're a jerk. This is what *you* play, and you're a jerk. And this is what you play, and *you're* a jerk. We have each other now, and screw you." At the end, we are the only two people left onstage who are free from that. So *The Teaming of the Shrew*, I guess.

A Midsummer Night's Dream (2014)

Crystian Wiltshire: I'm about to hate myself for how cheesy I'm about to sound, okay? I'm just saying that right now. My favorite Shakespeare is *A Midsummer Night's Dream*. It all started when I saw it done at the Shakespeare Festival when I first moved to Louisville. I wasn't sure where my acting career was going to go; I wasn't sure what theater would hire me, if this city would welcome me as an artist. I had no idea. I went to Central Park on one of those magical, magical nights where there's over a thousand people out there, the weather's perfect, and I had a couple of my friends from UofL that were in the show, that I was able to say hi to. But I watched that show, and it was such a fun experience at the theater. It's the most fun I've *ever* had seeing a play. And *Midsummer*, to me, is one of those shows where, if you do it right, it will bring in anybody to your theater. It will help anybody appreciate Shakespeare. To me, it's the perfect play. And my night seeing it at Kentucky Shakespeare, I was like, "Not only do I love this play but I have to work for this company. I have to know these people." I fell in love with the company that night. I really did, and with *A Midsummer Night's Dream*. To this day, it's my favorite. When I say *cheesy*, I just think about myself just sitting three rows from the front, just being so wide eyed, looking up at the actors doing all this amazing stuff, like Greg Maupin with his donkey costume piece on his head looking all hilarious. Just so rookie to the community, just so unfamiliar with everyone. That me knew nothing about really how amazing the company was and how great Louisville was.

Romeo and Juliet (2000 and 2021)

Georgette Kleier: I've done the nurse in *Romeo and Juliet* twice. You think going into it, "Well, I know this person. I know who she is. I get her." What an idiotic idea that you think you know this person or that the lines will come back. In 2000, when I did it with Tina Jo Wallace as Juliet, I was in the process of adopting Miguel and the process of becoming a mother, just in a nontraditional way. My only child. I have two stepsons whom I adore, but he's my only child. I was finding the connection with Tina Jo, as the person who raised her. The nurse talks about her daughter, having lost her own child. So that was very present. I was right there. It was in the forefront of my mind, being a parent, being a mother, the idea of getting to raise a child. I was probably the right age for her then in terms of Shakespeare. I love working with Tina Jo. I loved it. It was so raw. So now, doing it in 2021, after I've raised my son pretty much, now I'm doing it looking back on the raising of a child, which is probably more appropriate for the nurse. Maybe I'm too old legitimately in terms of Shakespeare, but I just feel a little more wise. My relationship with Juliet is always based on love for that child, for Juliet. Always. All of the nurse's decisions are because she just adores her. Two very different places in my life absolutely impacted the way I played her.

Romeo and Juliet (2016)

Casey Clark: My recent favorite performance has to be the *Romeo and Juliet* that we did in 2016. It was good. I won an award for it, Broadway across America Best Lighting Design in Louisville for that year. It's also one of my favorite plays, although the Scottish play's probably really my favorite. *R* and *J* is fun to light because you have street scenes, you have party scenes, you have nighttime courtyard scenes and balcony scenes and windows that light, and you have tomb scenes. They talk all the time about moons and stars in the night sky. It's a big imagery theme throughout the play.

The strongest lighting moments were the balcony scene and the tomb sequences. The tomb scene at the end of the show is a lot of pages. There's a whole lot that happens in that tomb. There are lots of fights. I owe Matt his bravery on this. He wanted it to really look like a tomb. At that time, we still had the old tiring house above that went all the way across.[7] We designated a door at the top to be the door of the tomb. I had just a tiny bit of light behind that door so that you could tell when it opened and you could see their silhouettes. The rest of the stage was completely dark. They did their fights with flashlights. The exception was Juliet on her bier was brilliantly lit, but you couldn't see the lights that were lighting her because I used beam projectors, which aren't made anymore. They're very bright and very tight so that I could light her from just the right angle that where the light falls off on the other side, it was hidden by the bier itself. She was bright as a firecracker, and everything else around her was pitch dark. There were two lights on in that scene and flashlights. When Romeo comes in, he's in that light too. But after their deaths, I talked Matt into letting us do some really low angled slots, pale blue that came in from the side without any front light. It filled the sides of their faces and left shadows down the front. They had the flashlights for their faces. I just crept that in really, really slowly because when the duke comes in, there's a long, long, long, long, long scene. It's hard on the audience to stay in the dark that long when somebody's talking. We just crept it up a little bit at a time and still kept the look of it. But it made the whole thing look sort of gray, which was really nice. It was good. It was powerful.

Braden McCampbell: We had a Black Romeo in *Romeo and Juliet*. They've been as diverse as they can possibly be, in my opinion, based solely on the fact that they tried to bring that issue to light pretty early on. Case in point: *Romeo and Juliet*. It is two feuding families, but one of the concepts was that all of the Montagues were Black. Romeo's entire family, all of his friends, were Black. Juliet's family was all white. So that immediate point that they're trying to make is like, "Hey, we can make this show about anything." Here's what's going on in America right now. This was based on—maybe based on—a racist-motivated attack at a Kroger or something. They were like, "We're going to put this in a light. Your kids really just want to get together, and the only reason you two don't like each other is because. . . ." Oddly enough, most people, [it] seemed like, didn't even pick up on it. All of the Montagues are Black, and all of the Capulets are white. People didn't pick up on it. Nowadays, if we had put that up, people would be like, "Oh, why is this all about race? This is clearly about race." Whereas when we originally did it, people didn't pick up on it. A grocery store just got shot up, and we're totally going to make sure it's still in your face because while some of you may have already forgotten that that happened, the people it affected, the Black community, totally remember that.

With *Romeo and Juliet*, one of the coolest things about that show was [that] to help people understand just what was happening, we started transitioning from old period-piece clothing into modern clothing in the middle of the play. My grandma came. Crystian Wiltshire, who played Romeo, walks out, and he's wearing Jordans, and she said, "I thought that that boy just forgot to change his clothes over after intermission," because that's when we start transferring into the standard clothing. But then everybody else is doing it, until at the part where they kill each other, we were all in regular attire now. Then she's like, "*Oh.*" That's when she got why they killed each other. It was two teenagers in love. But she had always thought *Romeo and Juliet* were these old people, even though they mention Juliet's birthday at some point in the show. She'd always just glanced over that. Okay, two goofy people decided they're going to kill each other because they're so in love. She said that that was the first time that she realized that these two kids killed each other, because they were wearing younger-looking pieces than everybody else, who's got like a suit or something on. So she's like, "Oh, they're kids. They're two kids who killed each other."

The intensity for that show was probably one of the worst. I remember hearing someone say, "I hope this reads." They were absolutely right that it would read. They were kind of right that it wouldn't read at first, because if my grandma's going, "Why's that boy out in Jordans? Did he forget to change clothes?" then you know other people in the audience are like, "Why is that boy out in Jordans? Did anybody tell him that he wasn't supposed to? Why's he wearing his regular shoes when he had on boots earlier?" Then as our clothing progressively changes into more modern things, it's like, "Oh! Oh." Because when people see Shakespeare in period clothes with all the ruffs and stuff, they're like, "This is a bunch of old-timey nobles doing old-timey noble things." Like these are the *Days of Our Lives* for old English people. But when you put it in the more modern clothing and you adapt it to modern day, it forces people's brains to go, "Nah, hold up. Remember when you were nineteen and were all in love and thought this was going to be the love of your life and you all broke up like three weeks later and you were heartbroken even though y'all dated for three weeks? That's this show right here!"

Crystian Wiltshire: I think any member of Kentucky Shakespeare would be really upset at me if I didn't tell you what happened at preview night for *Romeo and Juliet*; it's the night before opening. At the time, it was a record preview night for a show that Kentucky Shakespeare had done. There was over nine hundred people there for *preview*, which is amazing! The show was going so well. So, so well. We get to the end, where I am already dead, and Juliet wakes up from her poisonous sleep. She sees that I'm dead, and she is supposed to use the dagger that I used to kill myself to kill herself. She can't find the dagger. She's feeling around me, feeling around this set piece that we're on, and the audience is starting to get a little restless because they know that she's supposed

Crystian Wiltshire as Romeo and Megan Massie Ware as Juliet in *Romeo and Juliet*, 2016.

to be dead sooner than later. When I realized that she can't find it, I realized where I'd put it. I decide to tell her, "It's in my pocket" [*stage whisper*]. Because I'm assuming that since I'm dead, my microphone is certainly off at this point! She ends up digging in my pocket, and she finds it. I think the first line she says is, "Come, dagger," after she finds it, so the audience gives a big round of applause, like, "Yay, she found it; she can kill herself now," which is kind of weird. But she does do the deed. After the show, Matt Wallace tells me that my microphone was still turned on, and this audience of nine hundred people heard me say, "*It's in my pocket.*"

It was a fun little hashtag that started after the show. There were some comments on the Kentucky Shakespeare Facebook page where audience members were like, "Wow, that show was so, so good! #It'sInMyPocket." What Matt loved to do for the company at the end of every summer season is give away some form of swag, basically to show everyone his appreciation for all the work that they've done throughout the summer. Sometimes when the summer was really rainy, we'd all get a Kentucky Shakespeare poncho; sometimes we'd just get a Kentucky Shakespeare hat, anything like that. That summer, Matt gave out these little, tiny flashlights and on it, [it] said "Kentucky Shakespeare" and underneath it was "#It'sInMyPocket." After an embarrassing night like that, we obviously got all the kinks out, and opening night was just magical.

Much Ado about Nothing (2017)

Gregory Maupin: I think we probably agree on our favorite production. It was doing *Much Ado* together. That was one of those times when you actually get to play parts that you're well suited for. The part is recognizable and something that you know. This is one that I understand how it works. It's both a challenge, but it's not a weird "How am I going to do that?" There are parts that are a challenge because you don't see how you are going to do that, and there are parts that are a challenge where I have to meet what is asked of me, but I know that I am right for it. We really like performing together—it's weird. It's a thing that we legitimately enjoy and feel comfortable doing. You can get to deeper places more quickly when you finish each other's sandwiches. [*Laughs.*]

Abigail Maupin: My favorite role was Beatrice in *Much Ado*, partly because it was with Greg and partly just because it's a fan-freaking-tastic part. She's so smart, and she's so together, until the scene when she's not together, when she loses it after the wedding with Benedick. There again, it's the rage thing. It's being able to maintain, maintain, maintain, and then lose it completely. That's really fun. I'm a huge Jane Austen fan. So being able to do that production with the love of my life opposite me set in a beautiful Regency setting: this is my dream right here; this is it.

King Lear (2019)

Jon Huffman: Last year, I knew I was going to be playing King Lear; I knew it before December. As I read and read the play, I realized this is an eighty-year-old man but there is stuff in here that an eighty-year-old man cannot do. You have to play it when you're younger. A lot of it is pretty physical. I thought, "Well, I'm in pretty good shape." But among other things, once the character has been onstage doing everything an actor can be asked to do for two hours, then at the very end he is asked to carry the body of his daughter onto the stage and hold her while he emotes over her death. I thought that's a lot. That's a lot

In the Park   129

to ask. I began last year in January a really sort of strenuous workout regimen and diet regimen. Spent about six months really preparing hard for this summer because I knew it was going to be physically demanding. I knew I better be in shape because otherwise you'd get to the summer and you'd get the show blocked and you'd get to the end and you'd have to say to the director, "You know what, this carrying the body, I don't think that's going to work." You don't want that as an actor, especially when it's clear in the script that that's what happens.

That was my first time playing Lear, and it will probably be my last. It's not a role actors do much. It's by far the hardest thing I've ever done onstage. It's not a role an actor aspires to; it's a role an actor feels obligated to. After you've done so much Shakespeare and you reach a certain age, you think, "If I'm going to do it, I better do it now." It's really, really hard. I'm glad I did it. Don't know if I ever want to do it again.

Braden McCampbell: You can feel the way that people shifted when Jon Huffman walked onstage to do *King Lear*. You could *feel* the way that people suddenly were like, "Oh, hi, King Lear, hello. Hello." He had this royal, grand proclamation thing where he came on the steps. We're all standing at attendance. We snap our staffs into place. We stand and we look at him, and then somebody blows a horn. It goes *whoo*, and then everybody crosses and bows, and he comes out. You could see the way that everybody's head in the audience goes, "Oh, oh, well, should we bow too?" Then they all snap and look up at him like, "Hello, Your Majesty."

I got to play Edmund, who's one of the bigger villains. I will not lie: I had impostor syndrome terribly bad. Terribly bad for the first month and a half of rehearsal and even into the first week of the show. I came this close to being like, "Matt, I don't think you cast me in the right part for this, my dude. This is a big part. I do not believe that I should be here." The first two nights, after everything was done, I still felt that way. I was talking to Neill Robertson about it. We bowed together, as the brothers. We got a big roaring, rousing applause that night, and I'm just like, "Man, people really loved you tonight." And he's like, "They loved *us*. Why would you think they were just applauding for me?" I just brushed it off. But then I'm sitting there, and Jon Huffman, who was my mentor my first year there, walks up to me and says, "Hey, man, everything okay?" I say, "Yeah, no, it's good. I'm still really just in awe that I'm working with so many great people." And he's like, "Man, you're doing great out there! What do you mean? Why are you in awe? You're one of us." I felt completely out of my element, like I shouldn't have been there. He leaned over and said, "That's called impostor syndrome, and I had it for the first week of this production as well." Jon Huffman telling me that he had impostor syndrome, the man who literally makes the audience turn and look up at him like he is royalty, King Lear, telling me, "It's fine, dude; you're doing great. Don't let it defeat you." I took a little while to actually believe it, but I'm like, "Okay, if Jon Huffman can still get nervous, if Jon Huffman still has those moments where he's like, 'I am not supposed to be here right now,' well, the show's got to go on, and for some reason, somebody cast me in this, so I guess I'm going to go do the dang thing."

Later in the run, someone in the audience waited until we got done and everything was over with, and then they were standing off to the side. Someone said to me, "Hey, man, somebody out here in the audience wants to see you." I'm thinking someone like my friends or family, they came to encourage me with "Hey, we're about to leave, but you were great; good job." But it was some random person I'd never met. He's been coming to the show for years, he said; he was there with his wife and his two kids. He's like, "Hey, man, your Edmund legitimately made me feel sorry for Edmund." There will always be slimeballs that you're like, "Oh, okay, you're going to get what's coming to you. Your mom made you the bastard, or your dad made you the bastard, and he's been joking about it. Okay, fine. But you're going to get what's coming to you." But this guy was like, "Your Edmund legitimately made me go, 'Yeah, he's screwing over a lot of people, but he's genuinely doing it because he's tired of being the butt of everybody's jokes,'" which is how I played that.

My take on Edmund was Jon Snow. That's who I got my guide and inspiration from, from *Game of Thrones*. He goes through a lot of shit that he just takes on the cheek, being called Ned's bastard and everything. I decided Jon Snow is a decent person who's just always trying to do the right thing. Even though everybody's like, "You're the bastard; why would we listen to you? Oh, you're the bastard; you should be sent to the Wall. Jon Snow, you know nothing." What would happen if Jon Snow decided one day, "You know what, I'm tired of being the bastard. I'm tired of y'all talking shit to me. I'm going to be king, somehow or another, and I'm going to do whatever's necessary

Macbeth in a parking lot, 2020.

to get there. I'm going to go get a dragon, and I'm going to come back and have it eat you alive because I want to be king." I tried to work in that sympathy that was like if Jon Snow cracked off one day and was just like, "You're all dead; I'm done. You can all get eaten by the Ice Walkers." That was the approach that I used, and this random stranger said, "I genuinely felt sympathy for your character."

Macbeth [in the Parking Lot] (2020)

In fall 2020, after the summer season in Central Park had been canceled because of the COVID-19 pandemic, Kentucky Shakespeare did a production of *Macbeth*, not in a park but in a parking lot. A raised set was built in the middle of the lot, and the audience watched from their cars, listening through a local public radio station.

Elizabeth Siebert: In fall 2020, Matt just really wanted to produce something. The board only has to approve his choice of production if it's outside of the summer season. If he wants to do a spring show or a fall show, he has to get permission from the board. He brought it to us, and we were all like, "Yes!" Nobody hesitated for a second. We don't care how terrible it ends up being. We just wanted to see theater again. "Yes, let's do it." Nobody was hesitant. We were worried about safety protocols and making sure the city approved everything, that kind of thing, just to do our fiduciary due diligence as a board. But you know, what we often say is, "We don't even care if it makes money. We're a nonprofit. As long as it breaks even and doesn't hurt the company financially, let's take a risk and do something exciting." It felt like the right thing to do, to do theater in a safe way and let us be a company again.

I went three times, and my kids came with me. We sat in the car with the radio on. In fact, one of the times we thought we killed the car battery, and it was in my daughter's car. So we had a little panic attack. But that was extra fun, just because I love that show so much. And you got the radio-play sense of it, and the live action. You also felt connected again, human again, after having been quarantined for so long in our houses. To just have that communal experience with other people, even though they were in the next car, it was just so much fun.

Shakespeare in Love (2021)

Anya Bond Beckley is an African American woman from a theater-loving family. Bond Beckley was raised in Memphis, attended school and worked in several cities, and then settled with her family in Louisville. At first a longtime audience member, she then became a member of the board of directors.

Anya Bond Beckley: Favorite performance: As strange as it seems, I'd have to say this year. It has nothing to do with the play. It has to do with the audience's reaction because we got to come back to the park. You're doing *Shakespeare in Love*, and everyone seemed excited. Not just us geeks but everybody. You're talking about crushing numbers of people coming to see it. I'd have to say this one because it's like Matt picked the perfect play to put on this year. It really spoke to the audience, because I saw faces I had never seen before. People who had never seen it, but they were just so happy to be with someone else, whether it's socially distant or however it had to be, to be back in the park.

And one perhaps best-forgotten performance . . .

Back in the park with *Shakespeare in Love*, 2021.

Lizard *Lear* (1987)

Elizabeth Siebert: In '87, I went and checked the list of shows. I was at UK [University of Kentucky] in undergrad. I came home for the summer and went to one of the shows here. It was one of the worst shows I've ever seen. It was the *King Lear* that they called the lizard *Lear*. They had lizard tails. It was one of the worst productions I've ever seen. Lear, I don't know what kind of lizard it is, but he was the lizard that has the big thing, frill, like in *Jurassic Park*, and then each one of the daughters had an elaborate lizard costume with a huge tail that they would drag across the stage. It was most ridiculously overproduced. So I sort of had a bad taste in my mouth. I was like, ick. I never tried to get a job as an undergrad or grad student with Kentucky Shakespeare because I was just like, "That's not my thing. I'm not into that." To this day, we talk about "Did you see lizard *Lear*?" Terrible.

Gregory Maupin: There are several lines in *Lear* about animal imagery and stuff, and someone decided that everyone was an animal. There were lizards. I think there were some birdlike things going on. Very literal

134   Under the Greenwood Tree

costumes which had long tails hanging off the side of them. That's what people do with Shakespeare. There was an episode of *Mystery Science Theater* where they did a *Hamlet* sketch and they talked about, "Here's our storyboards for—this is the bucket-head *Hamlet*, where everyone has buckets on their heads. And it represents humanity. Here's one underwater. Here's one where we just put pieces of furniture as characters and no human actors are involved." It happens a lot with Shakespeare, so this was not the weirdest thing anyone has ever done in the world.

Act 4

"All the World's a Stage"

In spring 1961, before there was even a full season of Shakespeare in Central Park, the Carriage House Players launched what would become a long tradition of community outreach by performing a play for the senior class of the Old Kentucky Home High School in Bardstown. The next year, the Carriage House Players arranged a tour of Old Louisville and a production of *Macbeth* for Shepherdsville High School students.[1] These early events exemplified Doug Ramey's desire to bring Shakespeare to audiences who had limited access to live theater. Ramey himself came from a small town in Kentucky and wanted to serve communities like his childhood home. Even more important, he and succeeding directors were committed to reaching underserved audiences, whether they be in rural Kentucky or in minority and low-income neighborhoods in Louisville. Thus, when the summer season ended, Ramey and members of the company packed up their props, got into a bus, and headed to high school gymnasiums around the state. In addition, he and his successors experimented with performances and workshops in other venues, from coffee shops to libraries, other parks, and even a nearby prison. The shared belief that Shakespeare is for everyone animated all the outreach efforts over the years. The company acted on that belief by devising ways to draw people to Central Park; taking plays to audiences who, for whatever reason, could not get there; and engaging members of a wide range of communities in reading, studying, and performing Shakespeare themselves. The histories of these outreach programs illustrate how Kentucky Shakespeare became a model community-based and community-serving arts organization.

136 Under the Greenwood Tree

Scene 1: Shakespeare in the Schools

After that 1961 performance at the Old Kentucky Home High School, the Carriage House Players began traveling around the state to visit public K–12 schools as well as colleges and universities. By 1965, the troupe had given fifty performances in twenty-five schools. The program kept growing in subsequent years. By the end of the first decade, the company had entertained "287,000 people in 514 performances in 120 schools in 65 counties." And in 2013, on the eve of the recent renaissance, Kentucky Shakespeare could boast of having served its one millionth child.[2] These events included interaction between the cast and the students, many of whom had never seen a play, much less met an actor, and many former cast members fondly recall those interactions. Curt Tofteland expanded the youth outreach, hiring Doug Sumey as an education director because of his prior experience in Kansas teaching Shakespeare to young people. During Sumey's tenure, the program expanded beyond the schools to include summer camps and the development of the Globe Players, a troupe of high school students who underwent intensive training and put on professional-quality productions every summer.

Bekki Jo Schneider: Doug Ramey had a television show called *Songs of Faith.* Every Monday night, he would tape. Then, I got to get in a car with him at eight o'clock at night and drive to wherever the Shakespeare bus was going to perform for colleges. That was probably 1960 to '64. He performed all over the state of Kentucky, doing Shakespeare for colleges.

Monte Priddy: There were some great times and there were some interesting performances during the seventies. Doug would work up a tour. He'd find schools for us to play. I remember trips to the mountains of Appalachia. Typically, that would involve going to school in the morning, putting up our set in the middle of the gymnasium facing one of the sides where all the spectators usually sit at basketball games, and then blasting away to try to make ourselves heard and understood in these echoing gymnasiums. Occasionally we would be someplace where they had an auditorium where the acoustics would be a little better. But we couldn't depend on that.

Georgette Kleier: During Bekki Jo Schneider's time, we just did it with music stands. It was sort of like a readers' theater thing that we took

"All the World's a Stage"   137

to the schools. It was the fall of '84, and it was Mackers [*Macbeth*]. It's the show to do around Halloween. We took our music stands, and we took our scripts, and we sort of did readers' theater for students in local Jefferson County Public Schools. I'm not sure the student reaction was particularly effusive, to be completely honest with you. I think it's before we understood how to unlock Shakespeare for kids. I think it was our best attempt at that time with the tools we had to at least make them aware of what it sounds like, instead of just getting the assignment to read it in the book.

Hal Park: My vision for the company originally was to end the season and then literally pack up that costume trailer and the tech trailer and the control booth and pull out of town and pull into any town in the state of Kentucky that had a gym in it and be able to set up a show right there. That was my goal. That was my vision. In the state of Kentucky, there's not a small town that doesn't have a basketball gym in it. My vision was to be able to pull up to the back of a gymnasium, and if they had 220-volt power somewhere in the building, we would be able to put up a full-fledged Shakespearean production with set, lights, and sound and invite the entire community in to see it. I would have loved to have been able to go to Scottsville, Kentucky, or go to Whitesburg, Kentucky, or go to Pikeville, Kentucky, or wherever and be able to pull in and do a great production and maybe even stay around long enough to go into the school system and talk to the kids. Kind of like the circus.

Curt Tofteland: I wanted to be a year-round operation. We were the Kentucky Shakespeare Festival, and I wanted to serve the 120 other counties in the region. I was interested in getting out there. Every year when Doug Ramey did the summer season in the park, he loaded up a school bus he painted red, and off they went to Appalachia to go up and down those mountain roads and take Shakespeare to his homeland. I felt the same.

It became my passion to take Shakespeare to the schools. I heard so many people say they had a very bad experience with Shakespeare. I said, "Yes, I hated Shakespeare because our teacher read it and made us read it." It became my mission to be able to help English teachers who were not comfortable with getting Shakespeare up on his feet. I wanted to be the resource. I thought of being in service to educators as the secret of success. I created a program with Kate Brain, who is a local English teacher, a brilliant English teacher. We did a summer camp called Page to the Stage, where teachers would come for a full week and be taught how to use Shakespeare and how to play games and stuff. I was working with only the best teachers because they were teachers that wanted to go beyond sitting on your butt in the chair, teachers who recognized the value of Shakespeare, and they had some sense of performance in them. It was always being in service to others. We were there to do what it is that we do, and you do what it is that you do, and we can make you better at that, and your students can better understand it. It was my passion for every student who ever graduated from high school or middle school in the state of Kentucky that when Shakespeare was mentioned, they would go, "Oh, yeah. I remember when I was a sophomore this troupe of actors came to my school and did Shakespeare for us in the gymnasium."

In the education program, one of the shows they still do is *Boy Meets Girl Meets Shakespeare*, a version of a show I did when I was working with Moses Goldberg at StageOne. I just recreated that from my experience at StageOne. It was always two actors—one male, one female—and it was usually three scenes that were introduced with a prologue, and then the scene would be performed, and then there would be a post-scene discussion with the students, and they would get a study guide. We developed the study guide. A few years down the road when the Kentucky Education Reform Act (KERA; 1990) came into existence, we began to rebuild the tenets of what an education in Kentucky meant. I was on the committee that was fighting for including the arts. When KERA was passed and implemented, twenty percent of your high school grade was connected to the arts. That's what we were asking for. It made us more mandatory.[3]

We took it to the high schools, but it didn't take very long before the middle schools right next door said, "Hey, well, what about us?" So, by invitation, I started serving the middle schools, and then it wasn't very long before the upper elementary said, "Hey, what about us?" So I created a program for upper elementary, and then the surprise of surprises came when the kindergarten through third grade teachers said, "What about us?" That really challenged me because what can I do with kindergarten through third graders using Shakespeare as the core? It couldn't be *Boy Meets Girl*. I created a one-man show called *Shakespeare's Clowns and Fools*. I did that primarily

Curt Tofteland performing *Shakespeare's Clowns and Fools* for a school group, 1993.

because I wanted to continue acting. I've done over four hundred performances of that show.

Now we're serving the entire education system. We could go into a county and set up base camp and then go to elementary, middle, and high schools within a sixty-mile drive. That's how we were able to serve more students in more counties. I always looked at it from the standpoint of "you can't appreciate Shakespeare reading it on the page." It's only appreciated up on its feet. Around these performances came workshops where kids participated. They weren't audience members. They were actually participants. Rather than doing art for an audience, you do art with an audience. That's how the programs began to expand. I ended up doing *Shakespeare's Kings*, *Shakespeare's Queens*, one-person shows to be able to serve the schools. Every year in *Boy Meets Girl Meets Shakespeare*, the scenes changed, and we developed a range of study guides.

Turning it from a summer season only into a year-round outreach was a huge challenge. But it's proven to be our survival. It was the education program that dug us out of debt and then began to build a cash reserve. It was our education program that got the most visibility because we were out in the state. You can raise more money when you

140   Under the Greenwood Tree

serve more counties. I remember telling the board in 1990 that we will have taken our programs to all one hundred twenty counties within ten years, and they sort of chuckled and laughed and didn't think it was possible. We accomplished [it] in early 1999. Year after year, we will be back out there serving the whole state because we're still connected to the historical memory of Doug being from Appalachia. It was a great joy for us the first time that we took our workshops back out into Doug's homeland.

Doug Sumey: We had two vans. I would hire touring teams, usually kind of an A team and a B team, but not that one was better than the other. One male and one female on each team. We would usually book them for a full week in a geographic zone, and they would do two to three shows a day, usually an hour long. It might be a day of *Boy Meets Girl Meets Shakespeare* shows, or it might be two *Boy Meets Girl Meets Shakespeare* shows at one school, then they take a lunch break and go to another school and do maybe a couple *Staging Shakespeare* workshops. There's either a performance-based workshop, which was the *Boy Meets Girl Meets Shakespeare*, or *Shakespeare's Clowns*, which is what Curt did, or the teaching-based workshops that were *Staging Shakespeare* or *Teaching Tolerance*. The one thing I really liked about our educational performances was that we never performed for more than one hundred students at a time. It was never a big assembly for three hundred kids because we wanted to keep it interactive, and we wanted to be able to have the actors engage with the students and for them to ask questions and respond to the work that they were seeing on the stage.

For many people at the educational tours that were going out to the communities, this was their first experience seeing live theater. That is a huge amount of responsibility, which I would communicate with the staff and the actors in the training process. What an honor, to be that first experience, and a privilege to be able to share that and to be the ones to share it. Some of the kids who came and did Camp Shakespeare said, "My first experience of seeing Shakespeare is when *Boy Meets Girl Meets Shakespeare* came to my school, and now I want to do Camp Shakespeare." Then they graduate along and do Globe Players. That right there means everything.

Tina Jo Wallace: Our artist educators are the hardest-working people in show business. It was only a few weeks that we would rehearse. You'd have to learn *Boy Meets Girl Meets Shakespeare*, which is a guy and a girl doing scenes from Shakespeare and then teaching about Shakespeare in between. You'd have to learn your scenes and create those and rehearse those. Plus, all the interaction part—practicing what information you have to get out and how you get the kids to be involved in that and how you get them to stimulate the conversation, so it feels like they're the ones who are directing the conversation.

Then you have what we call Bard Buddies, where you learn one Shakespeare show that you kind of create. You create the props and costume pieces that you're going to take out to them. You get into a classroom with a kindergarten, first-, or second-grade class, and you basically tell a Shakespeare story—maybe it's *The Tempest*—and you cast the kids as you're telling it. It's advanced storytelling because you get the kids up and you get them to say some Shakespeare lines and act out the show. But you have to know that show so well so that no matter what a kid says to you or how the classroom is shaped, you can still get that story across to the kids. It's also a very creative, fun thing to do. I even brought in my guitar and made up a song! That was part of my Bard Buddies. The kids always think the guitar is the coolest thing ever, so you immediately get that validation. They love you!

Then there's conflict resolution programs, where you use Shakespeare's conflict scenes to motivate the conversation about conflict resolution. I did a program that was through the Girl Scouts. It was about abusive relationships. We did several scenes—like a Kate and Petruchio scene—and we would then talk about what were the warning signs. We'd play it to the nth of him being an abuser or potential abuser. Then we would say, "Oh, okay, what are the warning signs?" and try to get the kids to recognize when relationships are unhealthy. We use several different scenes from Shakespeare to get them to be like, "Oh yeah, when he's trying to tell you that you didn't see what you saw." Things that kids could identify and then say, "Oh, I see that. My friend has got a boyfriend, and he's always saying, 'No, I didn't do that. No, you didn't see that on my texts!'" That kind of thing. That was a great workshop. You learn all of these before you even get in the van and start going out to the schools.

You work intensely with your touring partner. It's usually a guy and a girl. Then you usually get to workshop it at, like, one local school. We would give a workshop away for free. You get to go try it out with them, and then you're on the road for four months just in every corner of Kentucky. Sometimes in Tennessee. Matt and I toured to North Carolina. What's awesome about it is sometimes you are the first theatrical experience kids have had. They think that you're famous. They think that you know all the famous people because you're an actor and you're in front of them. You're showing them what professional theater is and that this is something they can and should enjoy, and maybe this might be something that they want to do. In some of these places in Kentucky, they don't have exposure to a lot of that. It's not Peace Corps, but it really felt like we're going out there and showing them different ways to think about things and really making a difference.

It's not just about creating the next artist, because only so many people are going to do this for a living. It's that theater can teach so many things. It teaches empathy; it teaches conflict resolution, how to have a disagreement and then come out of that, through positive and negative examples. It teaches confidence and just so many things even for those kids that are never going to pay to go see a show. I don't care that they don't give us their money. If I can spark in them a new thought—putting themselves in somebody else's shoes for five seconds—that will make a difference. I've worked with at-risk kids who've already gotten in trouble. One of the things that I hear, and Matt hears this with the work that he does in the prison, is they never learned to see things through other people's eyes. If we can do that, we're going to make the world a better place. It's not necessarily going to help the theater, but it might!

Abigail Maupin: The reaction of the students depends sometimes on the time of day. Are we at the end of the school day? Are they not awake yet? Are they hungry? Mostly, we thought the seventh and the eighth graders were the most difficult audiences. They don't want to be taught anything. Even if we're taking them out of the class that they hate the most. They still just are, "I'm at school. I hate this." It was hard finding the balance between "we don't talk to you like the elementary school kids, but we don't talk to you like the high schoolers either." They're tough. They're a grumpy audience who slouch in their seats and cross their arms, and you have to win them over.

I'll tell you my favorite story. We did the *Boy Meets Girl* for a high school in an extra-large classroom. We had an AP English class. They were probably juniors or seniors. We also had the wrestling team at that very same performance. The wrestling team, I think, wanted to be wrestling. I don't know if they were supposed to be in class or at wrestling practice. They did the slouching and the arm crossing. Our last scene for the high schoolers was Brutus and Cassius in *Julius Caesar* the night before they go off to battle knowing that things are probably going to go badly. They argue, and then they get over it. I was playing Brutus. We get to the end of the scene. Greg goes back to change. I'm the one who said, "Okay, what happened in that scene?" It's not an easy scene. It's wordy, and it's subtle. Their relationship is subtle, and why they're clashing with each other at this moment is subtle. One of the wrestling boys sort of shifted in his seat and said, "Well, they love each other like brothers, and they're saying goodbye." I'm like, "My work here is done. We have nothing else to talk about. That's it."

Braden McCampbell: We travel all around Kentucky with the education side, including Ohio and a few other places, even. There was one moment that will always stick with me, and that's because it was somewhere in Kentucky, very rural. We're at a school. There is a kid. We're doing a two-person show for these kids and talking about conflict resolution and things like that. There's not very many African Americans in this school. So few, in fact, that this little African American kid immediately latches onto the fact that he's seeing me. We're starting to pack up and everything, and the teacher's like, "Hey, there's not many Black people in our town. Like, very few." At this point in time, I had my hair cut short, and my beard was nicely trimmed, and I kind of looked like Chad Boseman from *Black Panther*. It was kind of an intentional look, yes. She was like, "He's just really happy he got to see someone like you onstage. He thinks you're actually Black Panther, and he wants to know if he can have a picture with you." I'm like, "You said there's not that many Black people?" She said, "No, you're the first one he's ever seen onstage, apart from the Black Panther, so he thinks you're Chadwick Boseman who just came to his stage to do a play for him." He runs up, and he gives me a hug. He's like, "I'm really happy I got to meet you." Part of me thinks I should really not be claiming to be Chadwick Boseman right now, but, "Hi, kid!" I talk in the Black Panther voice for him. "How are you doing? Are you good today?" I'm sitting here trying to do my best Black Panther voice and everything with him, and he asks, "Can we take a picture?" So there's a picture of me and this little Black boy doing the "Wakanda forever" symbol. He's smiling with this big grin on his face. He's screaming out, "Wakanda forever," while they're taking the picture. It looks absolutely amazing.

Having that moment with that kid gave me some insight. If when I was younger there had been more people of color that were coming to my school doing theater, I might have been into it a lot sooner. I might have invested more time in it. I might have invested more work in it, versus "Oh, that's that thing people do that's weird." That's one of those moments that stuck with me. The teacher said there weren't that many Black people in the surrounding area, and for him to see so few Black people and suddenly immediately believe that I'm Chad Boseman, that I'm Black Panther, is . . . [*sighs*] it's heartwarming, but it's also a little painful. Man, there is so much out there in the world for you, my dude. There's so much out there in the world for you that you have not yet realized, that you do not know. But I got to introduce him to Shakespeare; I got to introduce him to theater. I got to pretend to be Black Panther. [*Laughs.*]

Doug Sumey: The thing that I found to be the most unique about Kentucky Shakespeare, and the reason why I left Kansas City Shakespeare to come to Kentucky, was their mission towards education and the incredible work that they were doing all throughout the state to bring Shakespeare to these rural communities all over the commonwealth. That really inspired me. What also inspired me was the work within the prison program and what Curt was doing there and how he was wanting to generate that same type of programming for—for lack of a better phrase—at-risk youth. The same kind of models of teaching tolerance and conflict resolution and using theater and the works of Shakespeare for the intrinsic value of it. The other thing that intrigued me was that they didn't have the summer camp programming yet, and Curt had asked if I could bring that model from Kansas City, which I had been doing for three years, to Kentucky. I was really excited to spearhead that and bring that year-round education programming through the summer months as well.

The first season, we had one site, and it was amazing. We had forty kids in the program, and that was the fortieth year of the festival. It was a great experience. I was the manager of the camp, and I hired three other instructors; that way there was a ten-to-one ratio. We had students from eight years old up to eighteen years old all in one camp together, where they would work together at times, but then we would

Globe Players in rehearsal, 2004.

parcel them out to age groups so each group could have more lesson plans that are geared a little more to what their level might be. It was fantastic. We put together a show at the very end that got rained out, intense rain. It was a monsoon. We had to move over to a nearby church that had agreed to open up their space for us and have all of these drenched kids put on some Shakespeare.

We had a partnership with Louisville Central Community Center and did a camp with them.[4] We had all these kids who normally wouldn't be on the stage at the Kentucky Shakespeare Festival performing. Then one of the little brothers or little sisters, maybe about four years old, came charging up on the stage during one of the Camp Shakespeare arrangements, dancing and chanting and singing with her big brother or big sister. It was just a part of it.

Then I wanted to make Camp Shakespeare a little bit more of a high school program. So I created the Globe Players, which is still running now. It's the high school conservatory type program that culminates in a performance on the Shakespeare Festival stage on their own given night. They put on a full-length Shakespeare play.

Casting for that was unique because it's pretty much based on enrollment or those who sign up for the program. We would assemble that group and decide on a show that would fit with that particular

146   Under the Greenwood Tree

group. Then auditions would happen once we got all assembled as a group. That's usually cold readings from the play, or they bring in a monologue and recite that. Everyone gets a part; everyone gets to have an experience on the stage because that's what they sign up for. Then we would have at least a month of a daily rehearsal schedule, maybe a half-day rehearsal schedule. We would kind of fast-track the performance. I wanted them to believe that they were part of something more than just being actors, that they were part of creating the whole show. So students were also doing props, and students were also creating the costumes and doing publicity and the set. I thought that was important for them to get a good experience on and off the stage.

Scene 2: Taking to the Road

In addition to schools, over the years Kentucky Shakespeare took performances to different stages, with the goal of reaching new audiences where they lived. An early precedent was in 1968, when the Carriage House Players traveled to Shawnee Park, on the northwestern edge of the city, to perform in the Art and Talent Festival sponsored by the West End Community Council, a civil rights organization that was working to keep the neighborhood around the park racially integrated.[5] Over the years, the company performed in coffeehouses and libraries. One of the most successful and popular ventures has been the more recent addition of a spring season that takes one play to public parks around the county and nearby communities. In 2022, the park tour visited a record thirty-five spaces, targeting low-income neighborhoods or those with few arts amenities available. The park tour also hires more young actors, recruiting performers from underrepresented communities to heighten the racial and gender diversity on the "stage"—in this case, usually a grassy field or small amphitheater.

Brenda Johnson: One time—it was generally on the weekends—we did a show called *Shakespeare Unplugged*. Curt started it. They would come to someplace like a coffee shop. The actors would talk the play in regular clothes. It's amazing how interesting it is and how forceful it can be to hear someone actually talk the play. We did that for three or four years, and it was really neat. We went to a lot of coffeehouses and a Jewish community center. I can't even begin to tell you the different places. I went a lot. Now they go around to the libraries, and that's kind of like what they did, only this was with the full company.

Doug Sumey: I like theater that can have not only merit within the way it's presented and the skill and the quality of the work professionally but that you can also break down all the walls and just offer it at a library for people who want to just hear it. *Shakespeare Unplugged*, which we would do a lot, took the actors to a community space. There may be only five or six people there, but those actors are bringing it and giving everything. They've got to be able to share the works in a unique way. It just strips it all down to just two people talking, in a way, and making it about speaking the speech. Shakespeare's words are so global and so human. We as a company, I felt, needed to make that a part of our action statement and give Shakespeare in multiple ways to as many community members as we can, without it breaking the bank or having social barriers be the reason why they can't see it.

Abigail Maupin: When Matt came in in '14, part of it was his "This is your Kentucky Shakespeare" thing, his push to make it available to all communities. But also there was a little bit of logic that said, "Wait, if we do a parks tour and a school tour of this play with the actors who are going to be in it in the summer, that will shave off some rehearsal time." He's a smart man. Our first year out, with *Hamlet*, we all played the same parts. It was me and Greg and Jon Huffman and Jon O'Brien and Megan Massie Ware and Kyle Ware and Tony Milder. We all went directly from that into the summer season, already feeling like we had a handle on the play. It was great because the beginning of the rehearsal process was in February, and it wasn't a whole lot of time.

Granted, the touring play is cut down to ninety minutes, but it's a lot for about three weeks, learning not just your lines and the play but, because we are the crew as well, it's learning all the scene changes and the costume changes and figuring out as you move from school to school or park to park, "Are we on grass? Oh, this auditorium is much smaller than the last one." Or "Oh, we're in the gym, and the fans are on overhead." There is a day-to-day sort of reconfiguring of how we're doing this in the time limit. You'll learn a lot about your own performance and how the play works. It's really valuable in that.

But it's rough. Greg and I haven't done the tour since '15. We did the '14 and '15 tours, and then we got busy. We did other things. Coming back this year [2021] to tour again, we both realized that, six years later, we are much older and that perhaps the touring is for the young people. Because we are very tired, and we hurt.

Mollie Murk as Juliet and Tony Reimonenq as Romeo in *Romeo and Juliet* in the park tour, 2021.

In the park tour, the audiences are so energized and hyped up to be there. The first few small audiences, they were leaning forward and so engaged, and that makes a huge difference. When you feel that coming at you from the audience, it just makes you want to pump it up and give it back a little harder. I enjoy how close the audience is in the park tour. I think once you are an actor with the experience of working in small black boxes and gigantic amphitheaters, you learn how to adjust to that: "Oh, I can see faces here; that means I can pull my performance in a little bit and be a little more subtle because everybody's right here."

Georgette Kleier: The touring company is a young person's gig. The only reason I was able to do it this year [2021] is because when Amy presented it, she said, "Look, it's COVID; we're maybe going to have five or six shows. You're in shape." That's what she thought. She said, "It'll be relatively easy." I signed on sort of thinking we'll have five or six shows, and there was like twenty-five or something!

The temperature change from two weeks ago even to now is— gosh, we all drank tons of water and had umbrellas on top of us because of how hot it was. It was just relentless. The tour runs from April.

"All the World's a Stage"   149

Think about Louisville weather from April to the end of May. We were performing in fifty-something degrees on the river in New Albany [Indiana], in the rain. There were people with their little umbrellas. We were like, "They'll all go home." It was during the wind and the rain. It was kind of magical. You're onstage thinking, "They are going to call this thing, and we're going to go home. We're going to call this thing any minute." Then you see the umbrellas go pop, pop, pop, pop, pop. And we're like, "Oh my God. They're going to stay? Well, okay, then I guess we're all going to do this play." It was in the middle of a play. I guess people were so starved for live theater.

Scene 3: Shakespeare in Service to the Community

From interns to producers, the artists associated with Kentucky Shakespeare agree that engaging with the Bard's plays can provide not only a creative outlet for people who may not otherwise have one but also a way to get audiences thinking about issues such as racial representation, healthy relationships, and conflict resolution. They are not alone in this. There is a long history of Shakespeare being performed and discussed outside of formal theaters and with an eye to social impacts.[6] The outreach programs of Kentucky Shakespeare both continue that tradition and forward the company's mission of using the Bard's works to serve diverse communities. In that spirit, they bring wordless short scenes from plays to immigrant and refugee groups at the Backside Learning Center, involve cancer patients in discussions and performances through Survivorship Shakespeare, and cooperate with the Clark County Juvenile Detention Center on a youth justice program.[7]

Two initiatives have received particular accolades and support: Shakespeare Behind Bars, which was founded by Curt Tofteland in 1995 and became an independent nonprofit in 2010, and Shakespeare with Veterans, run by Amy Attaway. Tofteland launched Shakespeare Behind Bars at a time when other similar programs were running in penal institutions around the country, following the lead of the pioneering model by Jean Trounstine in a women's prison in Massachusetts. The leaders of these programs share the belief that engaging with the Bard's work can bring both psychological and social benefits to the incarcerated, and in scholarly studies of their results, the participants often talk about the life-changing chance to "be themselves by playing other people." The Kentucky Shakespeare program, one of the longest-running of this cohort, was the subject of a multi-award-winning 1995

150   Under the Greenwood Tree

documentary by Hank Rogerson and Jilann Spitzmiller, which followed the
nearly yearlong process of producing *The Tempest* at Luther Luckett Correctional Complex. While Matt Wallace continues to direct the Kentucky
Shakespeare Behind Bars, Tofteland has replicated the model in his new
home in Michigan, where he sponsors programs in a number of correctional facilities.[8] Another population that is a common target of outreach
by Shakespearean theater companies is veterans, perhaps not surprisingly
given the prevalence of soldiers in the Bard's plays. In programs around the
country, theater professionals cooperate with returning military personnel in
the study and performance of Shakespeare as a way to help them process
their experiences. Psychologists have found that such programs ease post-
traumatic stress disorder symptoms and help veterans to make an emotional
return to the civilian world. Attaway's program downplays the therapeutic
element, however, stressing the social and intellectual stimulation of working
together to present Shakespeare's works.[9]

Curt Tofteland: I read an article about Dr. Curtis Burkestrand, who is a so-
ciologist at Bellarmine University, and he had created a program called
Books behind Bars. He took troubled and challenged middle school
students that had the highest dropout rate to the prison to show them
what prison was all about and to hopefully dissuade them from dropping out of school and turning to crime. His wife was a psychologist
in Luther Luckett Prison in LaGrange, Kentucky, and she handpicked
prisoners, and they formed that group. Each group was in their own
environments. They read a book. Then they came together, and they
facilitated a discussion.

I quickly called him up and said, "May I take you to lunch? I'm
Curt Tofteland, producing artistic director of Kentucky Shakespeare.
I want to know more about your Books behind Bars." We met, and he
talked about the program and why he founded it. I said, "Have you
ever thought about doing theater?" Theater is the closest art form to
the human condition. It's reality up there onstage. I said, "I want to go
one step further: Shakespeare." And his nose wrinkled up. I thought,
"Okay, had a bad experience with Shakespeare." He said, "I know even
less about Shakespeare [than about theater]. I'm scared of it." Shakespeare writes about the human condition and anything that's happening in any human being's life. He got really excited and said, "Will you
partner with me?" I said, "Absolutely."

"All the World's a Stage"   151

What they would do was read a play by Shakespeare, pick a scene, and then produce the scene. The students would come out and perform their scene for the prisoners, and the prisoners would stand up and perform their scene for the students. Then it was just a free-for-all in the discussion because the Romeo prisoner could sit down with the Romeo eighth grader and they could talk about Romeo. Anyway, it was a huge success.

This is in the early nineties, and then couple years go by, and I dropped out. I handed it over to him and a wonderful other psychologist at the prison named Julie Bartow. Julie Bartow happened to be a gift in that she was an undergraduate literature major. She adored Shakespeare, but she decided to explore the human condition through psychology and was a prison psychologist. Just a brilliant, smart, caring human being. A couple more years go by, and they call me up and say, "We've really flatlined. We've taken this as far as we can take it. What can we do now?" I said, "Let me come in and teach [a] master class to take you to the next level." That was the first time I went into a prison. It was the women's prison. They were working on *Macbeth*. I watched the students do their *Macbeth*, and I watched the prisoners do their *Macbeth*, and then I taught workshops, and I coached them, and I worked on it. I just fell in love with the work in the prison.

Back at Luther Luckett, they were working on *Romeo and Juliet*, and their actors were much further along because Julie Bartow was their coach and she was so smart. They were really far along and deep into the scene. It was the death of Mercutio and the murder of Tybalt. When the students came in, they just seemed more nervous than I thought they should be. Coming into prison is nerve-racking when their doors are closing and razor wire and all of that. I pulled one of the kids aside, and I say, "What's going on; how are you doing?" He confessed right away. He said, "Our teacher didn't rehearse very much with us. We're really not prepared. We're scared because we don't know our lines and our blocking, and we don't want to be embarrassed." I said, "I'll take care of it. Don't worry; thank you for sharing." What I did is I started with the prisoners and started coaching them, watching the scene. I watched the kids be able to speak the line as the character because their character was up there onstage speaking it. It took away some of the fear, and they got to see how we blocked it and all of that. Then I brought two kids up, and I coached them. I never had them

152 Under the Greenwood Tree

perform it from start to beginning. I started to coach them right away, and so it was a good success, huge success.

I had so much fun. I said to Julie, "Can I come back and work with these guys?" She said, "Sure." She went to the warden and said, "Curt Tofteland, the producing artistic director of Kentucky Shakespeare Festival, is going to come in and teach some workshops." The warden said okay because he trusted Julie, so she was my key to come in. Maybe the sixth or seventh time I came in, I said to her, "Julie, can I just keep coming back?" She said, "Sure, we'd be loved to have you. I'll sponsor y'all." That was twenty-five years ago.

One production that sticks in my mind is when the guys picked *Othello* to be the next play. An inmate named Sammy chose the role of Othello. We don't cast. They pick their own roles. We sometimes picked the play, but oftentimes the prisoners pick the play, or we have a collaborative effort. I just was blown away by the courage of that because Sammy was in prison for a third time and this bit was because he had strangled his ex-mistress who was threatening to tell Sammy's wife about their affair. Something snapped, and Sammy strangled her. Well, if you know Othello, he smothers and suffocates Desdemona with a pillow, which is much like strangling. How much courage does it take for a human being to pick out the worst thing that he ever did and to reenact it and to relive it?

I had a young man who joined Shakespeare Behind Bars, and he told me flat out he would never play a woman. Never, ever. He's in his early twenties. He's worried about what others think of him. He doesn't want to be thought of as gay, the worst thing that you can call a human being in prison. It's because it attacks the very core of their manhood, they think in their ignorance. He played a comedic character, a tiny little role, in our first production, and in the next production, he played one of the best comic roles in the canon, Sir Andrew Aguecheek in *Twelfth Night*. He came up to me after it was announced that we were going to do *Othello* and Sammy had chosen his role and other guys are choosing their roles. He came up to me privately, and he said, "I'm going to play Desdemona." I said, "Wow. Well, oh man, why the change of heart?" I'm always interested in transformative experiences and cataclysmic events. What's your epiphany? What's your discovery? He said, "Sammy is one of my best friends, and I know he's going to be playing that role, and I know how hard and how deep he's going to dig. I want to be there for him.

Julius Caesar by Shakespeare Behind Bars, 2017, at the Luther Luckett Correctional Complex, LaGrange, KY. Photo by Holly Stone. Courtesy of Shakespeare Behind Bars.

I want to play opposite him so that I can serve him." Empathy came in, and he thought, this is not about his machismo. He only thought about his friend, and he only had compassion and empathy for where he knew his friend would go and how emotionally difficult it would be to play that role at the depth of truth that we play in Shakespeare Behind Bars.

Matt Wallace: In 2001, Curt said to the acting company, "Hey! I'm bringing you out to the prison to see *Titus Andronicus*," Shakespeare's bloodiest play. I was not really that crazy about going. I had a prior experience with the criminal justice system from somebody that I loved in high school. That really lent a bias to me, to thinking people should be locked up and the key thrown away. But this really opened my eyes to that gray area. I fell in love with that program right away and just the honesty and the rawness from their performance. The *truth*—the search for truth. Tina and I would go out and visit with the summer company, and we would come share some material once a year, and then in 2008, when Curt was retiring from Kentucky Shakespeare and I was applying for the job of producing artistic director, he asked me if I would be interested in being the artistic director of Shakespeare Behind Bars, and I said yes. I did that for a couple years when it was still a program of Kentucky Shakespeare.

154   Under the Greenwood Tree

We spend about two hundred hours a year at Luther Luckett. I now have cofacilitators to assist. In a typical session, we'll check in; we'll talk about how they are, really just listening, sharing anything in the circle. We might do a theater exercise, and we will jump into the text. Over the course of two hundred hours—or over a school year—we will work our way through a Shakespeare play, and it culminates in performances at the end of the year. We do three performances for inmate audiences and then public performances.

It's not really an acting troupe. It's very different. We're reducing recidivism; we're reducing future crime. We see that it's developing empathy. By playing characters, they're able to reflect on what they've done in their life. We're changing the outcome of what they're going to do in the future. We see people change. When you're there that many hours and you see this growth in people, it's astounding. You've got guys letting down their masks. You've got to keep in mind that we're in the one safe place in an *unsafe place*. If somebody loses a family member, the only place that they can express emotion without judgment is in our group. When I've worked with somebody for twelve years, I know in the past they would get mad, and they would storm out, and they would curse or something and just walk out. That guy a couple years later is able to breathe and not tell the other person to eff off. It's those kinds of changes. I had a guy that I was warned about him coming into the program because he was such a high risk, the things he had done. He ended up being the most beautiful Juliet. He really wanted to play that role. It was just a beautiful discovery. There's so many of those moments where a guy shares something that you never would have guessed or when they break down and they realize the pain that they've caused their mom. It's constant like that.

When I did a residency of *Julius Caesar*, I went in, and I talked about the Cinna the poet scene when Cinna gets jumped on the street. "Has anyone been jumped on the street before?" Talk about violence and kind of get to that action point in the story and get them hooked on the story and the conflict and the stakes and the drama. Then we'll get into the language. But empowering them and saying, "You know what, these are *your* words." These plays have been done for four hundred years—we don't care how they've been done. There's no right way. They've been done every which way. What we care about is how *you* do it. What do you have to bring to it? I might get them playing with that. I'm not maybe working in a linear way; I'm trying to hook them with the part that they might want to explore. Then maybe the next week, we'll come back, and we'll do the scene right *before*, then we'll do the scene before, then we'll do the scene before, over a couple months. All of a sudden, we've just talked about the escalation of violence *backwards*.

Donna Lawrence Downs: Shakespeare Behind Bars is now a big part of my life. I'm blessed to do it once a year with Matt at the prison here. It's a transformative job, for sure. It's people who have done terrible things in their lives and are trying to be better. They're my favorite people to work with because they have so little and they expect so little because of the way that they've been conditioned. That art that we're doing with them is saving their lives and helping to rejuvenate them and get them back to society. Never in a million years sitting there in high school, thinking, "Should I make this for Peter Pan or Cinderella?" or whatever we were doing, would I think I'd be working with inmates doing theater.

The first couple of years that we did it, the show was done outside in the visitation room. I was not on lockdown with the guys. I come in, and I have a list of information from the prison, things I'm not allowed to take in, like leather jackets, sunglasses, wigs, belts. I can only cover about thirty percent of their uniforms. Once or twice, I've gotten away with covering up almost one whole person, like Shylock from *Merchant of Venice*, we were able to cover up a whole uniform. But they have to be able to see the inmate's prison uniform underneath it. I can't take in anything they could hurt themselves with or someone else with or use to possibly escape. No safety pins. No scissors. None of that sort of thing. I'm not allowed to have any physical contact with the actors, the inmates. It's hard to dress somebody when you can't physically touch them. I have to touch someone to fix their hat or re-pin something on. But it's just not like huggy, touchy, feely. I have to say, they are the most gentlemanly and most wonderful of my people.

Amy Attaway: Shakespeare with Veterans started because Fred Johnson, who's a retired army colonel who used to work for the Fund for the Arts, came to see Shakespeare behind Bars, thought it was exciting, and came to Matt and said, "Do you want to do something like that with veterans?" Matt said, "Of course I do." That was in 2016. Matt brought me and Kyle Ware in to facilitate the classes. We just started doing two classes, partnering with the Louisville Vet Center and Athena Sisters, which was an organization for female service members. He said to Kyle and I, "Just take Thursday night and Saturday." Kyle picked Saturday, and I picked Thursday, and Thursday is the one that stuck. So that's why I do it. That was before I worked here, so I was just a guest teacher. Shakespeare Behind Bars is something that Matt is still a really big part of. When they were starting the program, they did a lot of work with the Peace Education Program, learning about consent circles and these sorts of things.[10] That foundation is the basis of all our outreach in Kentucky Shakespeare, and so that foundation was what we used to start teaching with veterans. The first thing I did was go learn from Matt and Kyle because they already knew how to do that kind of work. I learned it, and then I went and did it.

Because of Fred, we have, like, a little bit of street credit in veterans' world. People came to the first few sessions, and we did a light-touch start. Let's play some games. Let's figure out what you know about Shakespeare. Let's talk about things that aren't Shakespeare. People kept coming back. That first year, we performed about a ten-minute compilation of choral pieces on the big Kentucky Shakespeare stage. That's a Shakespeare teaching thing. Our education team uses it. They use it in a lot of the outreach programs, not so much anymore at Shakespeare Behind Bars. It's a way in which you take a piece of text monologue from Shakespeare and you work through the meaning of it with a group and then decide what the important parts are. You create a new piece of text based on the Shakespeare words. Then you divide it up in a way that makes the whole group involved. Some pieces are spoken in unison, and some lines are repeated. We did those the first year. Then we kept performing wherever people invited us. And then the next year, we did a twenty-minute cutting of *Julius Caesar*.

Then it just became a thing. We meet every Thursday night, forever and always. Every Thursday night for the past five-plus years. It's free to participate in. It's open to any veteran of any age, any gender, any branch of service, any rank. We've had people all the way from draftees from Vietnam to a brigadier general in the air force. When we get in the room, when we get in the circle, rank doesn't matter. Age doesn't matter. Gender doesn't matter. We do not talk about politics, because, holy cow, do we all have very different politics.

It's a group of people who trust each other now. It will get new people. They come in, and they sort of learn the ways, and they trust

"All the World's a Stage"   157

each other too. We have just a very few rules about what we do in the group. One is that we keep the confidence of the group. The other is don't say no, which means try everything, and also there are no wrong answers in Shakespeare. Yes, you can interpret a thing how you want to interpret it, and that we respect each other. And we laugh a lot.

A normal session, which doesn't exist, would be I would come in with an opening question, which sometimes would be about military service and sometimes would just be like, "What did you have for dinner last night?" Or "What would you dress up as for Halloween?" That would always lead to a conversation, whether people making fun of each other for their Halloween costumes or having serious conversations about what basic training was like for them. Then we would play silly theater games. There's really nothing like it . . . when you have a seventy-year-old Vietnam vet playing group juggling. Then we would tackle a piece of text. At the beginning, I would bring in a different piece of text every week, and we would read it in the circle, interpret together, and I would usually give some context about the play. Then we would decide what it means to us. We still do that part of it, the text part. We don't usually play games too much. But we still interpret texts that way.

We've evolved over the past five-plus years. At first, we spent a lot more time on the conversation parts. Then we started to spend a lot more time on the Shakespeare part because a lot of them started to really love performing and the act of putting together the performance.

That part of what we do has gotten bigger every year. The last time we were onstage before COVID, which was 2019, we did an hour cutting of *Macbeth*, with everybody playing one or two roles. The first year we did *Julius Caesar*, we still did some choralized parts, dividing up the parts. The next summer we did *Henry IV, Part 1*, and we still had two people playing Falstaff. But when we did *Macbeth*, there was one person playing Macbeth. We still do the choralized pieces for anybody that invites us.

There are a lot of people who are there who were there the first night, who still come. There are a couple of guys who joined a year in who still come, and some people who joined later and still come. We had a new guy a month ago. They come because of their friends, mostly. We had some counselors at the vet center who were really into what we were doing, and they would recommend it for clients. The program is for people who are looking for another unit, to belong.

158   Under the Greenwood Tree

People who aren't averse to the arts, of course. People who aren't averse to sitting and talking with other people. What I've learned is that what people get out of it the most is the unit. I had no idea. I've learned so much. Something that people miss when they leave the military service is that camaraderie and the sense of purpose. The people who always have your back, and the reason for going forward. We have our tribe, the good of the people who always have each other's back, and performing Shakespeare is just hard enough that it feels like a real mission.

They recognize the people in the stories. They recognize themselves in the stories. They recognize their friends in the stories. We do a lot of Shakespeare's war plays together. When we look at the war plays, or the king monologues or the soldier monologues or the kings-rallying-their-troops monologues, they're like, "Yeah, this is the speech that we would give." Mark Antony's speech, "Pardon me, thou bleeding piece of Earth," over Caesar's body. "I've said these words. This is how I felt when my buddy was killed. I wanted revenge immediately." Some of the great conversations we've had have been around how the soldiers in the plays talk to their spouses. We do the Lady Percy and Hotspur scene, where Hotspur is rushing off to battle and not telling her where he's going, and she's pissed, and they have this big scene where they fight.[11] We do this scene in the group, and then they all say, "Yeah, because of what you see out there. You can't just come home and tell your family; there are no words for it." That's why he's not talking. It's not because he's trying to be an asshole. It's because he can't. That was mind blowing to me. But that scene is in a lot of the plays. That scene is in *Julius Caesar*. Portia in *Julius Caesar* says, "Why won't you tell me what's going on? Look at me, look, I'm cutting my thigh to show you how brave and smart and noble I am." And he [Brutus] says, "You are brave and smart and noble. But I'm still not going to tell you." Being in this group every Thursday night with these soldiers and corpsmen and sailors and airmen has completely changed the way I look at the history plays. It's completely changed the way I see those scenes.

Darryl Stewart is a Vietnam War veteran and member of Shakespeare with Veterans.

Darryl Stewart: I was down there at the park about five years ago, and I had seen the play once, but it was so good I decided to go back and see

"All the World's a Stage" 159

Shakespeare with Veterans performance, 2016, with Amy Attaway.

it again. I was talking with this couple from Indianapolis, and I was telling them, "Oh, you're just going to love this. It's a wonderful play." And the lady says, "Well, if you think so, you should go tell that lady right there. She's the director." Well, it was Amy, of course. I went over and complimented her on the play. She said, "Well, do you come down here pretty often?" I said, "Oh, I've been coming down here since 1968, before I went in the army." And she said, "Oh, you're a veteran?" And I said, "Yes." And she said, "Well, do you ever do anything at the vet center?" And I said, "Yeah, I do several things down there." And she said, "Well, you know, we have a Shakespeare group. I'm the director." And I said, "Well, I knew that you had it. But I haven't come because I didn't want to come in in the middle of something, like in the middle of the play." And she said, "No, no, that's not how we operate. Please come on down." I did, and that was how I got hooked up with them.

The thing that drew me in is that Amy would open each session with an opening question. We would go around the room, and everybody would answer that question. It didn't necessarily pertain to Shakespeare. But something to help us get better acquainted and help her get better acquainted with us. As we went around that first time, I realized these are some of the smartest, funniest people that I ever met in my life. I was really, really infatuated with it. I thought it was great. I made up my mind that I was going to come back, and have consistently down through the years. We had two retired army colonels, retired air force general. I mean, these are not stupid people. Everybody in the group was smart and had a sense of humor, which I really liked. I just kind of stayed.

I told Amy, when I joined up, "Look, I am best suited for a non-speaking role that requires sitting. I can walk onstage and sit down. Anything beyond that, no, we don't want to do that." Well, she went right along. My first role was as Julius Caesar after the assassination, so all I had to do was lay there, dead. Let me tell you, I was good. I mean, you couldn't find an actor in the world who would have been any better. Don't swallow. Don't visibly breathe. Don't open your eyes. Yes, I was really good. [*Laughs.*] We did that for a month or so. Then Amy backed us up in the play where Caesar had lines, and I said, "No, this is not what I agreed to. This is not sitting or a nonspeaking role." And she said, "You're already Caesar; get used to it."

When I started coming to the vet center—I had not been coming long before I joined the Shakespeare group—I was talking to my younger brother, and he asked me, "Well, if you go down there, are you going to talk about Vietnam?" I said, "I don't know. Why would you ask?" And he said, "Well, because it's been forty-six years and you've never said a word about it. Not one word. I still don't know where you were, what you did, who you served with, what it was like. I think it may do you good to talk about it." One of the reasons people don't talk about it, and there are a lot of us who are like that, is because I don't want to sit there and rehash my own trauma and hear other people rehash. There's enough who do it. But the beauty of the Shakespeare group is you go in with feelings that you think are exclusive to you. Nobody knows what this is like. Nobody knows what these feelings are. But as you get into Shakespeare, you get a big surprise. Shakespeare at one point or another has written about most of those feelings. I mean, some things are obvious, like the speech from *Henry V* before Saint Crispin's Day. We do that, and we all know that we love that because when you're in a combat zone, and you're getting your ass shot, and you've got four people in a bunker, your sole concern at that point is those four people. They are your family. They are your friends. As Shakespeare so aptly put it, we are a "band of brothers." You begin to think, "Gee, maybe this is common to mankind." You get to the point where you don't feel so isolated. You don't feel like those feelings are exclusively yours. You can begin to talk about things a little bit. I've gotten to where I can talk about Vietnam reasonably well now. It is therapeutic. It's very cathartic, even though it's not meant to be a therapy group. It's cathartic, and it is good therapy, I think. But it's not designed to be that way.

I like Shakespeare because I don't think there's a human emotion anywhere that Shakespeare doesn't deal with in one of his plays; I think that's why he is such a great and gifted author. He has an ability to elucidate human emotion and to portray it in a nonthreatening way that everybody can relate to. That is what I like about Shakespeare; he brings out my feelings in a very positive way. And this program has been an opportunity to release a lot of feelings that were pent up in me for forty-six years. It has taught me that they're not exclusive to me. There's nothing wrong with them. Everybody at one time or another has had those feelings. It has been a wonderful release emotionally for me. Also, I would like to think that on the occasions when we do perform in the community, it gives people an opportunity to be a little more aware of what veterans are about. Maybe a little more receptive to us as veterans. I think our program helps them to understand that we're just like you. We're all the same here. We're all just people. Let's get together and have fun. I think that's the value of the program for the community.

Scene 4: Sharing Art, Building Community

Under Matt Wallace, Kentucky Shakespeare's efforts to use art to build community became a two-way street, literally. From the beginning, the company has brought performances and workshops to venues, organizations, and audiences all over the city and state. Then, beginning in 2014, they began inviting community arts groups to the Central Park stage. In this section, narrators reflect on the significance of both, ending with the story of one of the most successful collaborations, with the Louisville Ballet. In telling these stories, narrators emphasize not just what these partnerships mean for Kentucky Shakespeare but what they do for the community.

Phil Cherry: I think what Matt's doing is good in terms of some performances of Shakespeare in the Parks, where they don't just perform in Central Park. It's more of a touring thing, where they take a scene or a play to the West End, or to the East End, or to Iroquois Amphitheater. I think that's wonderful. I think that hiring actors of color so that all audiences get a chance to see people who look like them, that's always important. I think that when you have a vision, you have to give it time to work. You have to give it time to ferment. You have to cultivate audiences, also. When I say *cultivate*, it means give them a chance to appreciate your work and bring them to their neighborhood as well as them coming to the park. I think that that's a real big deal. Give the kids in the neighborhoods a chance to perform Shakespeare through Globe Players. That's all really good stuff. It enhances what they do in the community. The more you can do to break down the walls, so people don't necessarily have to come to the theater to see you: send a couple actors to the community center, do a scene, then teach an acting workshop. Same way with Kentucky Shakespeare. You know, do a scene, do some acting with the kids, or whomever your audience is. Those are all wonderful ways of connecting with community.

Doug Sumey: I think we were always wanting more diversity and wanting more of an audience so that it felt like it was a kaleidoscope of our world. I think a lot of organizations strive for that and struggle with that. Where we were serving that purpose, within my world, was these partnerships that we would have with community centers and with organizations like Brooklawn and Maryhurst and Tenbrook, where we were working with kids who were just a little bit more disenfranchised or from a part of our community who wouldn't maybe make that trek to Central Park to see free Shakespeare.[12] One night at the Louisville Central Community Center, we had a wonderful, diverse audience because we had so much from the West Louisville community coming to see our show. I think it was always that we strived for it, but we struggled with it. Again, we did that within the rural communities, where it isn't an ethnic issue but sometimes there's social parameters that hinder people from being able to experience professional theater. We would go to the rural communities within Knox County, Pike County, Harlan County. In the hollers.

Interconnectivity, I think, is what Louisville is all about. We should never be an arts community that fights or works against each other. I've always believed that. One of the things that I really loved doing was partnering with the Peace Education Program, which is not in the arts at all, and Squallis Puppeteers.[13] We would put on residencies at elementary schools around the community and put on *A Midsummer Night's Dream*. But we also do conflict resolution work with the works of William Shakespeare. That's where the Peace Education comes in because that's their trade. We would have an instructor from Peace Ed with an instructor from Kentucky Shakespeare partnering to do these conflict resolution workshops. Again, it's a way of bringing in all these different connections around the community.

Abigail Maupin: I feel like Matt did good by not only bringing in community partners for free shows in the summertime, but he's really extended the educational stuff by putting a spring tour out, not just going to the schools but going to parks. I think that brings a lot of the community into shows and the theater. Just being able to have it in their own neighborhood, that's a huge difference as far as sharing the arts. Matt is one of the people who really put forward the idea of "Let's work with the ballet; let's have the orchestra work with this other company." He's been at the forefront of that. We've been doing our little shows for some of the immigrant groups in town. Little short pieces that are Shakespeare without words, where we keep it language free. We've done it for Backside Learning Center and the Kentucky Refugee Ministries.[14] I know Huffman has done some work with recovering cancer patients and that sort of thing. I think Matt has really been making such a difference in Kentucky Shakespeare's ability to reach out to as many parts of the community as he can.

Elizabeth Siebert: Getting all of the preshow groups to come and give those organizations a chance to be in front of an audience really helps build up the whole community of artists, because then that small dance troupe that maybe only got to perform in front of their family members now gets to perform in front of our audience of one thousand people on a Saturday night. I think that's one of the great things about that opportunity is that it gives other arts organizations the chance to grow. They grow their audience through us. It just makes the whole arts community in the city stronger.

Amy Attaway: The preshows were all part of Matt's "make a big splash." When he took over the company and everything was in shambles, he made an insane decision to make a giant splash. The company had been doing two plays or one play for the past however many years, and he was like, "No, I'm going to bring the company back together. We're going to do three plays. We're going to do a week of community partners. And we're going to do preshows." It was like all at once, everything,

164 Under the Greenwood Tree

because he's crazy. That was his idea. Let's just throw the doors wide open. We're all about accessibility. This is "your Kentucky Shakespeare." That was his tagline. We're back, and we're here for you, and we want not just for you to come and see us onstage; we want to see you onstage. We want not just to open our audience to you but open up our stage to you. Come be in the park with us. Enjoy the summer. Bring your kids. Bring your dogs. Enjoy the food trucks. Here's some poetry.

Matt Wallace: We have a huge pool of talent here in Louisville. It was really important to me to utilize that and to open up our doors to everyone in the community. I wanted everyone to feel welcome here. I got this position following a time when I had left the company and had resigned and did not go in the park, and I didn't feel welcome. I moved on in my life and let Kentucky Shakespeare go. When I got the opportunity to come *back*, I wanted everyone to feel like I did. That's when we decided every night is going to have a different community preshow group. We're not going to screen them. We're not going to audition them. We're going to make sure that it's family friendly content-wise, but we want a diverse array of performers on our stage. We also want to reach out to partners, to share the space with other people! So that first year, we had four guest companies. Each year, we have multiple guest companies. We're only going to be stronger from these collaborations. We're going to diversify our audience. Bringing somebody like the ballet to Central Park is *perfect* for us. It furthers our mission of taking something that some people may see as something that's not for them—and guess what? Come here; it's professional, and we're going to give it to you for free because we believe you deserve it and you're entitled to it. We have tons of collaborations, including indoor plays that we do during the year. We haven't yet partnered with Pandora Productions, which is Kentucky's only LGBTQ+ theater company. We're going to do a coproduction of a four-person adaptation of *Romeo and Juliet* called *Shakespeare's R and J*.[15] For our indoor shows, we've partnered with Louisville Visual Art, and Play Louisville, and Louisville Public Media to present our radio plays.[16] It's always more exciting when you're partnering with somebody, and it's also a way to share resources.

Brenda Johnson: I was so thrilled when the ballet came there, because I had a lady, an older lady, come up to me a couple years ago when they first started it, and she lived in the neighborhood. She said, "I've always loved the ballet, but I could never afford to go." She came every night. It was like she was getting to see her dream come true. The Cincinnati Shakespeare Company comes, and they do a neat job. They're fun. They're always doing something kind of fun. I think that's good. Matt is bringing other things for people to get to see. He's sharing, which I think is wonderful. I don't think somebody in Actors [Theatre] would be willing to say to a small theater company, "Come use our stage for free one night. Put on a play, and we'll all watch." I just don't think they would do that. Matt feels comfortable enough to show off what we have to someone else and let someone else show what they have.

Amy Attaway: Another crazy artist genius man, Roger Creel, was in the corps of the Louisville Ballet. He is super intellectually smart, as well as being a great dancer and choreographer. He created this piece for their Choreographer Showcase called *William's Folly*, where he incorporated the text of the sonnets into the dance. He put [it] on our stage with a short *Othello*. It grew from there because Roger is really into Shakespeare and he wanted to keep doing it. So the next year was a full-length ballet, *The Tempest*. The next year was *Julius Caesar*. And 2019 was *King Lear*.

Roger Creel is a former dancer with the Louisville Ballet. He has been the choreographer of the Louisville Ballet performances at the Kentucky Shakespeare Festival.

Roger Creel: Choreographer Showcase has been around since, I think, Helen Daigle, who is now ballet master, was in the company. There was no pipeline for dancers to learn how to choreograph, so they started this kind of out-of-the-truck production. I applied to choreograph. There was this long application that we had to fill out, which had some parts which were really helpful, including the suggestion that we tie this into Kentucky somehow. I had just read an article about some hypothesized—or perhaps real; depends on who you talk to—links between Elizabethan English and Appalachian folk dialects. I thought, well, great. In this artistic world, you don't need strong evidence; you just need a plausible connection. So let's make a ballet, an Appalachian folk music ballet, with Shakespearean sonnets. That first iteration was twelve minutes. It had four or five sonnets. It was kind of a skeletal creation. I think I called it *Sonnets in Blue*. Like sonnets in bluegrass. All prerecorded music.

I used a friend, Tony Milder, who was at the time acting with Kentucky Shakespeare. Matt Wallace came to see Tony. Matt saw that and said, "Hmm, that was interesting. What if you all did a season on the main stage?" Simultaneously, Robert Curran, as the new director of Louisville Ballet, fielded a cold call from a Louisville-based, Kentucky-born composer, violinist, and performer named Scott Moore. Out of the blue, Scott said, "I'd love to work with you all." So Robert paired us up. We decided that we would expand *Sonnets in Blue* to be *William's Folly*, a forty-minute one act for the main stage in the park.

That summer, Robert sent me off to the Australian Ballet to guest for six weeks, to be in the Corps de Ballet in their *Swan Lake*, which was extraordinary. I'm in Melbourne, and I'm going to the Victoria library, sitting looking through the Shakespeare research collection. I print out all the sonnets. I'm sitting in this Melbourne coffee shop, one of those big oak tables, and have all the sonnets spread out, and I'm trying to stitch together a story from the sonnets. If you start digging into the critical literature on Shakespeare's sonnets, it's not just a rabbit hole; it's like a badger hole. It's some big hole. You can start going into the Oxford theories and all the different conspiracy theories about who wrote them, who are the people in the sonnets? If you just read them as is, you see a middle-aged, forties, fifties Shakespeare, your old Shakespeare, falling in love with a young man. First twenty-six or twenty-four sonnets are Shakespeare saying, "Young man, you're so beautiful; you really should procreate. You should pass your genes on." Then he has this love affair—Shakespeare with the young man—that traces most of what we feel when we love: jealousy, adoration. "Darling, you're keeping me up at night. It's not your love for me. It's my love for you. Why are you doing this to me? Let me confess that we too must be twain"—like we have to break up. "To me, fair friend, you never can be old. You're going to live forever." Yeah. Then the young man cheats on him with this Dark Lady, and then Shakespeare himself has a thing with the Dark Lady, and that really doesn't go well. That's the story that I told with sonnets.

I've had extraordinary freedom in these pieces. This is, I think, one of Robert's strengths. He basically just says, "Go do the thing." There's been a lot of trust, and I appreciate that. Up until this year, I've designed the lights for these productions, which was its own learning curve. You make the piece, and then you go in the lighting booth several days ahead of time from ten thirty to midnight or one, whenever, and you visualize what the piece is. You see the dancers in your mind onstage, and then you build lights to illuminate them. I love doing that. That's the final creative part of the ballet. At the point where the lights are done, well, off it goes toddling away. The audience loved it.

In addition to being artistic director of the Louisville Ballet, Robert Curran danced the role of Prospero in *The Tempest* at the Kentucky Shakespeare Festival.

Robert Curran: I think Matt would back me up on this. I believe the ballet's performances at Kentucky Shakespeare are the highest-attended performances. I think that's a testament to what a collaboration can do. When the ballet audiences come down and sit side by side with the Kentucky Shakespeare audiences, we get a really fun experience. There's nothing better than being in a sold-out or packed house to witness something. I think that's because of the collaboration. I really, really, really enjoy working with Matt and Amy and the whole crew at Kentucky Shakespeare. They take such good care of us. They are so excited to be working with us, and we feel exactly the same. I felt nothing but positive, joyful feelings towards our Shakespeare. It is the opening of our season too, so it's our audience's first look at the dancers.

The collaboration with Kentucky Shakespeare means we get to create new work. Only our first presentation at Kentucky Shakespeare featured existing choreography. Everything else since then has been new, which means we've gotten to work with Roger and give Roger an opportunity to create new work. We've gotten to work with Scott Moore to create new music. It's new interpretations of existing works, the Shakespeare works. It is definitely deep in our mission to create new interpretations of existing classics that are relevant to the community that are seeing them, are witness to them. We get to show an audience that doesn't have to pay and doesn't have to even think about worrying that they weren't fitting in[to] what we do, and hopefully make ballet feel more familiar to them so that those kids sitting in the front row would be like, "Yeah, I'll go to *Nutcracker*, or I'll go and see the ballet." Because it's more familiar, and they've had an experience, they don't feel so alienated by it. I feel like the other opportunity that this collaboration gives us is the chance to give more to our community than we can always give when we're in our traditional proscenium experience. I feel like there's a community-building, a dance community-building, an arts community-building opportunity that you get with an event like the Kentucky Shakespeare Festival. I know that Matt and Amy and I kind of share that desire to exponentially grow that community. Finally, I hope it makes Louisville a better place to live, better place to raise children, a better place to work knowing that you have these opportunities to come together as human beings and witness a finely crafted piece of art. Not every place in the world has that, and we certainly have it here. I hope that makes Louisvillians proud of the city that they live in. I hope it encourages or grows a sense of the need for investment in that part of our city, of our life.

Act 5

Reviews and Reflections

Shakespeare's final words are spoken; the cast dances a jig (if the play was a comedy) or does one last bow and waves. The lights come up, and the voice of Monte Priddy thanks you for coming and bids you to return. The audience members gather their belongings and begin to make their way to their cars, and the cast and crew secure the costumes, props, and sets for the next night. If you wait around long enough, you will see the actors walking out of the park and back to their lives in neighborhoods around the city. You exit, ambling along the darkened pathways under the trees, with a line or scene still running through your head. Perhaps you engage in a conversation with others about the merits of the performance or the meaning of the play. But now it is time to go home and to anticipate the next time when you can come back to Central Park.

And people do come back. Audience members have demonstrated their fondness for Kentucky Shakespeare by their repeat attendance, financial support, and formal and informal reviews. Since the renaissance, the summer season has attracted an average of 28,600 people a year to Central Park. Moreover, in the 2022 season, audience surveys revealed that 75 percent of attendees saw more than one performance; indeed, 15 percent braved the heat for six or more. They also return season after season, as the same survey reported that over half of the audience had been fans for at least four years, with 10 percent of people coming back for over two decades. Festivalgoers show their appreciation for the company not just through the extended ovations but through enthusiastic contributions to the barreling and, perhaps more important to the sustainability of a nonprofit, through year-round donations. Since Matt Wallace's tenure began, the number of annual donors has tripled. In addition, the company has

A final jig, *Taming of the Shrew*, 2015.

consistently benefited from funding from foundations and granting agencies, including the National Endowment for the Arts and Arts Midwest.[1]

Positive reviews, both those in the press and those spread by word of mouth, play a large part in bringing people to the park. Critics from the local public radio station, arts publications, and news media regularly give rave notices to individual cast members, the summer season, and the more recent indoor productions. The comedies have always been popular, drawing praise, for example, for the "comedic timing and pure joy" of the "delicious romp" that was *Twelfth Night* or the chemistry and innovative use of local music in *As You Like It*. But the histories, though "shrouded by the misconception that they are dry stuff," proved to reviewer Marty Rosen that "this company is operating at an extraordinary level of excellence." New takes on well-loved tragedies have also impressed; as reviewer Allie Fireel noted about *Shakespeare's R and J*, "I highly doubt there will be anything on stage in Louisville as beautiful, moving, and ultimately as socially important as this play." In Rosen's essay on the summer 2022 season, he called the festival "the best theater Louisville has witnessed in many, many years." He also hearkened back to a theme in the early reporting about Shakespeare in the Park: the audience's contribution to the whole experience. Concluding that "it's been one of the great pleasures of this summer season to sit amongst people whose alert interest and uninhibited

Reviews and Reflections   171

enthusiasms punctuate the action with spontaneous cheers and applause,"
Rosen brought the attention back to those whose opinions matter most to the
company: the people on the benches. In social media comments that cap-
ture the heart of what Shakespeare in the Park is all about, those amateur
reviewers applaud the chance to "sit under the stars" and watch a great
play, take in a "wonderful performance in such a beautiful setting," and
have "lovely summer experience" complete with fireflies that "add some
sparkle" to the occasion.[2]

In this final act, members of the company have a chance to review Kentucky Shakespeare. They reflect on the artistic and personal significance of
participating in the work, with many of them emphasizing the connection
they feel to the audience and to one another. They also ponder what
makes Shakespeare in Central Park special. Here they affirm an idea that
has been fundamental to the mission since Doug Ramey began producing
plays in Central Park: the value of free Shakespeare and of the resulting
heterogeneity of the people gathered under the trees. They also note the
expansion of that mission. In recent years, the company has acted on its
commitment to diversity on the stage, behind the curtain, and in the audience by drawing on local talent, cooperating with other arts groups, and
bringing Shakespeare to a wide range of constituencies. Though it all starts
with the Bard's words, the company's outreach initiatives, programs, and
performances are each a means to the goal of creating an inclusive arts
experience.

Scene 1: What Kentucky Shakespeare Means to Me

Amy Attaway: Coming to see Kentucky Shakespeare as a teenager at a
really important artistic and life-formative time for me and seeing
those two actors who I revered so much follow those roles through the
Henry plays was so important to me as a young person. Then getting to
come back and do *Henry V* twice with the same company and getting
to do the journey of those four plays in the Henriad, again with the
same actors, is really important. It just happened that I've stayed in
Louisville to make my career, and to be a part of this organization that
believes in the city so much, and that the city believes in so much, has
been huge for me. I feel like Kentucky Shakespeare and I, personally,
are positioned to be a leader in our community of peer organizations
in making Louisville a more cooperative arts town. All the performing
arts companies now are working together in a way that they never did

172   Under the Greenwood Tree

when I was growing up, and it feels amazing. The mutual respect and mutual desire to work together feels amazing. I think it's good for the arts, and I personally find it very rewarding.

Phil Cherry: Kentucky Shakespeare Festival has provided me, on a personal level, as an actor, as a person in this community who loves the arts, a very unique opportunity to perform in plays that helped me to grow in confidence with every performance. I connected with a local audience here in Louisville in a way that has always been important to me and always will be. I see people all the time who remind me of how important my performances were to them in the park. We had great audiences, people who love Shakespeare, who love the company. Ken Pyle, the guy who owned the Rudyard Kipling, [which was a popular pub on the edge of Old Louisville], also helped with our costumes. We'd all go over there for our costume fittings and everything and all our cast parties. Ken is just a great friend of the arts. I want to give him some mention because he is a dear, dear friend. So having the opportunity to connect with such a wonderful audience of people for so many years and work with amazing performing artists in every show, it was just a wonderful learning experience beyond any I've ever had in my career. We didn't get paid a lot of money. It wasn't about money. It was about the camaraderie. It was about doing something that we love and respect. I don't think there's a better place for me to have been over the years—and over these thirty years that I've been a part of Kentucky Shakespeare Festival. They were always there with open arms, giving me wonderful opportunities.

Abigail Maupin: Being here with Kentucky Shakespeare has meant so much to my thoughts and feelings about myself as a person, my self-confidence, my growth and comfort, and my love of myself. That's because of the security and the trust and loyalty that they show to me—Matt, especially, and Amy. They have become a family for me. They give me things to do, and they stand by me doing them. That has meant a lot to me as a person and as an artist. They keep throwing stuff at me and saying, "Well, we're not going to give up on you just because you're too old to be Juliet now." But then they say, "Okay, but we want you to work with us. Here's a challenge: Mercutio." When Amy said that, when I got that little email from her, I laughed for days. "Really? Really—Mercutio? Okay, we'll see." Now I love him so much, and I'm

Reviews and Reflections 173

having so much fun. I think that's the thing that I definitely appreciate about Kentucky Shakespeare, is that they've entrusted me with some really wild challenges. Definitely, I feel like there's not anything they can throw at me that will—it may make me laugh for about three days, but it won't make me say, "Oh, no, I can't take that job. I can't do that." I feel so much more confident.

Casey Clark: Kentucky Shakespeare is a creative through line for me. It is a connectivity for me that I am not willing to give up. It's an artistic home for me. Very few places have what you would call a repertory company, a company that stays together over time. We have a version of that that is very comforting to me. What that does is increase the rapport that you have on each of your shows because you know each other as artists. I love that. Also, for me, it is a loyalty thing, because I promised Curt Tofteland, I think in my second or third year, that I would always come and do Shakespeare in the Park when needed, and I've done that. When he found somebody else, or the other artistic director found somebody else, yes. But other than that, as long as there's a need for me, I will come back here and do these shows. We talk about a world now where we don't work for the same employers for long periods of time. If you're an artist, you travel a lot; you work for a lot of different companies. There's value in that because it keeps you fresh. But Kentucky Shakespeare is a commitment for me.

Crystian Wiltshire: Kentucky Shakespeare was the first theater company that made me believe that I could do this crazy thing called acting for a living. They not only believed in me once; they trusted my work over the course of several years. As the company has grown and has come out of some really tumultuous times, I was a small, very small, piece of the overall whole that has become this really successful company. That's really, really cool. I do not take that for granted one bit.

Donna Lawrence Downs: This company for me has been gracious and loving and a very hard master. Matt makes me want to be a better designer. Amy makes me want to be a better designer. Working with Carl Anderson or Paul Owens as set designer makes me want to be a better costume designer. It makes me want to raise the bar on my abilities. I want to give my actors things that make them happy. It's important to me on a lot of levels. It's so cool to say I'm part of this company. It has

174   Under the Greenwood Tree

a huge history. It means a lot to me. A lot more than I thought. I tried to stop doing it the last couple of summers to move on to different aspects of my life, and it's very hard to let it go. I actually want to go to work every day, and I appreciate everything they do every day because I know they're trying to do so much with so little for so many people.

Doug Sumey: I really have a fondness for some of the earlier years. That company, there was just a great bond and a great feel of that general group all together. They were just spirited and lively on and off the stage. That's what I kind of look for. It's much more than just the performance itself. For me, Kentucky Shakespeare was about this family of people, both production-wise and acting. It was more than a job. It's about people who care deeply about each other and care about the community and want to give that as a gift, basically to each other and back to the community. Kentucky Shakespeare took me away from my first home but created for me a second home, personally and professionally.

Braden McCampbell: Being in the company has meant establishing some relationships with friends who genuinely care about me. I constantly get reminded by the people in this company, "Hey, you're not just an actor we hired, or continue to hire; you are a human being that we do worry about." I'm already a little antisocial when I'm not busy doing a lot of things, because I'm just me. During COVID, I kind of just was like, "Oh, I can't do anything, can't go anywhere, so I'm not really talking to people." But then my cat died, so I was suddenly truly alone in the middle of a pandemic. People were trying to get a hold of me. Kyle Ware and Megan Massie actually showed up at my door: "Hey, are you okay? Are you alive? Is everything all right?" They literally showed up at my house to make sure I was still alive and breathing.

It's also the stuff I've learned. I've changed from being, "Oh, I don't really like Shakespeare that much; I don't understand it," to, "Hey, I'm helping other people understand Shakespeare." That is pretty impressive and awesome to me. Learning from Jon Huffman, Jon O'Brien, Greg Maupin, Matt Wallace, Amy Attaway, and having the opportunity to work with them has taught me a number of things about the industry and myself and has been a big blessing in that way.

So that's what Shakespeare means to me; that's what the company means to me: the understanding that these people legitimately have my back and are here for me and here for each other. That makes

Kentucky Shakespeare different from all of the other companies that I've had the chance to work with, one of the things that makes it the best—well, I hate to say that—one of the best companies to work with. Instead of "We're about to run you through the wringer" style nonsense, it is, "Hey, fellow thespian! Come and be a part of us. You are here now. You are one of us. You have joined the family."

Tom Luce: [My wife] Charlie passed away just after Thanksgiving in 2018. Her daughter said, "Why don't you come to England for Christmas so we can be together as a family?" Matt made arrangements, because he's very good friends with the woman who runs the Shakespeare Birthplace Trust in Stratford, for me to be able to meet with her with Heather, Charlie's daughter.[3] While I was thinking about Shakespeare things to do in England, I remembered that you could purchase a bench in Central Park to memorialize someone. I emailed Matt. I said, "I'm going to ask Heather if she would like to go in and purchase a bench with me to honor Charlie." This was maybe a couple weeks after Charlie had died. I really just didn't want to open mail. I had a stack of mail on this counter for about two weeks. Matt responded to my email, and he said, "You should have gotten something in the mail by now." I went and looked, and there was a packet from [Kentucky] Shakespeare, and I thought, "Well, I don't know if this is an offer for the coming season or something," but I hadn't opened it. I opened it up, and Matt had arranged for people to donate and had already purchased a bench for Charlie. I remember I opened that up, and, oh, my poor cat, I scared the crap out of her because I just couldn't stop crying. Just a beautiful thing for him to have done.

Tina Jo Wallace: Working for Kentucky Shakespeare was a turning point in my life. I really feel like it was my place where I grew up. Then getting to meet my husband there—well, that's just insane. That first year of love—all of the romance and stuff—that happened in that park. There's that connection that will *never* go away. Then watching my husband taking over and the hardship and then the joy and the elation! Because when you work hard and you have success, it's even *better*! [*Laughs.*] That has meant so much to me. Even more than that is watching my kids gain confidence, make new friends and feel pride, and learn lots of Shakespeare and spend summer nights out under the stars watching Shakespeare. That means the world to me.

176   Under the Greenwood Tree

Amy Attaway: My daughter Maisie was a baby when we started rehearsal in April. Sometimes I would bring her with me to rehearsal, and mostly she would sleep, or one of the actors, like Abigail, would come over and roll her in the stroller for a little bit while I did other things. This one time, she was with me in the room. Toward the end of the rehearsal process for *Taming the Shrew*, we had done a run, and I was giving notes to the actors. I was sitting in a chair holding her. She was hungry, so she was fussing. I don't know if I would have said this or if I would have brought my infant to any other room. But these are my family. These are my close friends. I'm looking at this group of people—a lot of them don't have children. I was like, "Listen, you guys, somebody else needs to hold her, and she'll settle down." Tony Milder took her and walked over to the window and rocked her, and she stopped crying. I will never forget that because I felt like I was in a loving place enough to be able to say that and just hand my baby off to someone who I knew I could trust.

Jon Huffman: There's nothing better to me as an actor than working with people you know. You know they're good. You know you can't slack off a bit because they're bringing their A game and it's as good a group of actors as I've ever seen anywhere or worked with anywhere, and it's exciting. I guess if I were a professional athlete and I played for the New England Patriots and I knew everybody on the team was the best and we had a chance to be the best of all time, it's kind of like that. Being onstage and looking around and knowing everybody onstage with you is the best at what they do, and you can't imagine someone better at what they do. It's just exciting and gratifying, and as an artist, you can't ask for anything more. It's amazing. A whole lot of us, especially us over forty—and there are a few—were at one time members of Actors' Equity, the professional actors' union, which is what you have to belong to to work at a lot of the theaters across the country. We've been around. We have chops. We know what we're doing, and we love working together. It's wonderful. I feel like I'm at home.

Casey Clark: I love the company. I love the spirit of the company. I love the fact that we approach it as "We're doing quality work, but by golly, it's going to be fun doing it." Our production teams usually do not butt heads. It's remarkably civilized. There's a genuine enjoyment of each other's work that is actually kind of rare in theater. Because if

Reviews and Reflections   177

you think about it, you get hired to do a show; you're working with a company, with a staff, creative staff, that you don't know. Everybody's a little bit cautious; everybody's a little bit protective of their area. Scenic designers are worried about lighting designers ruining their work, and lighting designers are worried about scenic designers doing things that make it impossible for them to light a certain area on the stage. There's a lot of that sort of angst that goes into a normal production process. It can still be civilized by dint of discipline and professionalism, but it doesn't have that sense of sharing and comfort that we have.

Abigail Maupin: I talk a lot about the beauty of being with this company of people who've been the same over a handful of years. Taking on something like *King Lear*, which is so dark and so emotionally difficult, and playing Goneril and Jon Huffman as Lear with a wrenching scene where we are digging into each other. I feel like we dove into it on the first day of rehearsal because we're safe with each other and we've worked together and we already have our love and respect. There is no question about what's the work and what's not. Being able to do stuff like Beatrice and Benedick with Greg, like when we did Kate and Petruchio together, even Goneril and Albany, we can just get to the deeper places that much quicker.

Gregory Maupin: There is safety in an emotional connection. We have our actual relationship, so when we need to scream awful things to each other as Albany and Goneril, then I don't have to say, "Are you okay?" If we had just met and were playing those roles, we'd have to establish our safety. Jon and I and Abigail can all shout blue murder at each other, and no one is going to think, "Are you an abusive, terrible person that I've just met and I don't know it?" Your job right now is to spew vitriol at me, and my job is to take it really hard. So great, we're good.

Abigail Maupin: On the other end of that, for *Comedy of Errors*, there was a point early in rehearsal, I'm doing the big, long Adriana speech at Crystian, and I said, "Can I take your hand and put it on my boobs here?" and he's like, "Yeah, okay." Because it was funny. It was for comedy. So I did. Then he made silly faces, and there was never, ever any moment of this is weird and sexual and uncomfortable because he's

178   Under the Greenwood Tree

Left to right: Gregory Maupin, Tom Luce, Abigail Maupin, and Jon Huffman in *King Lear*, 2019.

Crystian and I'm Abigail and this is going to be a funny thing. Neither one of us felt inappropriate. It was all about the work and trust for each other. That, again, is part of the joy of having Matt bring a group together. I don't know if it's just because he is a nice person himself, who senses other nice people, but he manages to hire nice people. He manages to surround himself with good, nice people.

Like a Shakespearean comedy, there's even a wedding.

Tina Jo Wallace: It was my second summer—so 2001—and I actually got to meet Matt the day before rehearsals started. I had stopped by the office, and he came in because he had a fitting. He didn't know how to get there. I think the fitting at that time was somewhere down at UofL. I was like, "Oh, I'll drive him. I don't mind!" And I drove him down, and then I said, "Well, you know, if you want me to hang out, I'll give you a ride back!" And he was like, "Oh, no, I'll walk." I thought he was a really nice guy, but I was like, "Oh, he's obviously not interested in becoming friends because he would have said, 'Oh yeah, if you'll wait for me.'" I think it was the first day of rehearsal, which would've been the next day; he was up doing a monologue. I think it was from *Merry*

Wives of Windsor. He was *so funny*, and he was so ridiculous! I mean absolutely ridiculous and *fearless!* Fearless in his comedy. I remember turning to a new friend that I'd just met and saying, "I need to know that guy. I *need* to get to know him!" [*Laughs.*] It was pretty instant for me. I don't know when he knew. I think it was within a week that we started dating. I know for me it was the first day of rehearsal. It wasn't the first sight, but it was the first day of rehearsals, seeing him work and being like, "Oh yeah. We're going to get along." I didn't even know then that we were going to date, but I was like, "I *understand* him, and I *admire* him already. I *get* him."

Matt Wallace: I certainly was not looking to be in a relationship—that was for certain. I had been single for a while, and I certainly was not getting into a relationship. I was looking to just come for the summer, do the contract, and met her and thought she was great and so nice. I didn't think we were going to start dating right away, but things started to move really fast! [*Laughs.*] I do think we were dating, like, at the end of the first week of rehearsals. I remember I was adamant when we started dating that we keep it very professional in front of people. I didn't want to be the couple holding hands in rehearsal. We did make out in the back of the church. [*Laughs.*] I definitely think we had an attraction fairly soon. I just think it was like an instant chemistry. It's like meeting your other half, your soulmate or something. There was a little bit of a dance there at the beginning. We were all going out to a restaurant. We all went as a group, and then we went to do laundry afterwards, and we were doing laundry together. And then we ran down and did a shot at the Mag Bar. It's so romantic. [*Laughs.*] I think we kissed that night or something. We were working lines. I do think from that night, I don't think we spent another night apart, that whole summer. It was perfect for us. It just seemed right. We've been together ever since.

I kind of knew in 2002 that I wanted to propose. But I *really* wanted it to be a surprise. I got her a ring. I was so poor I would pay like ten dollars a week just to still keep it on hold. In 2003, Curt Tofteland cast us as Beatrice and Benedick in *Much Ado*. I'm going to do this role where he's swearing he's going to die a bachelor. It was just kind of perfect timing. So I finally pulled the trigger and paid the rest of the ring through some *horrible* infomercial that I did for a fishing lure retrieval system called "The Go Get It." That helped me get the rest of

180   Under the Greenwood Tree

the money to buy the ring. I really thought about doing it that summer. I knew with nerves there is no way I'd get through a show, knowing that I was going to propose after the show. And I really didn't want to share it with an audience.

We were doing shows at Derby Dinner Playhouse, but we were both in different shows. We had our first day off . . .

Tina Jo Wallace: And he took me to Buck's for lunch, which is a decadent and wonderful restaurant in Old Louisville. It's such a great restaurant and *romantic* with all the flowers. Later he admitted he wanted to take me to dinner, but it was so expensive at the time, and we were both actors, so he took me to lunch. I don't know how he arranged this, but he has magic. It was a gorgeous day. It was March 24, 2003. He drove by the park, and he knew I would say, "Hey, let's go for a walk!" It was off-season, so we hadn't been on the stage for a while. So we went to lunch, and we went back to the park, and we walked through the park. We *started* to head down towards the stage, but in the off-season there are a lot more homeless people or people who are just living in and around the park, especially during the day. As we were going towards the stage, there was a homeless person on the stage, and Matt said, "Let's do one more loop!" When we came back around the second time, the stage was empty. We get up there, and I can't remember at *all* the exact words, but I know he got on his knee, and I *lost* it. It was just beautiful and—*perfect* . . .

Matt Wallace: And she said yes!

Scene 2: What Makes Kentucky Shakespeare Special

Crystian Wiltshire: I think what makes Kentucky Shakespeare really unique is the relationship that the company has managed to build with the community. I think the reason it has done that is because they're averaging, what, thirty thousand people a summer coming out there? I think that those people are accustomed to seeing some of the same top-notch actors year after year after year. The Jon Huffmans, the Greg and Abigail Maupins, the Monte Priddys. I could go on and on. That relationship is really special. You don't get that at every theater. At Actors Theatre of Louisville, you may not necessarily see the same actors year after year after year. They're flying in people from all over the country. But at Kentucky Shakespeare, the incredible talent that you see, not only are they really good individually, but part of the reason why the shows are so fantastic is because of the chemistry that those actors have, working with each other year after year. There's something really special about that.

Gregory Maupin: There's a sense of being a festival. That sense of having a core group of players that Matt keeps hiring back. When I was growing up, I remember going to Actors Theatre, and they used to have an acting stable. There was a resident company that was there for years. That's a difficult thing to do because people age out of roles and it changes what you can do. But there was a sense that I—a person who wasn't even that involved in the local theater community—knew those people by last name. Like they were a ball team. You could say, "What did O'Brien do? What did McNolty do? What did Sawyer do?" We could talk about them in that way because we were familiar with them. That's sort of starting to happen again. We get randomly recognized at coffee shops because of Shakespeare. In a very nice "Thanks, we love what you guys do, bye" kind of way. In a way that feels like a community in the best possible way.

Brenda Johnson: I like that Kentucky Shakespeare draws from local people. I think that's really good. Over the years, they've gotten people from other places, and that was fine; I'm not saying that season was any different or any worse or any better. I like that it's accessible to anyone because it's free. A lot of people are going to say, "If I go to that free, that's not going to be very good." Once they get there and they see it's such a professional company, they are just flabbergasted. They love it. I've had people every year come, even from out of town or people that have never been here before that lived here all their lives, and they will say, "That's so good." The actors and Matt, everybody is friendly and accessible to everyone. That's another thing that's really neat too. Are you going to go to Actors Theatre and meet the guy that runs Actors Theatre? No. These people are accessible to anybody, whether it's a little kid or people who've got a lot of money to give. Whether you give or not, it doesn't matter. You're treated equally. I like that.

Amy Attaway: It's the accessibility. It's the fact that we're there every night, consistently, doing excellent art for everyone. We have no doors.

We have no tickets. Bring your dog; bring your picnic; bring your kids; show up late. No problem. Leave early, no problem. Come back tomorrow and see the second half. There's no guilt associated with it. There's no dressing up needed. There's no preparation needed. Just come as you are, and we hope that you'll want to keep coming back. We hope that what you see will catch you. I love that we can make it be about both things—that we don't have to sacrifice one for the other. I think a lot of companies have to do one or the other. You can make great art or make it for the people. I think that we are constantly striving to do both and never let one suffer for the other. That's so important to me. It feels so special. We can have Shakespeare scholars come and find something enjoyable, and we can have somebody walking their dog who has never seen a Shakespeare play come and sit down and enjoy it. That's what I hope.

Georgette Kleier: I think Kentucky Shakespeare has lasted here because of the commitment and the passion of the people who lead it. I think it's been here because of its location. I think it's been here because of the fact that it's free. I think that it's been here because there's a hunger for experiences that don't involve, necessarily, technology. Everybody can't afford to spend whatever it costs to go see shows at Actors Theatre or the Kentucky Center. You can walk down to a park and see a professional company doing some of the greatest stories ever told, and you're welcomed. It's like being at a baseball game, only baseball games aren't free. You could sit next to somebody who's this big Wall Street tycoon, and then you can sit next to somebody who's using government assistance. There's a level playing field for everybody at the park. There's no hierarchy to the seating. You do really good stories told by really wonderful artists, and it's free. That's rare, really rare.

Crystian Wiltshire: If you have a theater company that is offering non-ticketed productions, that audience will most likely be a really diverse audience. As an actor, quite often, when I am performing, I look out into the audience and I only see white people. Or people that just don't look like me. And that gets straining emotionally. You want to share the work that you've committed so much time to with people who look like you. Then I come to Kentucky Shakespeare in the summertime; it is always the most diverse audience that you can look out and see. You can see the energy. You can feel it. There's just nothing like it.

The company knows that if we're going to be putting on plays in Central Park in Old Louisville, that we don't want to be this company that is clearly for upper class or people that—how can I say this—people that might be willing to spend more than one hundred dollars to come and see a play. The openness is to show the community that if you're here, if you're in the area, please come see us. There is a seat for you. We want you here. Just come and enjoy what we're doing. There might be a plane that flies over at some point to distract you, but we promise, the play is still pretty good. [*Laughs.*]

Curt Tofteland: I love that when you sit in the audience on a summer night in Central Park and you look around, there are representatives from every zip code within a sixty-mile radius. There's every socioeconomic level. There's every education level. There's every race, color, and creed. There's every age. It truly is the only place where all human beings can, if they choose, come to see art. That's the greatest joy for those of us that commit our lives to Kentucky Shakespeare. There's no other arts organization in town that has the diversity of audience that we do. We've been around for such a long time, we now have third generation coming back. Kids who came because their parents brought them and then they grew up and had kids—they bring their kids. There's so many stories just in that audience. You can walk out there and ask, "Is this your first time? Is it your second time? How did you get here?" They're just marvelous stories. I would meet people who drove from other states. They now live in another state, but they came back in the summer because they wanted their kids to have the same childhood experience in Central Park that they had. That's what really gets artists going is being able to be of service to such a vast inclusive part of humanity.

Tina Jo Wallace: I think it's unique that you don't have to buy a ticket. Some places it's free, but you have to stand in line, or the donors get the first tickets. You can come as many times as you want. Louisville's such a great community! And there are so many talented actors, technicians, designers in this community. Kentucky Shakespeare is part of the reason that they still live here and that they can make a living and that they're not waitressing. It's not just creating a great experience for those people who come to the park but for people who come to see lots of shows in Louisville because these actors and designers are staying in Louisville. They're working at other companies, and so it's a bigger reach than even just the people that we reach there. Since Matt's taken over, we're going to the parks in all the neighborhoods and finding money to get buses to bring kids from other neighborhoods and reaching out to veterans and to cancer survivors—people who need to have these great breakthrough moments and need some uplifting and need some soul-searching and to find some humanity in the world.

Matt Wallace: The nonticketed part makes us so unique. Chicago Shakespeare's beautiful, amazing, state-of-the-art theater at Navy Pier does some great shows. In New York, you have to wait in line all day for a ticket. You can imagine how that cuts out a large demographic of people. What I love about Louisville is that we have neighbors coming over because there was nothing on TV that night. It's part of the culture, that access. We work to make it so easy. We're not going to ask for a ticket; we're not going to ask for your information—just come. I think the tradition, because it's been around for sixty years, is ingrained in people's lives. Louisville's really been open to it. So many people have been so open to the experience of Shakespeare in the Park. It comes back to the material. It's universal; it's timeless. Everyone can connect to stuff in it.

What drew me to Kentucky Shakespeare is that mission of the free Shakespeare. I think what made me fall in love with Shakespeare along with my wife that summer—and Louisville—is, "Oh my gosh, you are all welcome!" We're going to mount this professional play, something that some people say is elitist—an opera or a ballet or Shakespeare. But we're going to strip it down; we're going to make it accessible; we're going to make it fun; and we're going to give it away to you. And we're going to pay a lot of money to these actors. We're currently spending three hundred thousand dollars on a summer season, on all that. And we're going to give it all away to you. Because we believe you're entitled to it. We believe you deserve that. We believe Shakespeare belongs to you *all*. This is not something for the few.

Braden McCampbell: Louisville is weird. The reason Kentucky Shakespeare works here, rather than like New York or anything, is because if it becomes so much of a business, then it becomes a hoity-toity thing to do. Whereas here it's like, "Come! Sit your ass! Eat the sugar thing from the food truck! We'd love to see you!" That's it. That's all it is. Come as you are. We don't care what you look like, what you've done, who you are—just come. Come and spend some time with us. We'll entertain you. There's food if you want it—that's not free, but there is some food if you want it—all of that.

They put so much time and effort and love and work into bringing this to the community for free! For free! That is a big deal. I can't stress how big of a deal that one thing is. That means, "Come—bring your kids; bring your wife; bring whoever—this is free. Come and just enjoy it." And that takes a lot of work. This is a professional company. This is seven-hour rehearsals. This is money. It is a lot of money. There's all of this grant writing that goes into it. There's just so much effort, so much time. But it turns out an amazing product, and it's all for the audience, so that they can come and see a show for free! I know a lot of people probably do not understand just how much effort goes into this to make this thing free, to keep Will free.

It's a labor of love. We do this because we love this community. We do this because we love Louisville. It's all so that people can come and see it.

Elizabeth Siebert: Kentucky Shakespeare defines what it means to be a good citizen in this community. I hold them up. They do excellent work. They make everyone feel included. They are very welcoming. It just connects the city. It's really the heartbeat of the city. Central Park is in many ways the heart of the whole city, and Kentucky Shakespeare helps it beat.

Inspired by both the longtime goal of bringing Shakespeare to diverse audiences and the fact that most of the interviews were conducted in the spring and summer of 2020, at a time of the Black Lives Matter movement nationally and the struggle for justice for Breonna Taylor locally, several of the narrators spoke explicitly about the experience of being an African American artist or the quest for racial inclusion in Kentucky Shakespeare programs and in theater more generally.

Braden McCampbell: As an educator, as an actor, I'm trying to reach everybody. As a Black actor, I'm just like, "Look, I want the kids to understand that there's more out there." Because I hadn't realized there was more out there. I wish I had known there was more out there. As a Black actor, when I'm trying to reach children, if I try to say, "Hey, this is a message specifically for the kids," I always feel like I'm preaching at that point. I feel like, on one hand, I don't need to do that, because seeing me is sometimes enough. Like I said with that kid [who thought I was Black Panther], seeing me, knowing that I was there, knowing that I existed, knowing that there are Black people out here who kind of look like Chad Boseman, who are out here doing shows, and they can come to my school and do things—that representation is important. But it should already be a thing. I shouldn't need to claim ownership and say, "Hey, I'm going to make sure these kids know that theater is a thing." Kids should already be able to know that. A Black student should already be able to know, "Yes, I decided that I want to go into the theater department. It's not that weird thing that white people do." It should just be, "I'm a Black kid who decided to go into theater. There's already a version of me out here doing this, and they're enjoying their life."

Crystian Wiltshire: There are plays that I have seen done across the country where I've said to myself, "Oh, I don't belong in this show." And that's okay. This show doesn't necessarily speak to my experience, and in no way should I ever audition for this show. But that doesn't mean it doesn't have value to the theater or to other communities. But I don't watch Shakespeare plays and think to myself, "Oh, that's not for me." No, when I'm watching those shows, I'm wondering, "Huh, where can I fit in? I see myself in this in some capacity." So that's exciting. I think that is up to companies like Kentucky Shakespeare and theaters across the country to hear that the opportunities are very much present for diverse casting. There's that fine line you have to walk of not taking advantage of a specific time that we might be in. For example, because maybe the country is in a climate where racial tensions are high, you decide to put on a Shakespeare play that is incredibly diverse. But then in a year from now, when tensions have calmed down, you go back to the way that things used to be at your company. That's where you begin to feel inauthentic, and you have to avoid that. Kentucky Shakespeare is not one of those companies. I played Romeo years ago, now, and I have continued to be hired by that company. They have continued to diversify on- and offstage. And it is really, really beautiful to see. Have they reached their full potential in terms of diversity and inclusion? No. But I think the leadership that is in place right now is aware of that and is going to continue to strive to make those necessary changes.

Braden McCampbell performing *Taming of the Shrew* during a school tour, 2018.

In this moment that we are in right now, as a country, really, there is a lot of pain that is coming out. Not just in the theater world but a lot of different organizations and institutions are being called out for discriminatory practices. In the theater, there's a real movement right now for Black voices to be heard, for diversity in casting to increase, for diversity on the administrative side of these theater companies to be increased. There's just a real movement behind that right now. So when I think about strengths at a company like Kentucky Shakespeare, I have to give them credit for not just hiring people that look like me but rehiring people that look like me, while still maintaining a familial environment. It's really shaped how I expect other theater companies to be run. If I have an experience elsewhere that is not up to par, I'm calling it out based on my time at Kentucky Shakespeare, where I've seen how running a theater is done right.

I think what Kentucky Shakespeare needs to do, and they're already doing this, but they just need to continue to stay aware of where the country is in terms of what is the best practice. Kentucky Shakespeare should just continue to be consistent. It's one thing for any company to say, for example, that Black Lives Matter, or Black Trans

Lives Matter. You can post that on your social media account; that's great. That's great that you are, as a company, stating that you are aware of this moment. But we need to see more than that. Let's see some real policy change; let's see something change in your day-to-day business. That's, I think, what the company needs to be aware of.

Anya Bond Beckley: Elizabeth Siebert and I and a couple of other members of the board went to the performances that traveled throughout different parks. We went to the opening show. Initially, I didn't recognize I was counting people of color in the show—not meaning to, but I was. Is this real? Do you realize how many years I've been coming to Shakespeare plays, and that was the largest cast of people of color I had ever seen? I lost it in the park with Elizabeth. Elizabeth and I caught each other's eye contact. She knew exactly what I was thinking. The play was over; Amy was standing there. I said, "I've got to thank you for this because this play is going to go from park to park. People are going to see this. This now is the equivalent, is parallel to what our community looks like." And it was beautiful. Because Shakespeare's for everyone is what we say, and we truly believe it. When I looked on them performing on the grass, that mission statement was ringing true. Because when you're in the parks, we could be in Shawnee all the way to Norton Commons, people are looking at the actors—male, female, people of color.[4] I just told Elizabeth, "Give me a moment; I've got to take it in." Amy and I embraced and just looked at the stage together and the kids on the grass and just couldn't believe it. How far we've come.

This is just something that happened naturally, not something we forced. Kentucky Shakespeare gets it and continues to allow the stage to mirror the community and try to break down barriers at the same time. Matt truly believes, let's mirror the community. How do we get more people? How do we take away the barriers? There's a difference between equality, equity, and true inclusion. Inclusion is when you say, "Hey, everybody gets to not only participate in being on that stage but pick the music for that stage, pick the costumes for that stage." He gets that. That has nothing to do with the racial unrest of our city or any other city. This is something he's truly believed in. That piece is nothing new.

Matt Wallace: We pretty much think about diversity and inclusion every day. I'm never happy with as much as we have. I'm always trying to

Reviews and Reflections   189

push, push—how can we get more? Other than it's what we *all* need to do, it's the *right* thing to do. When I would be up onstage, the neighborhood African American kids would come and sit on the stoop and watch the show and give us notes afterwards about their favorite parts. Or they would come running when the sword fight would come because they *loved* that part! I want to make sure that those children are seeing themselves represented on that stage. I don't want it to be one African American in the show. It's a challenge when you're a professional company and you have limited funds. If you can't find all your actors locally, you have to bring them and house them, which we've done for several summers for a couple actors. But we're committed. I want those kids to see themselves on the stage.

In response to local and national events and to an anti-racism movement in American theater, since the time of these interviews, Kentucky Shakespeare has redoubled its commitment to its historic mission of creating inclusive arts experiences. The company partnered with the city's public bus system to distribute one thousand vouchers for free rides to Central Park through over thirty community organizations in low-income neighborhoods. With funding from the National Endowment for the Arts, it developed arts education programs with the Imagine Blind Players; Down Syndrome of Louisville; the LaNita Rocknettes School of Dance, which has been teaching dance in the West End for over sixty years; and the Louisville Youth Group, an organization by and for LGBTQ+ teens. The summer festival also welcomed to the stage arts groups from a wide range of racial and ethnic communities, who brought their friends and family with them to the park. The result of this outreach is that the demographics of the audiences for the summer season are getting close to mirroring the population in Jefferson County. New initiatives are planned to continue that trend and also to bring the spring tour to more diverse neighborhoods. Meanwhile, Wallace and Attaway have pushed for more inclusion onstage and behind the curtain. As Bond Beckley noted, the company has hired more people of color and queer artists for all of its programs. In the most recent year, more than 50 percent of the arts education team, spring tour cast, and summer season performers were people of color, while 20 percent of the cast and 42 percent of the crew were from the LGBTQ+ community. Finally, the leadership team, staff, and board have produced an IDEA (inclusion, diversity, equity, access) plan to lay out long- and short-term goals and institutionalize the new practices—all with an eye toward realizing Doug Ramey's vision that Shakespeare is for everyone.

190   Under the Greenwood Tree

The last word goes to Matt Wallace, who, when asked to reflect on the future of the company, promised ongoing work toward that vision but also the fun of discovering and sharing Shakespeare.

Matt Wallace: I want to keep making Shakespeare feel relevant and exciting. It's kind of funny that Amy is in this position as well because both of us came from doing new plays. Both of us came from looking at Shakespeare like a new play. When people see Kentucky Shakespeare shows, I hope that people walk away with that "Oh my gosh, it was so clean and clear! And I felt it!" You're not going to get every word—that's just how it works—that's Shakespeare. But if you'll breathe—you're going to get what's going on, and your ear is going to get used to it. And hopefully, if we're doing our work, it's going to be exciting and feel relevant. I think it's a pretty cool thing that a majority of the Shakespeare that this community is going to see is going to see *us* doing it. I think we have a great responsibility to do that truthfully and with integrity, onstage and off.

I want to continue to improve what we're doing and the stories that we're telling and expanding to the community further. Increasing the diversity—in all areas of what we do. Increasing financial strength and sustainability. You know I want to retire doing this job. This is what I want to do and what I want to continue to do. I also want to be open to inspiration about what we do next. You talk about barriers to Shakespeare: we added the microphones one year; then we did the bench campaign; we improved the restrooms; we added a police officer. What's keeping people away from coming to Shakespeare in the Park? I think we continue to find creative ways that we advertise it and remove barriers and *get* people to come to experience free Shakespeare. We have the infrastructure to have fifteen hundred people a night, in Central Park. We're just getting going! The festival is going to expand in the summer, so much more. I want to get the education program to all 120 counties in *one season*. We can do that! We're getting close. I think we will continue to produce interesting, out-of-the-box indoor productions during the year in interesting spaces with interesting companies. That's the great thing about working with some of the artists over and over is we're all growing and we're all continuing to learn about Shakespeare. If we ever have all the answers about Shakespeare, we're just going to stop doing it because it's not going to be any fun anymore. It's just a great, fun mystery, and we will continue to explore it.

Appendix

Methodology and Acknowledgments

The oral history project that led to this book began in a fangirl moment. I have been a professor of US history at the University of Louisville for over twenty years and have done extensive oral history interviewing in the community in my role as the codirector of the Oral History Center. I also periodically teach the Department of History's graduate seminar in interviewing methods. But theater and Shakespeare were a recreational, not a professional, interest. After having avidly attended every summer production since *The Taming of the Shrew* in 2015, I wanted to give something back to the company. I attended a meeting for volunteers with the thought of passing out programs at performances or the like. When producing artistic director Matt Wallace mentioned that the anniversary season was approaching in summer 2020, I spontaneously offered to put my expertise to work by conducting interviews to document the company's history for the occasion. I next reached out to students who I thought might be interested and quickly rounded up four to conduct and transcribe interviews as part of an independent study course: Timothy Chase Johnson, Arabella Paulovich, Emily Tingle, and Rebecca Wishnevski. At that point, I approached Amy Attaway, associate artistic director of Kentucky Shakespeare, for help with the project.

To get the project started, Attaway provided the names and contact information of some longtime cast and crew and came to class to give the students an introduction to the company. In the course, which was

191

taught in spring 2020, students learned methodologies for conducting and using interviews. We then developed a common interview outline. Each student completed three interviews of at least an hour in length. When the COVID-19 pandemic ruled out in-person meetings, students got creative, using their technological skills to conduct and record oral histories remotely with a variety of programs. They also completed the transcriptions of the interviews they conducted. When the semester was over, Wishnevski, a graduate student in public history, continued to work on the project as a summer intern and recruited and completed additional interviews, focusing on African American actors. Finally, in summer and fall 2021, I reached out to other narrators to enhance women's voices in the collection and to gain a more thorough account of some of the community outreach programs and partnerships. Professor Joseph Pearson donated his interview with Bekki Jo Schneider, which was conducted just before her death. All the interviews are transcribed, and both audio and print versions are in the University of Louisville Archives.

Two factors influenced the decision to produce a book based on these interviews: the limited opportunity for an in-person presentation such as an exhibit in the park or readers' theater piece because of the pandemic and the sheer richness of the memories, which seemed to beg for a more extended treatment than a digital presentation would allow. As I read and corrected the student interviews and rough draft transcripts, I familiarized myself with the content and with the narrators' storytelling style. The structure of the book arose from the material, reflecting the topics the interviewees spent relatively more time addressing. Once I had an outline, I sorted stories from the interviews into chapter files, then arranged them in ways that flowed logically and propelled the story. I next edited the segments to produce a readable narrative. On the most basic level, this involved not only adding punctuation and creating paragraphs but also moving material around and inserting some brief phrases to help the passages make sense. Unfortunately, it also required significant cutting to produce a manuscript of a manageable length. In the final round of refining the text, I sought to produce an engaging narrative while retaining the integrity of the interviews and the manners of speech. In editing and arranging the interview material, I followed strategies recommended by historians Linda Shopes and Michael Frisch.[1] My ultimate goal, however, was to craft a story that both illuminates the artistry that goes into producing a play and makes a night in the park come to life.

By its nature, any oral history–based project is a team effort and requires contributions and support from numerous parties. Most important, I would like to thank the narrators who gave their time and shared their stories so willingly. Their eloquence is the core of this book and made working on the project a joy. I could not have done the interviews alone, and so I am grateful to the students, especially Wishnevski, who went above and beyond and produced some of the best interviews. Amy Attaway and other Kentucky Shakespeare staff provided quick replies to questions and additional material to supplement the stories. I am especially indebted to Amy Attaway, who organized the hundreds of photographs held by Kentucky Shakespeare and then gave me access to all of them. I must acknowledge Gregory Maupin and the participants in his periodic Shakespeare off the Page seminars for brainstorming titles and helping me better understand the Bard's work. Professor Kathryn Nasstrom of the University of San Francisco has read and edited everything I've published, and her suggestions, as always, made this book better. More personally, thanks to my husband and fellow historian, A. Glenn Crothers, not only for reading and editing this manuscript but for putting up with my admittedly sometimes overly effusive enthusiasm for the project. Finally, I am grateful to live in a community that is home to and supports such a talented and visionary group of artists.

Notes

Introduction

1. William Shakespeare, *As You Like It*, 2.5. References are to act and scene. My thanks to Gregory Maupin for the title phrase suggestion.

2. The sobriquet "Bard," meaning poet, is often used to reference Shakespeare. It was likely first used in 1769 by poet David Garrick in *Ode Upon Dedicating a Building* and has become more common in the twentieth century. David Garrick, *Ode on Dedication of a Building* . . . (London: Printed for T. Becket and P.A. De Hondt, 1769). For full text see Eighteenth Century Collections Online, Text Creation Partnership, at https://quod.lib.umich.edu/e /ecco/004807629.0001.000?view=toc, accessed April 26, 2023. Sylvia Morris, "Bard of Avon Origin," *Shaksper: The Global Electronic Shakespeare Conference*, 2013, https://shaksper.net/archive/2013/339-april/29211-bard-of-avon -origin?acm=_360.

3. Regarding terminology, the Carriage House Players were referred to interchangeably as the Carriage House Theater in the local press. After the first summer season, Carriage House continued to host both Shakespearean and modern plays, but thereafter the summer productions were referred to as Shakespeare in Central Park or Shakespeare in the Park. In 1990, the latter became the Kentucky Shakespeare Festival, which in 2010 was renamed Kentucky Shakespeare. The narrators in this project occasionally referred to the Carriage House Players when discussing the very early years but for the most part used the terminology Shakespeare in the Park, Kentucky Shakespeare, the Kentucky Shakespeare Festival, and simply "the company" interchangeably regardless of the time period being referenced. I have followed that practice in my own introductions except when a specific term is required by the context.

Prologue

1. Priddy refers here to the Belknap Theater Playhouse, a theater on the grounds of the University of Louisville. The building has served as a theater

196 Notes to Pages 5–31

on and off since 1923. It is now part of Freedom Park and houses productions by the university's African American Theater Program.

2. The Louisville Children's Theater was founded in 1946. Between 1978 and 2002, it was directed by Moses Goldberg, who added StageOne to the name.

3. Equity refers to the Actors' Equity Association, which is the union representing actors and stage managers in live theater. An Equity professional theater is one that hires union actors and stage managers.

4. Iambic pentameter is a meter in English poetry. It means there are ten syllables in a line, organized in five pairs of a short beat followed by a long one.

5. Elder (1927–96) was an African American playwright and actor.

6. Jon Jory was the producing director of Actors Theatre from 1969 to 2000. He is credited with developing Actors into one of the top regional theater companies in the country. The Negro Ensemble Company was founded in New York City in 1967 with the mission of producing plays on the Black experience.

7. Actors Theatre is comprised of several spaces, including the Victor Jory Theatre, the Bingham Theatre, and the Pamela Brown Auditorium.

8. Here Luce uses dated language to refer to one of two characters in Cole Porter's play, Chinese immigrants Ching and Ling, who were played in the first Broadway production by Asian American actors Richard Wang and Charlie Fang. In productions since the 1980s the names are often changed to common English names, though the parts are usually played by actors of East Asian descent.

9. The Midwest Theater Auditions, held annually at Webster University, is a mass audition and employment event for summer theater positions throughout the region.

10. Adale O'Brien was a founding cast member of Actors Theatre's Resident Acting Company from 1970 to 2005.

11. Because the summer performances are free, to raise money the company collects donations at intermission, a practice they call barreling. Downs references here the colorful cloth bags she created, which are still used in the performances today.

12. United Professional Theatre Auditions is an annual audition conference for theater professionals.

13. The Blue Apple Players is a nonprofit theater in Louisville that focuses on musicals and educational programs for young people.

14. The Henriad comprises Shakespeare's history plays *Richard II; Henry IV, Parts 1* and *2;* and *Henry V* produced in a series, usually with the same actors continuing the roles throughout.

15. The Young Actors Institute was a two-week summer program run by the Youth Performing Arts School. It is now known as the Clint Vaught

Young Actors Institute. See Clint Vaught Young Actors Institute, https://ypas.jcps-ky.com/AboutYAI, accessed April 17, 2023.

16. *Romeo and Juliet* (1968), directed by Franco Zeffirelli, with Leonard Whiting as Romeo and Olivia Hussey as Juliet. Upon its release, critics hailed the film for the passion of its leads, and public high schools around the country used it in the classroom. More recently, it has been criticized for the exploitation of the young actors. Recent generations are more likely to know the 1996 Baz Luhrmann film with Leonardo DiCaprio and Claire Danes.

17. A two-person scene assigned for an audition.

Act 1: The Plot

1. Doug Ramey, quoted in Bryan Woolley, "Louisville's Bard of Central Park," *Courier-Journal* (Louisville), August 1, 1971; *"As You Like It* Tonight," *Courier-Journal*, July 1, 1895.

2. Woolley, "Louisville's Bard"; Helen Lawton, "Five New Theaters Start Here," *Courier-Journal*, December 11, 1949.

3. On outdoor Shakespeare in the twentieth century, see Michael Dobson, *Shakespeare and Amateur Performance: A Cultural History* (New York: Cambridge University Press, 2011), 152–96; Alden T. Vaughan and Virginia Mason Vaughan, *Shakespeare in America* (New York: Oxford University Press, 2012), 176–79.

4. Morgan Lawson, "Kentuckiana Will Have a Good Share of Summer Theater," *Courier-Journal*, June 14, 1959; "Birth of a Festival?," *Courier-Journal*, July 1, 1962; Morgan Lawson, "Carriage House to Present Plays at State Fair," *Courier-Journal*, August 2, 1959; "At Carriage House," *Courier-Journal*, June 4, 1961.

5. For histories of Old Louisville, see John Paul, "Old Louisville History: More Than a Monument: A Learning Experience," October 2012, https://www.jpaul.us/history/; Louisville (KY) Historic Landmarks and Preservation Districts Commission, *Old Louisville Preservation Designation Report* (Louisville: Landmarks and Preservation Districts Commission, 1974); David Domine, Franklin Schmidt, and Esther Schmidt, *Old Louisville: Exuberant, Elegant, Alive* (Savannah, GA: Golden Coast Publications, 2013), 16–19.

6. Under a parks commission order, only Chickasaw Park in the west end of the city had been opened to Black patrons before the integration of city parks in 1955. See Tracy E. K'Meyer, *Civil Rights in the Gateway to the South: Louisville, Kentucky, 1945–1980* (Lexington: University Press of Kentucky, 2009), 28–33.

7. "Saving 'Old Louisville' Homes Aim of New Committee of 12," *Courier-Journal*, June 16, 1961; "Groups to Aid in Restoring Old Louisville," *Courier-Journal*, June 21, 1961.

198   Notes to Pages 43–45

8. "At Carriage House," *Courier-Journal*, June 4, 1961; Sarah Landsdell, "Both Shakespeare, Set Glow in Festival Opener," *Courier-Journal*, July 9, 1961; "Birth of a Festival?," *Courier-Journal*, July 1, 1962; Logan Pope, "Central Park to Have All Year Amphitheater," *Courier-Journal*, March 31, 1963; "More Shakespeare in Central Park," *Courier-Journal*, May 8, 1963; Vincent Crowdus, "$32,265 Left in Mayor's Money Box," *Courier-Journal*, July 13, 1963; Phyllis Funke, "Shakespeare-in-Central Park to Launch Season on July 7," *Courier-Journal*, May 23, 1965.

9. Sir Arthur John Gielgud was a longtime star of the British stage and screen, recognized in the post–World War II period for his Shakespearean roles.

10. William Mootz, "Nearby Noise Hampers 'Othello' Performance," *Courier-Journal*, July 7, 1962; William Mootz, "Shakespeare in the Park Up, Down, in 'The Tempest,'" *Courier-Journal*, July 12, 1963; William Mootz, "Bard-in-Park Needs Shot in the Arm," *Courier-Journal*, August 1, 1965.

11. Jean Howerton, "Out, Out Brief Candle for Plays in the Park?," *Courier-Journal*, June 3, 1966; Woolley, "Louisville's Bard."

12. Norma D. Henry, letter to the editor, *Courier-Journal*, July 26, 1965; Mrs. Richard Hayes, letter to the editor, *Courier-Journal*, August 13, 1965; Dick Hunter, "Bard in the Park Provides Fringe Benefits," *Courier-Journal*, August 13, 1967; Phyllis Funke, "Bard-in-Park Audience Gives Good Shows, Too," *Courier-Journal*, August 16, 1964; K'Meyer, *Civil Rights in the Gateway*, 118; Lawrence Pryor, "Shakespeare Lovers Turn Out," *Courier-Journal*, July 6, 1966; Woolley, "Louisville's Bard"; Brenda Henderson, "To Actors, Shakespeare in Park's a Labor of Love," *Courier-Journal*, July 10, 1969. Note that the *Courier-Journal* referred to the Committee for Shakespeare in the Park as Committee for Shakespeare in Central Park or the Shakespeare in the Park Committee, but they were all the same body.

13. The question of whether a white or Black actor should play Othello has a long and contentious history. Historically, the role was performed by whites, though Black actors have been cast since the nineteenth century. After Paul Robeson performed the role in 1943, it became more common to cast Black actors in the part. Nevertheless, white performers, including noted Shakespeareans John Gielgud and Laurence Olivier, played the part in the 1960s. By the 1970s, that became increasingly rare. When she directed the play in 1983, Bekki Jo Schneider hired an African American actor from New York named Victor Love to come to Louisville to perform the role. Andrew Carlson, "Not Just Black and White: 'Othello' in America," *Theatre History*, December 27, 2016, https://www.americantheatre.org/2016/12/27/not-just -black-and-white-othello-in-america/; "*Othello*: A History of Performance," *Internet Shakespeare Editions*, accessed December 26, 2022, https://internet shakespeare.uvic.ca/m/doc/Oth_PerfHistory/; "Shakespeare in the Park to Stage 'Othello,'" *Courier-Journal*, July 3, 1983.

Notes to Pages 46–65   199

14. Schneider is referring to Vietnamese refugees who were resettled in Louisville in the 1970s.

15. Cherokee Park is to the east in the Highlands neighborhood, which at the time was more middle and upper-middle class than central Louisville. Shawnee Park is along the Ohio River in the northwest corner of the city. In the late 1950s and early 1960s, it was in a neighborhood transitioning from working-class white families to working- and middle-class African American homeowners. Jenny Wiley State Park is in eastern Kentucky, near Prestonsburg.

16. A dramaturg is a staff person in a theater who helps actors, directors, and designers to understand the text of a play. Roger Fristoe, "Bekki Jo Schneider: The Woman Who Came to Dinner Theater," *Courier-Journal*, June 23, 1985; Roger Fristoe, "What's in a Name? Hal Park Switches Theatrical Parks," *Courier-Journal*, May 26, 1985; Joan Kay, "Professor Loves Pointing Out the 'Live Issues' in Shakespeare," *Courier-Journal*, July 20, 1986; Andrew Adler, "The Shakespeare Institute: The Bard off the Pedestal," *Courier-Journal*, August 2, 1987; Roger Fristoe, "Shakespeare's Apprentices," *Courier-Journal*, August 3, 1986.

17. Regional mass audition and employment events held throughout the year for actors and other theater professionals.

18. A Catholic church dating from 1896, located one half mile east of Central Park in Old Louisville.

19. William Shakespeare, *Richard III*, 1.1.

20. "Old Louisville Neighborhood Council," meeting announcement, *Courier-Journal*, March 4, 1992; "Charities Are Giving More, but Receiving Less," *Courier-Journal*, April 6, 1992; Curt L. Tofteland, letter to the editor, *Courier-Journal*, May 19, 1997.

21. Judith Egerton, "Festival Marks 40th Season with 'Romeo and Juliet,' 'Twelfth Night,'" *Courier-Journal*, May 28, 2000; Judith Egerton, "New Director Has a Passion for Shakespeare," *Courier-Journal*, September 21, 2008; "Adieu, Fare Thee Well," *Courier-Journal*, December 3, 2009; "Dunaway Helps to Restore Kentucky Shakespeare's Financial Standing," *Courier-Journal*, June 16, 2013; Erin Keane, "Ex–Kentucky Shakespeare Employees: Former CEO Brantley Dunaway Abusive, Financially Irresponsible," July 16, 2013, https://wfpl.org/ex-kentucky-shakespeare-employees-former-ceo-brantley-dunaway-abusive-financially-irresponsible/; Harold J. Adams, "Actress Gets Protective Order, Play Ends," *Courier-Journal*, July 12, 2013; Elizabeth Kramer, "Kentucky Shakespeare Leader Has Resigned," *Courier-Journal*, July 16, 2013.

22. A colloquial expression meaning to stop communicating without explanation.

23. The Rudyard Kipling was a bar/restaurant and performance space at the northern edge of Old Louisville.

200   Notes to Pages 66–107

24. Dathan Hooper was an actor with the company during this time period. He is over six feet tall. Abigail Maupin is petite.

25. Mark's Feed Store is a barbecue restaurant in the Highlands neighborhood.

26. Attaway's husband, Brian Owens, is a set designer who specializes in flight special effects.

Act 2: Putting Shakespeare on Its Feet

1. The Magnolia Bar, commonly known as the "Mag Bar," is a tavern in Old Louisville just two blocks from Central Park.

2. Theater expression referring to a rehearsal of just portions of scenes for light and sound cues.

3. In theater folklore, saying the name of *Macbeth* aloud is considered to be bad luck. Instead, many people will refer to the "Scottish play" or "Mackers."

4. In honor of the Kentucky Shakespeare Festival's sixtieth anniversary, Matt Wallace planned to present an adaptation of the film *Shakespeare in Love* in the summer season. It was postponed by the COVID-19 pandemic from 2020 to 2021. The play is a fictional story of a young William Shakespeare being inspired to write *Romeo and Juliet* by falling in love with a woman whom he cannot marry. The *Shakespeare in Love* script includes several passages from *Romeo and Juliet* and other Shakespearean plays.

5. Aqua Net is a hair spray used to keep hairdos smooth and in place.

6. In preparation for performing or reciting Shakespeare, actors will "scan" the lines, or look for the rhythm of the verse. Scanning enables the speaker to understand where the emphasis lies in the lines.

7. Scansion is the analysis of the meter of a piece of poetry.

8. John Barton was the cofounder of the Royal Shakespeare Company in the United Kingdom. He produced a series of videos called *Playing Shakespeare*, which gave lessons for actors and directors.

9. Regency period refers to 1811–20; Elizabethan refers to 1558–1603, Shakespeare's own time.

10. A spit take is a sudden comic motion, originally a sudden spitting of water in response to something funny.

11. The First Folio is the first collected edition of Shakespeare's plays. Published in 1623, it contains thirty-six of his thirty-seven plays. Scholars consider it closest to the original performed language that Shakespeare intended.

Act 3: In the Park

1. Christine Eade, "Bard in Shirtsleeves—That's Central Park," *Courier-Journal*, July 21, 1967; Phyllis Funke, "Bard-in-Park Audience Gives Good Shows, Too," *Courier-Journal*, August 16, 1964.

Notes to Pages 112–150   201

2. William Shakespeare, *Henry IV*, *Part 2*, 4.3.

3. During Bard-a-thons, the company performed all three of the summer season's plays in one day, back to back, with only a short break between them.

4. Pedialyte is a drink with a mix of electrolytes and sugar, usually given to children when they are dehydrated from illness.

5. In *Shakespeare in Love*, Queen Elizabeth repeatedly asks if the play she is seeing is "the one with the dog," a reference to *The Two Gentlemen of Verona*, in which there is, indeed, a dog.

6. Grand Guignol refers to the horrific or sensational entertainment found in performances at the Grand Guignol Theater in Paris.

7. Traditionally, a tiring house is a room backstage where actors change and wait for their cues. In the Central Park stage at that time, it was a room behind a raised platform creating a second story for the stage.

Act 4: "All the World's a Stage"

This chapter's title is drawn from William Shakespeare, *As You Like It*, 2.7.

1. Sarah Landsdell, "Culture Caravan," *Courier-Journal*, May 20, 1961; "Carriage House Plans Tour," *Courier-Journal*, April 8, 1962.

2. Phyllis Funke, "Bard Unit Finds Avid Fans on Kentucky Schools Tour," *Courier-Journal*, February 21, 1965; "*Hamlet* at Elizabethtown Will Begin Carriage House Players' School Tour," *Courier-Journal*, November 1, 1970; Matt Wallace, personal correspondence with author, February 17, 2022.

3. The Kentucky Education Reform Act (1990) equalized school funding across the state and also established accountability measures.

4. The Louisville Central Community Center is an independent nonprofit institution that sponsors educational, community-development, and arts programs aimed at children and adults. It is located in a historically majority African American neighborhood just west of downtown.

5. Phyllis Funke, "Arts, Talent Festival Scheduled in West End," *Courier-Journal*, June 27, 1965.

6. For an overview of this history, see Andrew James Hartley, *Shakespeare and Political Theatre in Practice* (New York: Palgrave Macmillan, 2013). Hartley pays particular attention to Shakespeare in school and prison settings.

7. Backside Learning Center is an independent nonprofit that provides programming and services to the largely Latino and immigrant families of employees of the Churchill Downs Racetrack.

8. Hartley, *Shakespeare and Political Theater*, 111–14. For more on the documentary, see "SBB Documentary: Shakespeare Behind Bars," https://shakespearebehindbars.org/documentary/, accessed April 18, 2023, and "Shakespeare Behind Bars: The Award-Winning Cult Classic Documentary," https://www.shakespearebehindbars.com/, accessed January 2, 2023. For

202 Notes to Pages 150–171

more on the Kentucky and Michigan Shakespeare Behind Bars programs, see "Michigan Programs," https://shakespearebehindbars.org/programs/michigan/, accessed January 2, 2023.

9. Drew Wiggins, "Veterans Find a Path to Healing through Shakespeare," *Mad in America: Science, Psychiatry, and Social Justice*, October 13, 2019, https://www.madinamerica.com/2019/10/veterans-find-path-to-healing-through-shakespeare/; Jessica Toome, "This Veteran Is Using Shakespeare to Heal," *Guideposts*, https://guideposts.org/positive-living/health-and-wellness/healing/this-veteran-is-using-shakespeare-to-heal/, accessed January 2, 2023. For more on Kentucky Shakespeare with Veterans, see "Shakespeare with Veterans," https://kyshakespeare.com/programs/shakespeare-with-veterans/, accessed January 2, 2023.

10. The Peace Education Program is a Louisville nonprofit that teaches conflict resolution to youth. See, "Peace Ed: Resolving Conflict Peacefully," https://www.peaceeducationprogram.org/, accessed April 18, 2023.

11. William Shakespeare, *Henry IV, Part 1*, 2.4.

12. Brooklawn, Maryhurst, and Tenbrook are facilities in Louisville that serve the mental health and social service needs of children and adolescents.

13. Squallis Puppeteers is an arts organization that uses puppetry performances aimed primarily at young audiences to convey values of empathy, community, collaboration, and social justice. See "Squallis Puppeteers: Unleashing the Creative Mind," http://www.squallispuppeteers.com/about, accessed April 18, 2023.

14. Kentucky Refugee Ministries is a nonprofit organization helping to resettle and support refugees in the community.

15. After a delay due to COVID-19, *Shakespeare's R and J* was performed in collaboration with Pandora Productions in August 2022.

16. Louisville Visual Art is a nonprofit organization that supports current and future artists through community programming and education. Play Louisville is a nightclub that caters to the local LGBTQ+ community and hosts popular drag performances.

Act 5: Reviews and Reflections

1. Kentucky Shakespeare, *2018–2019 Season in Review* and Kentucky Shakespeare, *2021–2022 Season in Review*. Annual reports are mailed to donors. The most recent year is also available for several months after publication on the organization's web page at https://kyshakespeare.com/about/our-mission/. Past issues are available upon request. Donor records were provided in personal correspondence from Matt Wallace and are available upon request.

2. Annette Skaggs, "Viola/Olivia Is an Anagram," *Arts-Louisville*, June 1, 2022, https://arts-louisville.com/2022/06/01/viola-olivia-is-an-anagram

-kentucky-shakespeare/; Ashlie Stevens, "Kentucky Shakespeare's *As You Like It* Doesn't Miss a Beat," *Louisville Public Media*, May 30, 2019, https://www.lpm.org/news/2019-05-30/review-kentucky-shakespeares-as-you-like-it-doesnt-miss-a-beat; Marty Rosen, "KY Shakes's *Henry V* Is 'Stunningly Beautiful' Theater," *LEO Weekly*, July 14, 2021, https://www.leoweekly.com/2021/07/henry-v-closes-kentucky-shakespeares-game-kings-spectacularly/; Allie Fireel, "Review: *Shakespeare's R&J* from Kentucky Shakespeare and Pandora Productions," *Leo Weekly*, August 19, 2022; Marty Rosen, "Theater Review [. . .]," *LEO Weekly*, July 19, 2022, https://www.leoweekly.com/2022/07/theater-review-twelfth-night-richard-iii-and-the-merry-wives-of-windsor/; Jodi Smiley, July 25, 2019; Joanie Roger, July 15, 2022; Brandilyn Ray Duggin, July 31, 2021; Heidi Harmon Konynenbelt, June 23, 2021; all on the reviews section of the Kentucky Shakespeare Facebook page at https://www.facebook.com/KentuckyShakespeare/reviews.

3. Shakespeare Birthplace Trust is the independent charity that preserves and creates access to artifacts and places associated with Shakespeare's life in Stratford-upon-Avon.

4. Shawnee Park is in the northwest corner of the city, surrounded by a largely African American neighborhood. Norton Commons is a relatively new upper-middle-class and largely white suburb on the northeast edge of the county.

Appendix: Methodology and Acknowledgments

1. Linda Shopes, "Editing Oral History for Publication," originally published in *Oral History Forum d'Histoire Orale* 31 (2011): 1–24; Michael Frisch, *A Shared Authority: Essays on the Craft and Meaning of Oral and Public History* (Albany: State University of New York Press, 1990), 81–146.

Index

Page numbers in *italics* refer to photos.

Actors' Equity Association, 6, 8, 63, 80, 176, 196n3
Actors Theatre of Louisville, 3, 8–9, 11, 13, 15, 16, 23, 25, 31, 35, 41, 46, 67, 180–182, 196nn6–7
All's Well That Ends Well, 61
anti-racism movement, 189
As You Like It, 6–7, 21, 30–31, 39, 109, 115, 170
Attaway, Amy, 35, 67–68, 79–80, *83, 159*; on becoming an actor, 31–33; on directing, 89–90; on directorships at Kentucky Shakespeare, 67–68, 74–75; on Louisville Ballet partnership, 165; on meaning of Kentucky Shakespeare, 171–172, 176; on preshows, 163–164; on Shakespeare with Veterans, 155–158; Shakespeare with Veterans director, 149, 150, 155–158; on *Taming of the Shrew,* 120–121; on uniqueness of Kentucky Shakespeare, 181–182
auditions, 78–80, 146

Bard Buddies, 141
"Bard," use of the term, 195n2
Bartow, Julie, 151–152
Belknap Theater Playhouse, 5, 41, 195–196n1

Bellarmine University, 4, 150
Black Lives Matter, 185, 187
Blue Apple Players, 26, 196n13
Bond Beckley, Anya, 132, 188, 189
Books behind Bars, 150
Boy Meets Girl Meets Shakespeare, 138–142
Brain, Kate, 138
Burkestrand, Curtis, 150

Camp Shakespeare, 18, 140, 144–145
carriage house (in Old Louisville), viii, 1, 44, 47, 49, 51
Carriage House Players, viii, ix, 1, 3–5, 41–49, 135, 136, 146, 195n3
casting, 78–79
Central Park, vii, ix, 1, 4–5, 35, 39, 46; criticism of as performing space, 43; diversity in, 183; fondness for as performing space, 53, 70, 84, 106, 108–109, 114, 116, 123, 185; history of, 41–42; history of Shakespeare in, 39, 41–43, 47; Ramey, Douglas, and, 46, 49–50; threat to move away from, 60, 106
Cherokee Park, 50, 199n15
Cherry, Phil, 10, 103; on acting, 100; on becoming an actor, 7–9;

206   Index

Cherry, Phil *(cont.)*
  on directorships at Kentucky
    Shakespeare, 57–58, 161–162;
    on Kentucky Shakespeare, 172;
    on *Othello,* 118–119; on outdoor
    theater, 115; in *Twelfth Night, 9*
Cincinnati Shakespeare Company,
  165
Clark, Casey: on becoming a
  lighting designer, 16; on
  Kentucky Shakespeare, 173,
  176–177; on lighting design,
  92–93; on outdoor theater, 111,
  116–117; on *Romeo and Juliet*
  (2016), 124–125
Clowes, Jack, 45, 47, *48*
Comedy of Errors, 177–178
Committee for Shakespeare in the
  Park, 43–44
community. *See* Kentucky
  Shakespeare, community
  relationships and partners
costume design, 26, 68, 77, 93–95
costumes, 17–18, 25–26, 27, 39;
  changes, 147; fittings, 172;
  Halloween, 157; for history
  plays, 84; light design and, 91,
  92; for "lizard *Lear,*" 133–134;
  for *A Midsummer Night's Dream,*
  123; for *Much Ado about Nothing,*
  39, 42, 94; for *Othello,* 118; for
  *Rosencrantz and Guildenstern
  Are Dead,* 118; shops, 47, 87;
  student-created, 146; for *The
  Taming of the Shrew,* 121; trailer,
  56, 137; washing, 47
COVID-19 pandemic, viii, 131, 148,
  157, 174, 200n4
Creel, Roger, 165–167
Curran, Robert, 109–110, 166,
  167–168

Daigle, Helen, 165
DeWhatley, Michael, 67

diversity and inclusivity, 185–190;
  arts education programs, 171,
  189–190; audiences, ix, 42, 44,
  106–107, 162, 164, 182, 183,
  185; casting and hiring, 46, 79,
  90, 125, 146, 164, 171, 186–187;
  commitment to inclusivity,
  72, 107, 186, 188–189, 190;
  community relationships and
  partnerships, ix–x, 149, 162;
  IDEA plan (inclusion, diversity,
  equity, access), 189
Downs, Donna Lawrence: on
  becoming a costume designer,
  17–18; on challenges of costume
  design, 93–95; on Kentucky
  Shakespeare, 173–174; on
  outdoor theater, 111–112; on
  Shakespeare Behind Bars, 155
Dunaway, Brantley, 30, 60, 63–68, 73
Dunaway, Faye, 63

Eastern Kentucky University, 5
Education Program. *See* Kentucky
  Shakespeare Education Program
Elder, Lonne, III, 8, 196n4

Gatton, John: on becoming an actor,
  4–5; on Carriage House Players,
  49–51; on missing lines, 103; on
  outdoor theater, 113; on teaching
  Shakespeare, 95–96
Girl Scouts, 141
Globe Players, *19,* 136, 140, 145,
  145, 162
Goldberg, Moses, 8, 15, 138
Grand Guignol Theater, 119, 201n6

Hamlet, 50, 51, 53, 79, 98, 112, 113,
  115, 117, 134, 147
Harris, Connie, *110*
Henriad, 27, 31, 171, 196n14
Henry IV, Part I, 116, 157
Henry IV, Part II, 28, 116

Henry V, 31, 33, 85, 116, 120, 160, 171
Hooper, Dathan, 66, 112–113, 200n24
Huffman, Jon, 13, 163, 174, 180; on acting profession, 100, 102, 176; on auditions and rehearsals, 80; on becoming an actor, 10–12; on directorships at Kentucky Shakespeare, 53–54, 61–62, 69; on forgetting lines, 104–105; in *Hamlet,* 147; on Kentucky Shakespeare, 76; in *King Lear,* 94–95, 107–108, 128–130, 177, *178*; as mentor, 105, 129–130; on origins of Kentucky Shakespeare, 46–47; in *Othello, 54*; on outdoor theater, 107–108

iambic pentameter, 8, 50, 54, 96, 104, 196n4
inclusivity. *See* diversity and inclusivity
Iroquois Park and Amphitheater, 43, 50, 161

Jefferson County Public Schools, 137
Johnson, Brenda, *110*; on directorships at Kentucky Shakespeare, 64; on Kentucky Shakespeare's accessibility, 181; on Louisville Ballet partnership, 164–165; on park tours, 146
Johnson, Fred, 155
Johnson, Jack, 48
Jory, Jon, 8, 13, 15, 196n6
Julius Caesar, 2–3, 24, 35, 42, 50, 53, 143, 165; costume design for, 93; directing, 89; Priddy in, *4*; Ramey in, 45; Shakespeare Behind Bars performances, *153,* 154; Shakespeare with Veterans performances, 156, 157, 158

Kentucky Education Reform Act (KERA), 138, 201n3
Kentucky Shakespeare: Camp Shakespeare, 18, 140, 145; commitment to inclusivity, 72, 107, 186, 188–189, 190; donations, 44, 103, 169, 196n11; final jig or bow and wave, 116, 169, *170*; funding, 42–44, *48, 56, 57,* 60, 169–170, 189; Globe Players, *19,* 136, 140, 145, *145,* 162; IDEA plan (inclusion, diversity, equity, access), 189; nonticketed productions, viii, 39, 42, 182, 183–184; park tours, 90, 146–149; repeat attendance, 169; reviews, 43–44, 56, 106, 169–171
Kentucky Shakespeare, community relationships and partners: Backside Learning Center, 149, 163, 201n7; Choreographer Showcase, 165–166; Clark County Juvenile Detention Center, 149; Kentucky Refugee Ministries, 163, 202n14; Louisville Ballet, 161, 163–168; Louisville Central Community Center, 145, 162, 201n4; Louisville Public Media, viii, 164; Louisville Visual Art, 164, 202n16; Peace Education Program, 156, 162–163, 202n10; Play Louisville, 164, 202n16; preshows, 68, 72, 75–76, 163–164; Squallis Puppeteers, 162, 202n13; Survivorship Shakespeare, 149
Kentucky Shakespeare Behind Bars, viii, 13, 30, 52, 66–67, 69, 149–156; documentary, 149–150; founding and history, 150–152; *Julius Caesar* residency, 154–155; Luther Luckett Correctional Facility, 52, 150–154; *Othello*

208   Index

Kentucky Shakespeare Behind
Bars *(cont.)*
production, 152–153; *Romeo
and Juliet* production, 151; *The
Tempest* production, 150; *Titus
Andronicus* production, 153
Kentucky Shakespeare Education
Program, 18–20, 28, 36, 57,
136–146; Bard Buddies, 141;
Boy Meets Girl Meets Shakespeare,
138–142; conflict resolution
workshops, 141–143, 144;
free workshops, 141; inclusive
arts education programs, 189;
origins and history, 136–140;
outreach to all Kentucky
counties, 139–140; Page to the
Stage, 138; performance-based
workshops, 140; *Shakespeare's
Clowns and Fools,* 138–139, *139;
Shakespeare's Kings, Shakespeare's
Queens,* 139; *Staging Shakespeare,*
140; study guides, 138, 139;
teaching-based workshops, 140;
Teaching Tolerance, 140; touring
troupe, 140–142; workshops and
residencies, 135, 139–142, 162;
year-round outreach, 139–140
Kentucky Shakespeare Festival in
Central Park, vii–viii, 7, *22,*
106–134, 171, 183, 185;
attendance figures, 169; audience
inclusivity, 107; Bard-a-thon,
112–113, 201n3; challenges
of outdoor theater, 112–117;
community-building at, 108,
110–112; free rides to Central
Park, 189; future of, 190; Globe
Players performances, 145;
inclusivity of art groups at, 189;
King Lear (2019), 128–131;
King Lear [lizard *Lear*] (1987),
133–134; *Macbeth* (1986),
117; *Macbeth* (2015), 119–120;
Macbeth [in the Parking Lot]
(2020), 131–132; memorable
performances, 117–134; *A
Midsummer Night's Dream* (2014),
123; *Much Ado about Nothing*
(2017), 128; *Othello* (2004), 118–
119; *Romeo and Juliet* (2000 and
2021), 123–124; *Romeo and Juliet*
(2016), 124–128; *Rosencrantz and
Guildenstern Are Dead* (2002),
117–118; *Shakespeare in Love*
(2021), 132–133; *The Taming of
the Shrew* (2015), 120–122; tiring
house, 124, 201n7
Kentucky Shakespeare with
Veterans, viii, 149–150, 155–161;
Athena Sisters and, 156; cutting
of *Julius Caesar;* founding and
history, 155–157; *Henry IV,
Part I* cutting, 157; *Julius Caesar*
cutting, 156–158; Louisville
Vet Center, 156–160; *Macbeth*
cutting, 157; Peace Education
Program and, 156; typical
sessions, 154
King Lear, 50, 85, 165; costumes for,
133–134; Huffman in, 94–95,
107–108, 128–130, 177, *178;*
Luce in, *178;* Maupin (Abigail)
in, *178;* Maupin (Gregory) in,
133–134, 178, *178;* McCampbell
in, 113, *114,* 129–130;
memorable performances,
128–131, 133–134
Kleier, Georgette: on becoming an
actor, 12–13; on directorships
at Kentucky Shakespeare, 54,
58–59, 75–76, 90; on education
program, 136–137; on outdoor
theater, 108, 112; on park tours,
148–149; on preparation, 96; on
Romeo and Juliet, 123–124; in
Twelfth Night, 9; on uniqueness
of Kentucky Shakespeare, 182

LGBTQ+ communities, 189, 202n16
lighting design, 90, 92–93, 124, 177
Louisville Ballet, 35, 109, 161, 163–168
Louisville Children's Theater, 5, 11, 15, 196n2. *See also* StageOne Family Theatre
Love, Victor, *54*, 198n13
Luce, Tom: on becoming an actor, 9–10; on directorships at Kentucky Shakespeare, 63–64, 73; on first read throughs, 82; in *King Lear, 178*; on meaning of Kentucky Shakespeare, 175; on outdoor theater, 115; on *As You Like It*, 109

Macbeth, 13 , 38, *40*, 41, 42, 45, 51–53, 88, 107; memorable performances, 117, 119–120, 131–132; Shakespeare Behind Bars performance, 151; Shakespeare with Veterans cutting, 157
Massie Ware, Megan, *127*, 147, 174
Maupin, Abigail Bailey, 200n24; on auditions, 79; on becoming an actor, 27–29; on *Comedy of Errors*, 177–178; on community partners, 163; on directorships at Kentucky Shakespeare, 30, 64–66, 73–74; on education program, 142–143; in *King Lear, 178*; in *Macbeth*, 119–120; on meaning of Kentucky Shakespeare, 172–173, 177–178; on meeting Greg, 29; in *Much Ado about Nothing, 30*; on *Othello*, 61–62; on outdoor theater, 112–113; on park tours, 147–148; on performing Shakespeare, 97–100; on school tours, 29, 30; in *Taming of the Shrew*, 120–122, *122*

Maupin, Gregory: on becoming an actor, 26–27; on directorships at Kentucky Shakespeare, 65, 66, 68, 73–74; in *King Lear*, 133–134, 178, *178*; on marrying Abigail, 29; on meaning of Kentucky Shakespeare, 177; in *A Midsummer Night's Dream*, 123; in *Much Ado about Nothing*, 30, 128; on *Othello*, 61–62; on outdoor theater, 107, 112, 113; in *Romeo and Juliet*, 90; on school tours, 29–30, 61–62; in *Taming of the Shrew*, 120–122, *122*; on uniqueness of Kentucky Shakespeare, 177; on *As You Like It*, 30–31
McCampbell, Braden: on audiences, 102; on auditions and rehearsals, 82–84; on becoming an actor, 36–38; on diverse casting, 125–126; on education program, 143–144; on forgetting lines, 105; in *King Lear*, 113, *114*, 129–130; on meaning of Kentucky Shakespeare, 174–175; on opening night, 84–85; on racial representation, 185–186; on *Romeo and Juliet*, 125–126; in *Shakespeare in Love*, 86; in *Taming of the Shrew, 187*; on uniqueness of Kentucky Shakespeare, 184–185
Measure for Measure, 42, 63
Merchant of Venice, The, 103, 155
Merry Wives of Windsor, The, 52
Midsummer Night's Dream, A, 8, 91, 94, 114–116, 162–163; Maupin (Gregory) in, 123; memorable performance, 123; Wallace (Matt) in, *22*, 25; Wallace (Tina Jo) in, *22*
Midwest Theater Auditions, 10, 196n9

210   Index

Milder, Tony, *101,* 147, 166, 176
mistakes and missed lines, 102–105
Moore, Scott, 166–167
Much Ado about Nothing, vii–viii,
   4, 5, *30,* 37, 39–40, 42, 50, 94,
   97, 114, 179–180; memorable
   performance, 128

Norton Commons (Louisville
   suburb), 188, 203n4

O'Brien, Adale, 13, 196n10
O'Brien, Jon, 105, 119, *120,* 147,
   174, 181
Old Kentucky Home High School,
   135, 136
Old Louisville (neighborhood),
   vii-viii; decline of, 60; history
   of, 41–42, 197n5; revival of, 42,
   44–45
Old Louisville [Neighborhood]
   Association, 43, 60
opening night, 65–66, 84–87
Othello, viii, 42, 45, 165; casting for,
   45, 198n13; Cherry in, 118–119;
   costume design for, 93, 98;
   costumes for, 118; Huffman
   in, *54*; Maupin (Abigail) in,
   61–62; Maupin (Gregory) in,
   61–62; Maupin (Abigail) on,
   61, 62; Maupin (Gregory) on,
   61; memorable performance,
   118–119; Priddy in, 47–48;
   Shakespeare Behind Bars
   production, 152
Owen, Paul, 173; on becoming a
   set designer, 25–26; on Central
   Park stage, 74; on set designing,
   91–92
Owens, Brian, 200n26

Pandora Productions, 164, 202n15
Park, Hal, *55,* 60; on becoming
   a director and producer, 5–7;
   on directorships at Kentucky

Shakespeare, 51, 54–57; on
   education program, 137; hired
   as producing artistic director,
   51–52; leadership style of,
   51–52; on *Macbeth* (1986), 117;
   on producing Shakespeare, 77,
   87–89
Patton, Anthony, 60, 63, 65
Peace Education Program, 156,
   162–163, 202n10
play selection, 78
Priddy, Monte, vii, 49, 169,
   195–196n1; on becoming an
   actor, 2–4; on Carriage House
   Players, 47–49; on directorships
   at Kentucky Shakespeare,
   52, 60–61, 63; on education
   program, 136; in *Julius Caesar, 4*;
   on outdoor theater, 115–116
producing artistic director, duties of,
   87–90

Ramey, C. Douglas, ix, 7, 11, *48*;
   death of, 54–55; Kentucky
   Shakespeare's history and, viii,
   1, 3, 39–44, 48–49, 50, 51;
   leadership style of, 50, 54–55,
   106–107, 135, 171, 189; legacy
   of, 69; in *Macbeth, 40*; *Songs of
   Faith* (television show), 136
rehearsal, 79–80, 83–84
Restoration Inc., 43
Richard III, 5, 30, 65, 67, 73
Robertson, Neill, 113, *114,* 129
Romeo and Juliet, 23, 34, 37, *127,
   148*; casting for, 125–126;
   Cherry in, 7–8; costume design
   for, 93; directing, 89–90; Kleier
   in, 58–59, 123–124; lighting
   design for, 124–125; Maupin
   (Gregory) in, 90; memorable
   performances, 123–128;
   Shakespeare Behind Bars
   production of, 151; Sumey in, 18;
   Wallace (Tina Jo) in, 123–124;

Wiltshire in, 33, 36, 125, 126–127, *127,* 186
Romeo and Juliet (1968 film), 197n16
Rosen, Marty, 170–171
Rosencrantz and Guildenstern Are Dead, 117–118

Salyers, Mae, 47, *48*
Schneider, Bekki Jo, 5, 6–7, 9–12, *55*; on becoming an actor, 1–2; on Carriage House Players, 44–46; on education program, 136; hired as producing artistic director, 51; leadership style of, 51, 53, 54–55, 61, 68, 69, 75, 90; as mentor, 66; on producing artistic director position, 52–53; in *Taming of the Shrew, 2*
schools. *See* Kentucky Shakespeare Education Program
Schultz, Stephen, 52
set design, 91–92, 177
Shakespeare, William. *See individual plays*
Shakespeare Behind Bars. *See Kentucky Shakespeare Behind Bars*
Shakespeare Festival. *See* Kentucky Shakespeare Festival in Central Park
Shakespeare in Love (2021), *86,* 92, 132, *133,* 200n4, 201n5
Shakespeare's R and J, 59, 124, 164, 170, 202n15
Shakespeare Unplugged, 146, 147
Shakespeare with Veterans. *See* Kentucky Shakespeare with Veterans
Shawnee (Louisville neighborhood), 188
Shawnee Park , 50, 146, 199, 203n4
Siebert, Elizabeth, 188; on "lizard *Lear,*" 133; on outdoor theater, 111; on pandemic production of *Macbeth,* 131–132; on preshows,

163; on uniqueness of Kentucky Shakespeare, 185
sonnets, Shakespeare's, 165–167
StageOne Family Theatre, 8, 11, 15, 17–18, 31–32, 35, 138, 196n2. *See also* Louisville Children's Theatre
Stewart, Darryl, 158–161
Stoppard, Tom, 117–118
Sumey, Doug, *19,* 30, 62; on becoming an actor, 18–20; on diversity and inclusion, 162–163; on education program, 140, 144–146; hired as education director, 136; on meaning of Kentucky Shakespeare, 174; on outdoor theater, 114–115; on park tours, 147

table readings, 59, 81, 82–83, *83*
Taming of the Shrew, The, 2, 23, 33, 53, *170, 187*; memorable performance, 120–122
Taylor, Breonna, 185
Taylor, Pat, 8
Tempest, The, 52, 53, *75, 101,* 150; in arts education programs, 141; lighting direction for, 92–93; Louisville Ballet collaboration, 165, 167; Luce in, 10; Priddy in, 48
Titus Andronicus, 153
Tofteland, Curt, 4, 9, 18, 20, 21, 22, 24, 25, 26; on becoming an actor, 14–15; on education program, 137–140; in *To Kill a Mockingbird,* 8; leadership style of, 52, 57–58, 60–61, 62, 63, 81; on producing artistic director position, 57; retirement of, 60; in *Richard II, 14,* 116; on Shakespeare Behind Bars, 150–153; Shakespeare Behind Bars founded by, 149–150; on uniqueness of Kentucky

212 Index

Tofteland, Curt *(cont.)*
Shakespeare, 183; youth outreach
under, 136
Trounstine, Jean, 149
truss, 75, 116
Twelfth Night, 9, 50, 53, 99, 152, 170

United Professional Theatre
Auditions, 196n12
University of Kentucky, 6, 48
University of Louisville, 3; theater
program, 1, 10–11, 26–27,
33–35, 36–37, 52

veterans. *See* Kentucky Shakespeare
with Veterans

Wallace, Matt, 28, 30–31, 32, 35, 172,
174, 175; on becoming an actor,
22–25; community building under
tenure of, 161, 163, 164, 165, 166,
167; on directing after acting, 89;
director of *Richard III,* 30, 65, 67,
73; on diversity and inclusion,
164, 188–189; donations under
tenure of, 169; on future of
Kentucky Shakespeare, 190;
leadership style of, 73–74, 75, 76,
81–82, 90; in *Love's Labour's Lost,*
25; in *Merchant of Venice,* 103;
in *A Midsummer Night's Dream,*
22, 25; on missing an entrance,
103; on outdoor theater, 109, 114;
on producing artistic director
position, 69–71; on proposal to
Tina Jo, 179–180; in *Rosencrantz
and Guildenstern Are Dead,*
117–118; on season preparation,
77–78; on Shakespeare Behind
Bars, 153–155; Shakespeare
Behind Bars director, 150,
153–156; on uniqueness of
Kentucky Shakespeare, 184

Wallace, Tina Jo, 22, 25; on acting
Shakespeare, 97; Bard Buddies,
141; on becoming an actor,
20–21; on casting, 78–79; on
communal experience of theater,
110; on education program,
140–142; on forgetting lines,
103–104; in *Hamlet,* 117–118;
on Matt as producing artistic
director, 72–73; on Matt's
proposal, 180; on meaning of
Kentucky Shakespeare, 175; on
meeting Matt, 178–179; in *A
Midsummer Night's Dream,* 22;
on opening night, 85, 87; on
outdoor theater, 108–109, 110;
on preparation and rehearsal,
80–81; on renaissance runs, 59;
in *Romeo and Juliet,* 123–124;
in *Rosencrantz and Guildenstern
Are Dead,* 117–118; on
uniqueness of Kentucky
Shakespeare, 183–184
Ware, Kyle, 37–38, 147, 155–156,
174
Western Kentucky University,
Theater program, 7–8
William's Folly, 165, 166
Wiltshire, Crystian: on becoming
an actor, 33–36; on diversity
and inclusion, 182–183,
186–188; on interning as stage
manager, 95; on meaning of
Kentucky Shakespeare, 173; on
A Midsummer Night's Dream,
123; on outdoor theater, 106,
107, 116, 123; in *Romeo and
Juliet,* 125, 126–127, *127;*
on uniqueness of Kentucky
Shakespeare, 180–181

Young Actors Institute, 31,
196–197n15

Kentucky Remembered:
An Oral History Series

James C. Klotter, Terry L. Birdwhistell, and Douglas A. Boyd
Series Editors

Books in the Series

Conversations with Kentucky Writers
 edited by L. Elisabeth Beattie

Conversations with Kentucky Writers II
 edited by L. Elisabeth Beattie

Barry Bingham: A Man of His Word
 Barry Bingham

Crawfish Bottom: Recovering a Lost Kentucky Community
 Douglas A. Boyd

This Is Home Now: Kentucky's Holocaust Survivors Speak
 Arwen Donahue and Rebecca Gayle Howell

Burley: Kentucky Tobacco in a New Century
 Ann K. Ferrell

Freedom on the Border: An Oral History of the Civil Rights Movement in Kentucky
 Catherine Fosl and Tracy E. K'Meyer

Under the Greenwood Tree: A Celebration of Kentucky Shakespeare
 Tracy E. K'Meyer

Arab and Jewish Women in Kentucky: Stories of Accommodation and Audacity
 Nora Rose Moosnick

Voices of African Immigrants in Kentucky: Migration, Identity, and Transnationality
 Francis Musoni, Iddah Otieno, Angene Wilson, and Jack Wilson

The Coal Miner Who Became Governor
 Paul E. Patton with Jeffrey S. Suchanek

Washington's Iron Butterfly: Bess Clements Abell, an Oral History
  Donald A. Ritchie and Terry L. Birdwhistell

Bert Combs the Politician: An Oral History
  edited by George W. Robinson

Gatewood: Kentucky's Uncommon Man
  Matthew Strandmark

Tobacco Culture: Farming Kentucky's Burley Belt
  John van Willigen and Susan C. Eastwood

Food and Everyday Life on Kentucky Family Farms, 1920–1950
  John van Willigen and Anne van Willigen

Voices from the Peace Corps: Fifty Years of Kentucky Volunteers
  Angene Wilson and Jack Wilson